CONFESSIONS OF A PLAGIARIST

CONFESSIONS OF A PLAGIARIST
And Other Tales from School

Kevin Kopelson

COUNTERPATH   *DENVER*   2012

Counterpath Press
Denver, Colorado
www.counterpathpress.org

Printed in the United States of America

Library of Congress Cataloging-in-Publication Data

Kopelson, Kevin, 1960-
  Confessions of a plagiarist : and other tales from school / Kevin Kopelson.
    p. cm.
  ISBN 978-1-933996-30-1 (pbk. : alk. paper)
    1. Kopelson, Kevin, 1960– 2. Critics—United States—Biography. 3. Scholars—
United States—Biography. 4. Plagiarism. I. Title.
PS29.K65A3   2012
801'.95092—dc23
[B]
                                                                    2011052437

Portions of "My Cortez" first appeared under the title "Confessions of a Plagiarist" in *London
Review of Books* 30.10. "Bright One" quotes extensively from "Sentimental Journey," which first
appeared in *n+1* on April 29, 2009. "Kiss and Tell" and "Death to Gumby" contain portions of
"The Happy Wanker," which first appeared in *Urban Molecule* 1.1.

Text design by Michael Flatt

For E.K.S.

1950–2009

The bonds that unite us to another human being are sanctified when he or she adopts the same point of view as ourselves in judging one of our imperfections. And among those special traits there were others, besides, which belonged as much to Swann's intellect as to his character, but which nevertheless, because they had their roots in the latter, Odette had been able more easily to discern. She complained that when Swann turned author, when he published his essays, these characteristics were not to be found in them to the same extent as in his letters or in his conversation, where they abounded. She urged him to give them a more prominent place. She wanted this because it was these things that she herself most liked in him, but since she liked them because they were the things most typical of him, she was perhaps not wrong in wishing that they might be found in his writings.

—MARCEL PROUST

To write, you have to allow yourself to be the person you don't want to be (of all the people you are).

—SUSAN SONTAG

One writes in order to become other than what one is.

—MICHEL FOUCAULT

Contents

Acknowledgments

These so-called confessions of mine—satires, really—are almost entirely truthful, with some truths stretched to fit the story. Some people's names, likewise, have—along with identifying characteristics—had to be changed. (Two people here are in fact completely fictitious; another is several different people I know put together.) Names of most friends and family, however, have not been changed. And three friends not in the story should—with both love and gratitude—be mentioned here: Ralph Savarese, who has even more to satirize (if not to confess) than I do; Tina Bourjaily, who has always encouraged me to write what I like; and Robin Bourjaily, her daughter, who by careful editing has made this writing much better than it used to be. So too must one friend in the story, only under a pseudonym, be mentioned: Brenton Thompson, who I sense likes to think of me as a latter-day Walter Pater to his own Oscar Wilde. Or perhaps an Oprah Winfrey to his Gayle King.

CONFESSIONS OF A PLAGIARIST

My Cortez

I quote too much. Give me a good line—what am I saying? Give me a good
paragraph—even a Proustian one—and I'll shove it into my own prose regard-
less of how tiresome that is. Take my last book, on David Sedaris. Not only do
you get more Proust than you'd ever care for, you get an awful lot of Sedaris—
pure, unadulterated Sedaris.

It's not that I'm lazy. Or rather, it's not just that I'm lazy. I do much more
in *Sedaris* than quote Sedaris, much more in other words than simply "rhap-
sodize" him, to quote Frank Lentricchia. (Lentricchia, unfortunately, doesn't
indicate his own source: Plato's *Ion*.) I analyze the man. I synthesize him. I
provide what both Marxists and Freudians call "symptomatic readings." But be-
yond that, beyond what all literary critics (including Lentricchia) are supposed
to do, I—well, let me quote Winton Dean:

> There is a big difference between the comparatively rare occasions on which
> Handel passed off others' compositions as his own and the far more numerous
> instances of his using the ideas of others as a jumping off point for fresh compo-
> sition. It may seem strange that he needed to do this, but it involves a creative
> process, not simple larceny.

Or *is* there? Is there—for me—a difference between what Dean calls "creative process" and "simple larceny"? Or rather, between creative process and not so simple larceny. Between process, that is, and, oh—just *"write* it!" (to quote Elizabeth Bishop)—plagiarism.

The answer, by way of explanation for which I offer the following narrative—or confession—is "no." Now, I know what you're thinking. You're thinking that all such confessions are deceptive. To quote J.D. Salinger (lines I've already included in more than one publication):

> A confessional passage has probably never been written that didn't stink a little bit of the writer's pride in having given up his pride. The thing to listen for, every time, with a public confessor, is what he's *not* confessing to. At a certain period of his life (usually, grievous to say, a *successful* period), a man may suddenly feel it Within His Power to confess that he cheated on his final exams at college, he may even choose to reveal that between the ages of twenty-two and twenty-four he was sexually impotent, but these gallant confessions in themselves are no guarantee that we'll find out whether he once got piqued at his pet hamster and stepped on its head.

I *will* tell you about that hamster—figuratively speaking—and also about how I've brained it.

It all began in the fall of 1968. I was in fourth grade (PS 135, in Queens). Mrs. Froelich, for some reason, was spending most of her time speaking French. (I remember the line: *"Nous allons marcher ensemble."* [We will walk together.]) And then she went on strike, along with the rest of her union. No more French. No more marching *ensemble.* Parents set up an interim school in the "reform" synagogue within walking distance of our house. (As "Conservative" Jews—as atheists, that is—we drove to one miles away. Think of the Jew stranded on a desert island who builds himself an entire town: a library, a bath house, a synagogue, a second synagogue. "Why two?" asked the sailors who eventually came to the man's rescue. "Oh," he said, "we don't go *there.*") My new teacher—my first male teacher—was just some guy. First grade: Mrs. Berg (Jewish). Second grade: Mrs. Dorsey (Catholic). Third grade: Mrs. Solomon (Jewish). Fourth grade: Mrs. Froelich (Catholic). Fifth grade: Mrs. Keaton (Catholic). Sixth grade: Mrs. Kelly (Catholic). I don't recall the man's name. I can't even picture him. In fact, the only thing I remember is that he made us write an essay on some conquistador. I chose Hernando Cortez—probably because, like Keats, I like the name. (The sonnet "On first looking into Chapman's Homer" ends:

"Then felt I like some watcher of the skies / When a new planet swims into his ken; / Or like stout Cortez [sic] when with eagle eyes / He star'd at the Pacific— and all his men / Look'd at each other with a wild surmise—/ Silent, upon a peak in Darien.") But knowing that whatever I turned in wouldn't really count and also that Mr. X cared even less about this ridiculous situation than I did, I simply transcribed an encyclopedia entry. (So much for the notion that students plagiarize so as to please us teachers, to give us what they think we want but feel they can't produce.)

Now the thing is, this was no ordinary encyclopedia and no ordinary entry. The set, which came with the house my parents bought when I was born, was about a hundred years old. "Cortez" there was about twenty pages long. Clearly, then, my submission (of which I can't recall a single line) wasn't the kind of thing an eight-year-old could devise. Even a precocious eight-year-old. Even a *pretentious* one. So imagine my relief (surprise? indifference? contempt?) when this primal larceny came back marked "A." ("Nice work!" Mr. X commented. But of course, unless the man was being ironic, he probably didn't read it—lazy bastard.)

After that, I did well enough in school—even without plagiarizing—to get into both Harvard and Yale. Well enough on the SATs, as well. Nor did it hurt that I'd attended both Bronx High School of Science and Juilliard, where I studied piano. Not wanting to go where my brother Bob went, I chose Yale—where, like him, I majored in music. (A far better pianist, Bob left Harvard in the spring of 1968.) Ironically enough, several of my new teachers were friends of Bob: the composer Martin Bresnick, who'd known him at the High School of Music and Art (in Manhattan); the musicologist Craig Monson, who'd known him in graduate school (at Berkeley); the conductor Jon Bailey, who'd also known him at Berkeley. Other than that, though, they were fine.

Unfortunately, another teacher (no friend of Bob) was musicologist "Betty Boop" (or so I'll call her), who covered the eighteenth century. I forget the name of her course, but we called it "Clapping for Credit." The thing was that ridiculous, that contemptible. So when Betty had us write an essay, I stole a seminar paper that Bob—still in his "successful period"—had done at Berkeley. (It too was in the house, along with everything else he ever wrote.) That thing concerned the "Jeunehomme" Concerto, a work generally considered Mozart's first masterpiece. The piece was supposed to have been written for someone Bob called "the mysterious Mlle Jeunehomme"—the only line of his that I recall. But to quote Wikipedia (not a particularly "good" line, but what can you do?): "musicologist Michael Lorenz [has proven] that the woman was actually Victoire Jenamy, a daughter of Jean-Georges Noverre, a famous dancer who was one of Mozart's best friends."

Now, this was no ordinary paper. It was about fifty pages long. And there were extensive footnotes citing French, German, and Italian material. (On top of everything else, Bob's a polyglot.) Rather obscure material, I might add. Clearly, then, my submission wasn't the kind of thing an eighteen-year-old could devise—even one who spoke a little French. Once again, though, I got an "A." Either Betty was too stupid to recognize the larceny (my assumption at the time), or—having recognized it—too lazy to bring me up on charges. Or too indifferent. Or too kind. Or maybe, I now realize, *she* never read it.

Needless to say, I'm not proud of what I did—even though, to invoke Salinger, I'm proud of my power to admit it (now that I can't be charged). Why, though, did I do it? Why *else*, that is—apart from contempt. I did it because I wanted to be Bob. Because I wanted to "walk together" with him, only not at Harvard. And because—subconsciously—I imagined this outrageous theft would let me do so. Of course, readers already familiar with my published work will have known this. To quote my essay "The Sonic Mirror," for example:

> One thing you should know about me—maybe *the* one thing—is that I didn't always want to be an English professor. I used to want to be a pianist. But it wasn't until I was around twenty that I had to accept my now rather obvious limitations. I lack virtuoso technique—for which I'm still petty enough to blame Mrs. Graa [my first piano teacher]. And I lack musical intelligence—for which I don't even have genetics to blame. My older brother, Robert, is a successful pianist.

Or to quote my book *Beethoven's Kiss*:

> Dr. Train, the psychoanalyst my father had me see when [my brother] Steve killed himself, once told me, after having determined that my mother hadn't caused my homosexuality, that the terrifying, dominating, and truly monstrous woman who had done so was Diana Graa. According to Train, Mrs. Graa convinced me I couldn't satisfy her fiendish, feminine desires—convinced me I was no good. Or at least not as good as my older brother Bob. Bob the true child prodigy, Bob the one with perfect pitch, etc. Sad to say, I believed him.

This second passage, by the way, first appeared in a letter I wrote to the English professor (and critic) Wayne Koestenbaum—also Jewish. Wayne, too, is

someone with whom I've identified. (In his case, though, it's because he re-
minds me of Steve, my one openly gay yet truly mean brother. Or rather of
the nice brother I'd always wanted him to be.) He's also someone who, in what
I take as an explanation of why I keep writing about both siblings, contends:
"In any life, as in any invention, or any work of literature, however lofty or
pedestrian, there exists a fixed set of dominating themes, and mere diligence
cannot increase their number or alter their nature. Their substance, if not their
sequence, remains incorrigibly the same."

I graduated from Yale in 1979. As I didn't even play piano well enough to
get into medical school—or so we majors used to joke—I went to law school. To
Columbia, in fact, which I loathed. (I'd gone to please my father, an attorney,
and also because I had no idea what else to do with myself.) Steve died shortly
thereafter. I developed anorexia—which is neither here nor there, but I may as
well admit that too. And then I read *The White Hotel* by D.M. Thomas, an anti-
Freudian holocaust novel. My parents had it. I remember the passage on the let-
ter scene in *Eugene Onegin*. (The heroine performs Tatiana.) I also remember
the horrifying passage on Babi Yar, where not only the heroine but also many
of my own relatives—on both sides of the family—were killed. Thomas, we
later learned (about a year after publication), had lifted much of the latter from
Babi Yar, a novel by Anatoly Kuznetsov. My parents had that as well. Now, some
critics don't consider this plagiarism. They call it postmodern. And while I'm
in no position to judge—never having read the Kuznetsov—I do know a thing
or two about postmodernism. I know, for example, that any such citation—like
sarcasm, if not like (verbal) irony—should be immediately recognizable as such.
Figuratively speaking, it should be within quotation marks.

I graduated from Columbia in 1982, started eating again, and then worked at a
terrible law firm in Rockefeller Center. David Hyde Pierce, incidentally, worked
there too—as a paralegal. He went on, of course, to play Niles Crane on *Frasier*,
to win a Tony Award for *Curtains*, and to blurb *Sedaris*. "Charting a course from
Marcel Proust to Tony Danza," he wrote, "Kevin artfully captures the exquisite
pleasure and pain of reading David Sedaris." ("If I were to read a book on David
Sedaris," wrote Paul Reubens, "it might be this one.") Not that we first-year as-
sociates had much to do. The firm was in a slump. And so although I did some
research and wrote memoranda (one of which simply transcribed a law review
article), I spent most of my time reading Proust in English—unbillable hours
I called "professional development"—and hanging out with another first-year.
"Albertine Simonet" (or so I'll call her) had graduated from . . . well, I'll say

Berkeley, where she'd also gotten a masters degree in French. (Not having yet learned, from Proust, to be unpretentious, we liked to imagine—in fact, we *still* imagine—that Albertine is Guy de Rothschild and that I'm Marie-Hélène, his wife: fantasy escape from life at the firm.) One time, Albertine told me—one of her more amusing revelations—she'd turned in some essay by Montaigne as a seminar paper. Her professor—very kind—simply handed the thing back unmarked and then asked, in private: "What drugs are you on?" In reality though, Albertine now tells me—very ashamed—that she'd turned in a rather famous essay *on* Montaigne ("Montaigne: The Crisis of the Self"), that the professor confronted her in private, that he then told her parents, and that—unlike me—she's never done any such thing again. Or to quote her recent e-mail:

> [My professor] first called me in to discuss. Something was really amiss, he said, because you're not that type of person. Plus having done this on such a wholesale basis was pure lunacy—"not just a sentence, but the *entire* text!" Then he called my parents. This was, in fact, a "crisis" in my own life. The three of them determined that my contact with pot was not helpful, that it had altered my judgment. "What drugs are you on?" was a humorous paraphrase of the drama of the event. And there was a *lot* of drama. Unhappy me! Unhappy parents! Unhappy professor! Not a great thing for me to have done, certainly. [My professor], by the way, is still a friend. I may call to discuss this with him.

In 1984, I moved to a much better firm, one with actual work to do. But I loathed it as well. (I'm not the lawyer type, I realized. I'm creative, or rather re-creative: not Chopin, but someone who *plays* Chopin—and in both senses of the verb: to perform, to impersonate. I do not, however, enjoy representing other people's *interests*—especially when they're bad.) Looking around for something else to do, I thought of favorite teachers. Favorite English teachers, that is: Florence Dragnet (a sexpot), Joseph Scavone (a comedian)—neither of them Jewish. But having then heard what kids at ordinary schools were like—in New York City, at any rate—I considered the advice of various friends including Albertine. "Teach college," they said. "Apply to grad school. Get a *doctorate* in English." "Well, why not," I thought. "Maybe I'm smart enough. Maybe I'll like college students—Yalies, at any rate." Maybe, moreover, I'd like writing something other than legal memoranda. For having read Sandra Gilbert and Susan Gubar's monumental—nay, encyclopedic—*The Madwoman in the Attic*, I felt sufficiently "imbued with otherness" to imagine myself doing for so-called sexuality studies what these collaborators—and talk about walking together!—had done for feminism. Only instead of treating every single gay male novelist (those two do almost every female), I planned to work on Henry James alone. James, for me, came after Proust. And he wrote in English.

There was just one problem. My grades were fine. My GREs were fine, though I hadn't been able to identify the line "When lilacs last in the dooryard bloomed." (It's by Whitman, of course.) I could devise a personal statement. Mine associated reading literature with the lines: "Young chameleon, I used to / Ask how on earth one got sufficiently / Imbued with otherness. And now I see." (In other words, it associated such reading with both identification and escape—a conflation I'd also experienced in pretending to be Marie-Hélène.) They're by James Merrill, although I'd never actually seen them in *The Changing Light at Sandover*. I'd seen them (quoted) in my college friend Jesse Green's yearbook quote. Jesse—a wonderful writer (poetry, fiction, creative nonfiction), a bit like Proust in person (independently wealthy, hypochondriac, self-indulgent, snobbish, Jewish) not to mention the first person I *knew* in person who made me want to write—was an English major. I, as you know, was not. And so, with all the schools to which I'd apply requesting some kind of research paper as a writing sample, I simply couldn't submit one . . . of my own. As a music major, you see, the only such paper I had was that one for Betty. And so, once again, I produced—or rather, re-produced—Bob's work on the mysterious Mlle Jeunehomme. "Well," I thought, "at least I'm not *publishing* the thing." But this time around, I now realize, the outrageous theft—the identification with Bob, that is—was not untainted by what, if memory serves, literary critic D.A. Miller calls "all due aggression." (I think it's in *Bringing Out Roland Barthes*, a book on wanting to be both Barthes and Proust. But I'm too lazy to look it up. Oh wait, here it is: Miller's language there is "the usual vicissitudes of adulation, aggression, ambivalence.") For Bob never did get his PhD—in musicology. He left grad school ABD (all but dissertation). That identification, in other words, contaminated my desire to get such a degree (only not at Berkeley, and not in musicology) both *as* Bob and *instead* of him. I must have thought, subconsciously, that Dad might like that too.

I got into both Columbia and Brown—not Yale, though, and certainly not Harvard. (Once you reject Harvard, it seemed, they never let you back.) I chose Brown. Classes there were fine, for the most part. My course on James, though, was not. It was taught by a very old, very flatulent man—I'll call him "Grover Cleveland"—who despite the fact that this was to have been a seminar, recited lectures to us. To me, that is, along with only two other students—lectures that, to judge from the crumbling condition of the legal pads upon which they'd been written, couldn't possibly have been revised within the past two decades. This was utterly ridiculous, utterly contemptible. So when Grover had us write an essay, I stole an article on James that I'd seen in some collection, entitled "The Beast in the Closet." And not just a sentence or two, but *nearly* the entire text—minus, that is, some of its clear and accurate description. Plus, if I recall, I added a bit of my own (less clear, less accurate) description. Now you might think that even I, by this point, should have known better than to do such a thing. You might think that even I should have had *some* shame. But I probably recalled, with amusement, Albertine's Montaigne and thought: "Well, why not." And, too, I had already begun to develop an identification with the article's author, a Jewish woman called Eve Kosofsky Sedgwick—a cross-sex, cross-sexuality identification (she's not gay) that I'd first write about in "Fake It Like a Man." The woman, you see, would soon come to dominate sexuality studies. And that article would eventually reappear as the central chapter of her truly monumental *Epistemology of the Closet*. I got an "A." Mr. Cleveland even read it, which I could tell from his commentary. But it turns out, I now realize, that I was ashamed. Here's what happened. Shortly after this larceny, I actually wrote a paper of my own. It was for a seminar on Roland Barthes and Oscar Wilde. That professor (Robert Scholes) suggested I try to publish the thing. So I submitted it to *Genders*, which secured two supposedly anonymous readers. One, though, was D.A. Miller (possibly Catholic). And the other was Eve. The journal had neglected to delete their names from their reports—reports, I'm happy to report, that were rather positive. I forget what Eve said, but Miller, for some reason, called me "shy and lovely." Or to quote the line in full, to the best of my recollection: "Must this be so shy and lovely, in the manner of the usual seminar paper, when with just a little work it could become the essay we *really* need?" But I didn't revise. "Wilde, Barthes, and the Orgasmics of Truth"—my first publication—appeared just as I'd written it for Scholes.

I then—this was 1989—attended a conference at Yale. Wayne, who taught there, had organized the panel I was on. And so we met in person. I met Miller too—a hunk who taught at Berkeley, wouldn't give me the time of day (lovely or not), and (so) certainly didn't connect me to any "orgasmics." I met Eve as well, an incredibly kind woman who did make that connection, offering both to read anything else of mine I might care to send and to be of further assistance. What to send? What to send? Reader—*mon semblable, mon frère*—I sent her "The Beast in the Closet."

This, clearly, was lunacy. (Think of Beethoven claiming to have written the "Jeunehomme" Concerto and then submitting it to Mozart. Think, rather, of some Salieri-like *jeune homme* doing so. Or maybe not so *jeune*. I was practically thirty.) Unlike Albertine, however, I didn't have marijuana to blame. Like her, though, I too must have felt ashamed—ashamed, that is, of what I'd done to both Eve and Bob. And so I too—subconsciously—must have wanted to be caught. Caught and *punished*, in fact: ruined career in academia, ignominious return to law. But I wasn't caught, unlike Albertine. For as far as I know, Eve's never read the thing. (But what if she has!) Never seen *my* name above *her* work. Never noticed the plagiarism. Well, she will now. As will Bob, I expect.

I chose Scholes (definitely Catholic) as my dissertation director, in part because he told me he's an impostor. "So are most of us," he added. The dissertation, though, wasn't on James. It was on Wilde, Barthes, and several others in between. Scholes, once again, suggested I publish. So taking her up on that second offer, I asked Eve to help me place the thing. She wrote to Stanford University Press. Stanford, having gotten another set of positive reports, offered me a contract. This time I did revise. And then I asked both Eve and Wayne for blurbs—compelling people I love to quote (and with whom I identify) to both read and write on *me*. Wayne's, in part, reads: "Everywhere tenderly epigrammatic, Kevin Kopelson's voice—moving with a litigator's clean, panoptic brio—demonstrates that critique can be a form of courtship, even a form of love." Eve calls me "invitingly stylish and excitingly lucid," which is much better than "shy and lovely."

Getting that contract to publish *Love's Litany* helped me get the job I still have. But I'm not at Yale. I'm at some public school in Iowa. Iowans, of course, are very nice. (Barthes would call this statement *doxa*, a bit of conventional wisdom—like the notion that students plagiarize so as to please.) And I do like my colleagues. But the students! Or rather, the English majors! Our department, you see, is the only one in the humanities not allowed to require that majors have a minimum GPA. (I imagine administrators saying: "They've got to major in something—and they *speak* English.") So for the most part, we get the very worst students: students with GPAs of 2.0 or lower. (I shudder to think what their SATs must have been.) They are students, moreover, with no interest in either literature or literary criticism—much like those administrators. They have other, primarily visual means of identification and escape. Other means of becoming sufficiently imbued with otherness. One such major, for example, began my seminar on Modernism, but then changed his mind.

"I don't like to read," he explained. "What should I take instead?" I recommended our course on the haiku, or maybe the one on epigrams. Another student, in my seminar on criticism, turned in a paper (on Gilbert and Gubar) that began: "Feminists believe that women should reap what they sew." "Don't you mean, 'sew what they *rip*'?" I commented. A student in my seminar on confession—very PC—turned in a paper (on *Portnoy's Complaint*) that began: "Every mother wants what's best for his or her son." "This is so wrong and on so many levels," I wrote, "that I don't even know where to begin." As you can tell, my main way of dealing with this ridiculous situation—with these students, that is—used to involve both (verbal) irony and sarcasm. Not always, though. A student in my seminar on creative nonfiction—an inarticulate senior about to go to law school—plagiarized a rather articulate essay on some baseball player. I found it on the Internet in about two seconds. "You probably didn't *intend* to lie and steal," I wrote—invoking that *doxa* about pleasing teachers. "You probably didn't know how to do the assignment. In that case, you should have come to see me." He then did see me—and was incredibly belligerent. He was contemptuous, in fact.

Irony and sarcasm, of course, did nothing for me in the long run. Nor did they do anything for students—students, I decided, who really need not seminars but lectures. They need to be informed, truly informed—not to have fake conversations on subjects about which they know next to nothing with some middle-aged professor dumbing down the material and pretending to be their friend. I'm practically fifty.

There was just one problem. Well, there were three problems. It's not that I'm lazy. I'm simply not smart enough to improvise lectures. Nor do I have the kind of memory that would take. Nor do I have time to compose such things beforehand. *Love's Litany* (a lofty work) took me two years to write. So did *Beethoven's Kiss* (pedestrian). So did *Sedaris* (both lofty and pedestrian). So did my two books in between, one of them on Elizabeth Bishop and the other—in a way—on Jean-Georges Noverre. (Work in progress includes poetry on Niles Crane and Sviatoslav Richter—a Heinrich Neuhaus student. By "poetry," though, I mean limericks—as you'll see.) At that rate, it would take me twenty years per course. And so—like most academics, perhaps—I now "rhapsodize" aloud. I play, I mean I perform, I mean I *recite* other writers' work. I do so, however, without actually naming them. I do so, that is, without putting any such citation—or rather, any particular citation—within quotation marks. Of course, I do begin each course by telling students—in postmodern mode—that the lectures they're about to hear aren't very original. But they always seem to think they are—which, I must confess, is really my intent.

Which other writers? The list, I'm afraid, is far too long for me to name them all. Let's just say it includes Eve Sedgwick—but not D.A. Miller. It includes Jesse Matz (Jewish), a hunk who did give me the time of day at yet another conference and who—like both Jesse Green and Wayne Koestenbaum, not to mention David Sedaris (not Jewish)—reminds me of Steve. It also includes Vladimir Nabokov (not Jewish), whose own lectures (now published) were really written—and this is why I mention him—by Véra, his wife.

Have I, then, become Grover Cleveland? Will I do so? Perhaps. But it won't be because I'll have identified with him—not consciously. (It's Yom Kippur, the Day of Atonement. The rabbi stops the service, prostrates himself before the ark, and cries out, "Oh, Lord! I am *nothing*!" Moved by this demonstration, the cantor then prostrates himself and cries, "Oh, Lord! *I* am nothing!" And then some tailor, sitting in the very last row of the synagogue, cries, "I *too* am nothing!" The cantor turns to the rabbi and says, "So look who thinks he's nothing.") It'll be an irony of fate—if not a crisis of the self. For my conscious identifications—along with my classroom rhapsodies—will, I suspect, have remained constant. They'll still concern the various men—and women—I know who take my brothers' place. (No crisis.) And my father's place, of course—Scholes in particular. As for my unconscious identifications—well, really, who am I to say? Who, in other words, am I to read *myself* symptomatically?

Or rather, to read myself *that* symptomatically.

||||

After the *London Review of Books* (LRB), in May 2008, both published an earlier version of what you've just read (as "Confessions of a Plagiarist") and posted it on the Internet, a couple of things happened. But first let me say what did not happen. I did not get fired, despite the fact that someone in "exercise science" told our dean I should be. I did not get a call from Eve Sedgwick. Nor did I get one from D.A. Miller, who I've since discovered *is* Catholic. I did, however, get a call from Bob, who simply wanted to know where I found that paper (mahogany dresser, bottom drawer, under some other stuff) and to tell me he doesn't remember it having been very good. The so-called blogosphere, moreover, went berserk. But I won't quote any of that. I'll just say that although some people there took those "Confessions" to be not entirely truthful (which happens to be the case), more than a few—mean people, also anonymous—saw me as a deranged crack addict who despite these problems (both mental and physical) should really be punished. They also saw me—rather incoherently—as both self-hating and smug. But I'm neither, or at least not anymore. Another thing that happened is, LRB editors suggested I now review for them a novel by James Frey: the best-selling autobiographer whom Oprah Winfrey had in fact shamed—but later forgave—for being very untruthful. My first response was to suggest Sedaris for the job. But no, they wanted me. And so I accepted it, even knowing I might hate the book and thus have to break a promise—to myself—not to trash anyone anymore.

Well, I did hate the book. I did trash it, pretty much, shaming Frey not for having lied but among other things for having not been novelistic. This, I wrote, is really a film treatment. I then told him to read Salinger: both *Franny and Zooey*, as a model for what he seemed to want to write, and *Seymour: An Introduction*, for advice (from Seymour Glass to younger brother "Buddy") on how to write it:

> Do you know what you will be asked when you die? But let me tell you first what you won't be asked. You won't be asked if you were working on a wonderful, moving piece of writing when you died. You won't be asked if it was long or short, sad or funny, published or unpublished. You won't be asked if you were in good form or bad form while you were working on it. You won't even be asked if it was the one piece of writing you would have been working on if you had known your time would be up when it was finished—I think only poor Sören K. will get asked that. I'm so sure you'll get asked only two questions. *Were most of your stars out? Were you busy writing your heart out?*

But they were too "square," said one editor, to publish me now—by which she probably meant that like those bloggers *I* was being mean, too mean, even, for the LRB. If so, of course, she was right. And so the question now is: why *did* I break such a promise to myself? Why, indeed, would anyone?

Hatchet Job

"Listen, listen!" Kalganov was really bubbling over, "even if Maximov is lying—and he lies all the time—he's lying so as to give pleasure to us all: that's not mean, is it?"

—FYODOR DOSTOEVSKY, *The Brothers Karamazov*

All we want from celebrities, when encountered, is what we want from people both known and loved: some parent or sibling, perhaps, some teacher or classmate. We want to be looked at—looked back at, rather, both literally and figuratively. We ourselves would be if not admired then at least recognized. (What the celebrities want, other than to be left alone, I couldn't say. But when I finally met David Sedaris, after doing that book on him, he seemed to want a friend. And when years before that I met an older such writer—Charles Rosen—he seemed, in part, to want a son.) Of course when *not* recognized by celebrities, in person, we rarely act out—for fear of seeming foolish. But when not recognized—as writers ourselves—by *literary* celebrities, whether in person or in print, we do act out, and viciously. We trash them as people, on blogs, which just happened to me. We trash their work in book reviews, which I myself did to James Frey. Oddly enough, though, and even more shamefully, such acting out in reviews can also occur when we *have* been recognized, which I, as you'll see, once did to Rosen.

As a New Yorker, of course, I used to see lots of celebrities—maybe as many as I'd have in Frey's Los Angeles. I saw Marvin Hamlisch once, on Fifth Avenue, shortly after *A Chorus Line* opened. He, however, did not see me. (Hamlisch and I, by the way, share a teacher: Frances Goldstein, who—while chain-smoking—taught music theory at Juilliard. "She was the best," he's said of her. "I answered all the questions perfectly because I had perfect pitch and a great ear, but she decided that I had to know the reasons why I knew the answers.") I saw Christopher Reeve—another Juilliard graduate—on Central Park West, shortly after *Superman* opened. Nor did he see me. I saw Lauren Bacall in the Vivian Beaumont Theater, sitting across the aisle—though I don't recall the play. Nor did she see me. I saw Gavin MacLeod (Murray, on *The Mary Tyler Moore Show*) in Alice Tully Hall—or rather the men's room there. (I don't recall the concert.) I saw Aaron Copland—unlike Hamlisch, a great composer—in it as well, but on a different occasion. I saw Cleavon Little, the star of *Blazing Saddles*, in some Manhattan shoe store. (I'd grown up—in Queens—around the corner from Madeline Kahn, his costar, but without ever seeing her.) I saw John Malkovich on Fifty-Ninth Street. Nor did he see me. I saw Liza here as well—Minnelli—but, once again, on a different occasion. She, at last, did see me. So when I later happened to find Julie Hagerty—the star of *Airplane*—on the subway, talking to a friend, I actually interrupted a conversation they were having to ask if she, in fact, was Julie Hagerty. She looked alarmed, sized me up, must have seen I'm not a stalker, and then said yes. "Well," I lied, "I love your work." And when at some dinner party I met Colleen Dewhurst—unlike Hagerty, a great actress—I took the liberty of monopolizing or rather of mesmerizing her (as she was kind enough to let me think) with stories about myself.

But my first and—for the purposes of this story—most symbolic such encounter was at Harvard, where I didn't even know the guy. The year was 1968—when I was eight. The occasion was my brother Bob's graduation and in particular a post-graduation reception in Kirkland House, where he lived. My mindset—as was usual back then—was shy, pathologically shy. My body was oversized. And so my brother Steve and I—he was ten, and thin—had just had a lot of cookies, no doubt too many. Steve wandered off somewhere. (Shades of things to come, when—in the end—he wandered off to Israel.) And then my parents noticed John Glenn, who apparently was some kind of astronaut. (What Glenn was doing there, I haven't been able to determine. Perhaps he'd just gotten an honorary degree. Perhaps his own son—David—had just gotten a real one.) Would Mr. Glenn, my father asked, mind having his picture taken with me? (No one asked did I mind.) No, he wouldn't. And so I was told to stand over here—no, *here*, next to Mr. Glenn—who then said something kind, no doubt, to which, being shy, I couldn't respond. The picture was taken. And then, tossing those cookies, I vomited on the man.

| | |

Charles Rosen was my first "such writer," the first literary celebrity I not only met but also came to know. He was also, apart from Bob, the first great pianist. The year was 1991, when I was thirty-one and Rosen about sixty-five. The location was Manhattan, for although I had just gotten my PhD in English from Brown and also—with Eve Sedgwick's help—my book contract from Stanford, I'd not gotten a tenure-track job anywhere. And so I'd moved back home, or nearly home: over a river—the so-called East River—and through some buildings.

My apartment, over by the Museum of Natural History, was tiny—with almost no room for the piano: a Mason & Hamlin grand. My employment—apart from the work of revision, for Stanford—was catch as catch can: part-time work at the second of my two law firms; part-time nanny work for an associate there; teaching "lesbian and gay studies," as it was still called, at the New School over by NYU; making deposits at a sperm bank, about which more later in the chapter "G712." My body size—as Steve's had been—was now thin, post-anorexia thin. My mindset, despite the book contract, was both anxious and depressed—clinically depressed. For I didn't know I'd ever get any tenure-track job. And, too, a ten-year relationship with someone my age—about whom more later in various chapters—was falling apart. Neither Warren nor I, I'd joke—I'll call him "Warren"—turned out to be the other's idea of a top. (Too effeminate, among other things.) Neither of us, moreover, was the other's idea of a bottom.

It was a friend my age who, knowing Rosen, offered the introduction. "Maximov," as I'll call him, was someone with red hair and maroon eyes whom I'd met at a conference. (Not hunky—like D.A. Miller or Jesse Matz—but very handsome.) Rosen, I'd told him, was someone whose writing I very much admired. Here, for example, is something from *The Classical Style*—for which Rosen won a National Book Award. It's on Schumann quoting Beethoven—or rather, on Schumann doing something Romantic to a song of his:

> Robert Schumann's homage to Beethoven, the Fantasy in C Major, opus 17, is the monument that commemorates the death of the classical style. The beginning of the last song of Beethoven's cycle *An die ferne Geliebte* (a setting of the words "Take these songs then, my love, that I sang") is clearly quoted at the very end of the first movement of Schumann's work but also hinted at throughout the movement. Nevertheless, in all significant respects of structure and detail the Schumann Fantasy

is totally unclassical: even the appearance of Beethoven's melody is itself unclassi-
cal by its reference to a personal and completely private significance exterior to the
work—the words of the Beethoven phrase are surely present for Schumann as an
autobiographical reference—and by its exposition of the definitive and basic form
of the main thematic material only at the last moment.

Schumann's music, by the way, is present for *me* here as an "autobiographical
reference." Bob played that Fantasy when I was very young; nowadays I do.
Or to be honest, I play the outer, easier two movements. At any rate, here's
something else by Rosen, from *The Romantic Generation*. It's on Liszt doing
something showy:

> What Liszt's technical innovations enabled him to achieve were not only
> new kinds of piano sound but layers of contrasting sound. His arrangement of
> Schubert's "Der Lindenbaum," for example, in the last stanza presents the theme
> in the right hand in octaves simultaneously above and below a steady, delicate
> trill, which gives a continuously vibrant sonority, while the left hand imitates a
> *pizzicato* bass and, at the same time, realizes Schubert's simple flowing accom-
> paniment as if it were performed by a trio of French Horns. This is, one must
> confess, rather an awful thing to do to a Schubert song, but it would be churlish
> to refuse one's admiration for the grandeur and richness of the conception—or
> for the pianist who can play it and make it sound as vulgarly beautiful as it was
> intended—particularly the spectacular passage where the trill is transferred to
> the fourth and fifth fingers and the accompanying triplets must be played with
> the thumb and the melody by the left hand. To comprehend Liszt's greatness
> one needs a suspension of distaste, a momentary renunciation of scruples.

Rosen himself, of course—as I myself was about to hear—is one such pianist.
He's the kind who can play such Liszt almost to perfection.

Maximov knew Rosen from the *New York Review of Books*, where—after
working at *The Nation*—my friend had been an editorial assistant and *his* friend
a contributor. Rosen then helped Maximov get into Princeton. (The latter's
dissertation would concern "Seduction in Dostoevsky." The former had writ-
ten one there—in 1951—on "Morality in La Fontaine.") Maximov—although
no musician—stayed in touch. And Rosen, I imagine, must have encouraged
such contact for the same reason I did: Maximov is both handsome and clever.
He claimed, for example, to have seen graffiti at Princeton that read, in one
handwriting, "Desire is imitative" and then in another "I wish *I'd* said that."

The joke's on Sedgwick. He also claimed to have overheard Cynthia Ozick—at some symposium there—tell Toni Morrison: "Here comes Joyce Carol Oates, the three worst writers in America." These were lies, of course.

Katha Pollitt, by the way—a feminist I love—has written of Maximov in both the *New Yorker* and her book *Learning to Drive*: "When I was a magazine editor, I had an assistant who lied all the time. Once, on a slow spring day, he called up the NYU Jewish student center, pretended to be a British Jew stranded in New York, and wangled an invitation to its seder. Finally, he went too far, insisting that he had checked the price of a book on Buddhism we had reviewed in the previous issue, and it really was $18.03. 'I thought it was odd, too,' he mused. 'It must be a Zen thing.' By the time I worked up the courage to fire him, he had already talked his way into a much better job, and somehow arranged it that his new employers never called me for a reference. Some people just land on their feet." A feminist I hate—Camille Paglia—has called Pollitt, on the Internet, a "whiny troll, an unscrupulous and unreliable critic and a cultural philistine. She's a good example of the phony prep-school / trust-fund leftism suffusing the incestuously intertwined Ivy League cliques who run the corrupt East Coast literary and magazine establishment." Paglia—with all her fame, or notoriety, and even a *Yale* PhD, also in English—teaches at "The University of the Arts" in Philadelphia. Paglia, moreover, is Catholic, and Pollitt Jewish.

At any rate, Maximov picked me up at home, in my apartment, and then walked me up to Rosen's—just three blocks north. The writer in person, I remember thinking, looked avuncular: a bit tubby and somewhat bald. Nice blue eyes, though. He looked, in fact, like an uncle of mine who died when I was ten. (Uncle Lou himself was just fifty.) The apartment—a large one—looked a mess. There were books everywhere. There was music everywhere. There was food everywhere as well. "How can he *live* like this?" I wondered. "How can he *work* here?" Yet there it was: Rosen's desk. And there—the eye of this domestic storm—was his own grand: a Steinway.

I can't recall anything the three of us actually said that day, nor even what we talked about. I do, however, remember Rosen playing Chopin. "Perfect," I thought. For—to coin a phrase—it was love at first audition.

And then I played Chopin.

And then Maximov played "Chopsticks."

Chopin vs. "Chopsticks"—I should mention, here, the no doubt wishful thinking behind this story. This whole book, rather. It's not, you'll find, so much compare-and-contrast as . . . well, let me quote *Roland Barthes by Roland Barthes*:

> Everything seems to suggest that his discourse proceeds according to a two-term dialectic: popular opinion and its contrary, *Doxa* and its paradox, the stereotype and the novation, fatigue and freshness, relish and disgust: *I like / I don't like.* This binary dialectic is the dialectic of meaning itself (*marked / not marked*) and of the Freudian game the child plays (*Fort / Da*): the dialectic of value.
>
> Yet is this quite true? In him, another dialectic appears, trying to find expression: the contradiction of the terms yields in his eyes by the discovery of a third term, which is not a synthesis but a *translation*: everything comes back, but it comes back as Fiction, i.e., at another turn of the spiral.

Anyway, I now began seeing Rosen by myself—maybe once every few weeks, usually in the afternoon. Rosen might play more Chopin. Or he'd tell me about Josef Hofmann, explaining that pianist's technique, and then play recordings. (He first heard Hofmann at three. It, too, had been love at first audition, which I could understand. For I, too, now loved Hofmann—who by the way never had to practice.) Or he'd tell me about Maria Callas, explaining the singer's intelligence, and then once again play recordings. (He first heard Callas at twenty-three. It, too, had been love at first audition, which I could *not* understand. In fact, I've always hated Callas, something I of course kept to myself at the time.) Or we'd try duets, with me on top—playing *primo*. (*Secondo* pedals, making the part more difficult.) Some of these were easy, and at any rate I'd done them before with Bob. Others, though, were much too hard. "But you can do this, Kevin," Rosen might prompt.

This—"one must confess"—was rather intoxicating. No such celebrity, literary or otherwise apart from Colleen, had ever paid me such attention. But—like that love of Callas—I couldn't fathom it. Rosen, unlike Sedgwick, had never read anything I'd written (or claimed to have written). Nor could I—in person—tell him anything he didn't already know. (Unless we're talking gay studies, which the two of us never did.) Nor—being depressed—could I have been clever. My playing, like that of Maximov, was what it was—despite any such prompting. Maybe, I surmised, Rosen felt sorry for me. Maybe I reminded him of someone. Some nephew, perhaps. Or maybe he felt not so much avuncular as paternal. (Rosen—like me—was childless.) Or maybe he needed the company. For whereas Rosen, like me, did have a partner—some French professor, according to Maximov—the man was at Harvard.

Well, I did get a tenure-track job—in 1992, here in Iowa. This was not, how-ever, with our Writers' Workshop. It was with the English Department. (The two, though, were administered as one.) So I moved from New York City to Iowa City, at which point—reasonably enough—Warren dumped me. (Despite the name, Iowa "City" is in fact not one. It's a college town.) Then my father died—at seventy, back in Queens. I taught one somewhat dialectical course on James Joyce (vs. Virginia Woolf) and then another on Oscar Wilde (vs. Woody Allen). Stanford published *Love's Litany*, but, in part because Dad hadn't lived to see it, the thing felt dead to me. So I wrote a second book, *Beethoven's Kiss: Pianism, Perversion, and the Mastery of Desire*—sans Warren, this time, but more to the point sans anyone. In other words, to quote Freud, I was "sublimat-ing"—sublimating, moreover, like crazy.

Beethoven's Kiss, a reference to a so-called consecration of Liszt, is more "di-alogical," as scholars say, meaning conversational, than dialectic. (The year was 1822. Liszt was eleven, Beethoven about fifty—not much further apart in age than Rosen and I, just a bit less than Uncle Lou and I. Beethoven, supposedly, heard the boy play and then embraced him. It too was love at first audition—but of course the man, by now, was deaf.) I do have a chapter there on Roland Barthes vs. André Gide, both amateurs. I have one, too, on Artur Rubinstein vs. Vladimir Horowitz, both professionals. But I'm responsive throughout—conversationally speaking—to *The Queen's Throat: Opera, Homosexuality, and the Mystery of Desire* by Wayne. (He, by the way, is just two years older than I—Steve's age—as are both Jesse Green and David Sedaris. He too, moreover, plays piano.) I love that book, as well as Wayne himself. So I wrote some very nice things about him. I also—in a section of *Beethoven's Kiss* on sublimation—wrote something nice about Rosen:

> Many of us prefer the serious music Liszt wrote when celibate to the pyrotech-nical music he wrote when dissolute. And the few of us who don't, know what we're up against—elitist (or envious) devaluation of musical virtuosity. To quote Charles Rosen, a serious musician with technique to burn: "I've always thought him a very great composer, but I have, I must say, very odd taste in Liszt. The fashion nowadays is to like the very late pieces, the strange experimental pieces. But I prefer the early."

But then I did something awful. Something churlish. Something unscrupu-lous. Something *mean*, in fact—like that Frey review. Stanford—to which I'd submitted *Beethoven's Kiss*—had asked musicologist Lawrence Kramer for a reader's report. They'd also asked Philip Brett, who—like Jon Bailey and Craig Monson—had been a friend of Bob's at Berkeley. Both Kramer and Brett, not surprisingly, recommended publication. Kramer, moreover, asked me to review *The Queen's Throat* in a journal he now ran: *Nineteenth-Century Music*. I knew, of course, that I didn't want to be at all negative about *Wayne*. I also knew how "performative" he is. (By *performative*, here, I mean his work both says and does things to readers—different things, in fact, to different readers. The word can also mean both saying and showing things, novelistically, as with all the quotes in "My Cortez"—the Salinger two in particular. Put together, they show—I hope—that unlike most public confessors I'd be telling about *several* so-called hamsters throughout this book, despite some lies, and also that I'd make it the one piece of writing in all the world I myself want to read.) So I cleverly decided to do symptomatic readings of *earlier* reviews—all but one of them hatchet jobs. (I also decided to call the thing "Tawdrily, I Adore Him"—a quote, in part, from Wayne. But he, like Rosen, adored *Callas*. By "symptomatic" here, as in "My Cortez," I simply mean Freudian—kind of like dream interpretation.) The positive one, I'm afraid, was by Rosen—who, for some reason, I imagined had never even heard of that journal. (In fact, I later learned, he'd published there: a 1980 article on—of all things—"Plagiarism and Inspiration" and a 1990 article on Chopin's "Funeral March" Sonata.) And even if he *had* heard of it, I didn't know I'd ever see him again.

Here's the first thing I wrote, on Rosen: that he's "somewhat misogynist." Or rather, that his written work is. For where Wayne simply suggests Mae West "thought like" a diva, Rosen, to quote his own review, finds:

> The diva, like Mae West, presents an erotic charge with no sexual threat. The coarseness of Mae West's verbal comedy, combined with the way her appearance both represents and distances an erotic invitation at the same time, allows the homosexual to approach female sexuality without fear of aggression. The cult of the diva offers him a similar and even greater freedom. The diva helps him escape the shame with which society has characterized his inadequate response to the female anatomy. At last he can find genuine passion for a woman, not merely as a mother or as a nanny, but as an erotic object, for the sexuality embodied—or disembodied—in her voice.

"Koestenbaum," I myself then comment, "shows no such sense of threat or fear of aggression."

Worse yet, here's the second thing on Rosen: that he himself is rather effeminate. For where Wayne, I wrote, suggests we identify with both stars who remind us of the "successful selves" we'd like to be and ones who remind us of our truly *un*-successful selves, Rosen doesn't see himself as such—or as a failure. And so, to again quote his review, he finds that although Wayne writes well about Callas' faults, he doesn't "sufficiently acknowledge her purely musical intelligence." Nor does he "remark about what two conductors have told me—that she had an uncanny ability to take account of the orchestra and alter the timbre of her notes according to the accompanying harmony." "Personally," I myself then comment, "I'd rather read about those faults, because I've had it up to here with intimidating queens who prattle about her intelligence. And as long as I'm ranting, how could Koestenbaum comment on something Rosen himself had to be told?"

I'm not sure why—in effect vomiting on him—I did such a thing. Or I'm not completely sure. I do know that it's always fun to trash—to top, that is—writing you either can't or won't fathom on its own terms. Just ask Camille. (The critic Wayne Booth, incidentally, has written "A Hippocratic Oath for the Pluralist" worth quoting here: "Article I: 'I will publish nothing, favorable or unfavorable, about books or articles I have not read through at least once.' Article II: 'I will *try* to publish nothing about any book or article until I have *understood* it, which is to say, until I have reason to think that I can give an account of it that the author himself will recognize as just.'") That's the main reason why journals like the LRB or NYRB or worse yet the *Times Literary Supplement*—an autobiographical reference I don't yet care to explain—are filled with hatchet jobs. But maybe, to quote both Freud and Barthes, my repressed hatred of Callas couldn't help but return at that particular turn of the spiral. Or maybe—more likely—I was displacing any aggression I might otherwise have directed at Wayne. Call it an envious devaluation of Rosen's virtuosity—his critical virtuosity—in lieu of any such devaluation of Wayne. Or maybe, more likely yet, I was wrong to have associated Rosen with Uncle Lou who at any rate—like D.A. Miller—played not the piano but the accordion. (See his *Place for Us: Essay on the Broadway Musical*.) For just as Wayne reminds me of Steve or rather of the brother I wish Steve had been, Rosen—I now realize—reminds me, in fact, of Bob. Or rather of the musician that I imagine Bob should have remained. If only he'd finished his own PhD, in musicology. Or if only—no Hofmann, as I was starting to realize—he'd ever really practiced.

| | |

The one Writers' Workshop member I'd ever heard of, upon my arrival, was someone I'll call "Becky Thatcher." She'd been famous for the novel I'll call *Home Wrecking*. That, though, had been published more than ten years earlier. *Balm*, for which she's won a Pulitzer Prize, wouldn't appear until more than ten years later, and there'd be nothing else in between. I soon met Thatcher at a dinner party, where she argued that the Spanish Inquisition—even with all its let's just say *coerced* confession—wasn't all that bad. There are, I confess, other such characters throughout the rest of this chapter as well as book—much like "Betty Boop" and "Grover Cleveland" in the chapter "My Cortez." For I've found it very hard—impossible, in fact—not to attempt to disguise and then trash such people: the people themselves, that is, along with their work.

But other members were less productive. Workshop director "Tom Sawyer," for example, hadn't published anything since the memoir I'll call *Freeze Frame* back in the sixties. His novel *Hawk Eyes*—about a brilliant pianist improbably based on Sawyer himself—wouldn't appear until the following year. I didn't get it. The school didn't make these people *teach* much. But I then learned—at another dinner party—just how much they drank. Sawyer—our host—in particular. Not Thatcher, though, as she's Mormon.

I first met "Emmeline Grangerford"—another workshop member—at that second party, and she, like Sawyer, was intoxicated. (Grangerford, unlike Thatcher, is Jewish. As is Rosen. As is Maximov. As am I, of course. Warren, however, is not. And I've never been sure about Sawyer.) Unlike both Thatcher and Sawyer, however, Grangerford is productive. But her work could be thought of as a more, or maybe less, pretentious, postmodern version of stuff done by her namesake in *Huckleberry Finn*:

And did young Stephen sicken,
   And did young Stephen die?
And did the sad hearts thicken,
   And did the mourners cry?

No, such was not the fate of
   Young Stephen Dowling Bots;
Though sad hearts round him thickened,
   'Twas not from sickness' shots.

No whooping-cough did rack his frame,
    Nor measles drear, with spots;
Not these impaired the sacred name
    Of Stephen Dowling Bots.

Despised love struck not with woe
    That head of curly knots,
Nor stomach troubles laid him low,
    Young Stephen Dowling Bots.

O no. Then list with tearful eye,
    Whilst I his fate do tell.
His soul did from this cold world fly,
    By falling down a well.

Then again, I admit I can't understand (and thus stand) most postmodern poetry. As you might have inferred, from "My Cortez," my own taste runs more to Keats and Bishop—Elizabeth Bishop. Also to Yeats. And also to Robert Hass. And also to Richard Howard. This is not to say such poetry—like atonal music, which I both understand and loathe—couldn't possibly be a scam. For as a music major at Yale, I learned both tonal and atonal composition. On one exam, I had just twenty minutes to turn a twelve-tone row into a thirty-two bar etude. I figured out the various permutations and then just flung them at the page. I had no time to try the thing out at a keyboard and so had no idea what it sounded like—nor even if it was at all playable. I got an "A." My roommate at the time—a biochemistry major with whom I'd also gone to Bronx Science—had a similar experience in a class on poetry. He turned in something that read like he'd put "The Waste Land" in a blender—which happens to be pretty much what he did, as an experiment—and got an "A."

At any rate, Grangerford—thereafter—didn't remember me at all. For I'd see her again and again—mostly at meetings, sometimes at readings—and each time have to be reintroduced. I found this amusing at first. But then—my own vanity wounded—I found it insulting. So insulting, in fact, that—once again—I did something mean.

The year was 1996. "Jessie Weston," as I'll call her—a Harvard professor who'd first discovered Grangerford—was in town to receive a "Daddy" Warbucks Award. The award—in the amount of my then annual salary—was administered by the workshop and would usually be given to writers, whether academic or not, who, well, either were or might become close to Grangerford. At any rate, I ran into the two of them in Prairie Lights—a local bookstore—the afternoon of the presentation. "Hi, there!" I said cheerfully. Grangerford stared at me, said nothing, and then turned back to Weston. "You know, Emmeline," I said less than cheerfully—and probably because I both recognized Weston and could sense how much she just loved Grangerford—"you do know me. We've been introduced about twenty times. And we're in the same department." Or to be totally honest—fool that I am—I said "the same *fucking* department." And then I walked away.

That was fun—almost as fun as writing hatchet jobs. But I did wonder what would happen the next time I saw Grangerford, which—oddly enough—wasn't until almost two years later. In the meantime, she herself had won a Pulitzer. I'd been given a sabbatical for work—in France—on Proust. Having just taken a flight back from Paris to Chicago and then boarded one to Cedar Rapids—Iowa City, of course, doesn't even *have* an airport—I noticed Grangerford walking down the aisle. "Oh no," I panicked. "What if she's next to me?" And then she did, in fact, take that seat—sliding herself down there, like some Proust in my own prose, but as usual with no recognition of our having ever met let alone my having tried to shame her.

So I greeted her—"Hi, there!"—prattled about "our" department, pretended we were the best of friends, which she then did too, and showed considerable interest in what Grangerford herself, it turned out, had been up to in France. Well, after she got that Pulitzer, Issey Miyake had flown her over on the Concorde to sniff some new perfume he'd made and then come up with a name for it. (Marianne Moore—Bishop's mentor—had done more or less the same for Ford Motor Company.) Having already used, for prior scents, the self-referential names *L'eau d'Issey* and *Le feu d'Issey*, he now wanted something similar but different from this now world-famous poet. So far, though, he hadn't liked any of Grangerford's suggestions, all of which she proceeded to tell me. They were in French. I then made a few of my own, none of which she liked. "How about *Les jeunes filles en fleurs*?" I asked. "How about *Volupté*?" (I was thinking of a line from "*L'Invitation au voyage*"—"*luxe, calme, et volupté*"—but I knew this Baudelaire only from a song setting by Duparc, much as in "My Cortez" I'd known his "*mon semblable, mon frère*" only from its citation, by T.S. Eliot, in "The Waste Land." It's really from "*Au lecteur*"—"To the Reader"—in *Les Fleurs du mal*.) And then, thinking of Revlon's perfume *Charlie*, and also wanting to be clever, wanting, that is, something clever to later report to others, I made one she loved. "How about . . . *Emmeline*."

After that, she didn't really bother me. I soon learned, however, that Grangerford had mistreated a student of my own. Brown-haired, blue-eyed "Pushkin," as I'll call him, had been in my undergrad class on Joyce. He, too—like Maximov—was both handsome and clever. He's brilliant, too, and also rather campy. One time, over some meal, I'd offered him the salt. "No thank you," he replied. "I don't care for that *particular* spice." This reminded me of the novelist Ronald Firbank, a contemporary of both Joyce and Woolf who uses italics both to be suggestive and to indicate citation—but of no source in particular. (See, for instance, Firbank's *Flower beneath the Foot*, where the Countess of Tolga gives the Queen of Pisuerga "a glance that was known in Court circles as her *tortured-animal* look.") A few years after graduation, Pushkin entered the Writers' Workshop. Having, I'm afraid, now forgotten exactly what Grangerford did to him there, I sent for clarification via e-mail. This is his response:

> So many young students idolized Emmeline (I was one of them) only to be crushed when she decided to later ignore them. Essentially, I felt she built me up only to cast me aside on a whim. Also, read [So-and-So's] reviews of her books—when a particularly scathing review of his was published in the *New York Times*, she ran to Prairie Lights to purchase all of the copies so that none of us would see it.

But when "Confessions of a Plagiarist" appeared in the LRB—one must confess—I, too, ran to Prairie Lights to buy all the copies, and for pretty much the same reason Grangerford had.

Now I know, dear reader, what you're thinking—if that is you, like Pushkin, in fact, could appreciate even some of Grangerford's work. You're thinking: Who cares if she hurt a young poet? Or you're thinking something along the lines of what Yeats in the poem "The Choice" probably meant by:

> The intellect of man is forced to choose
> Perfection of the life, or of the work,
> And if it take the second must refuse
> A heavenly mansion, raging in the dark.
> When all that story's finished, what's the news?
> In luck or out the toil has left its mark:
> That old perplexity an empty purse,
> Or the day's vanity, the night's remorse.

Or you're thinking of what Nietzsche in *Human, All Too Human* did mean by:

The ceaseless desire to create on the part of the artist, together with his cease-
less observation of the world outside him, prevent him from becoming better
and more beautiful as a person, that is to say from creating *himself*—except,
that is, if his self-respect is sufficiently great to compel him to exhibit himself
before others as being as great and beautiful as his works increasingly are. In
any event, he possesses only a fixed quantity of strength: that of it which he
expends upon *himself*—how could he at the same time expend it on his *work*?—
and the reverse.

Well, you should care. Because unless a writer, like Nietzsche, does in fact have
some personality disorder, *not* including that of pathological liar, unless that is
he or she's *nuts*, there's no reason—I now realize—for him or her not to be as
good a person, not to be as kind as, say, Rosen.

| | |

One year after that airborne *Emmeline* pitch of mine, it was Rosen's turn—for
his book on "poets and other madmen"—to get a "Daddy" award. I thought I
should probably call him, see if he'd want to meet me when he arrived in Iowa.
But then, once again, I panicked. What, I wondered, if he *has* read that review
of mine in *Nineteenth-Century Music*? So I didn't call, planning instead to just
play it by ear.

I myself got a call the morning of the presentation. It was some workshop
secretary. Would I care to have dinner tonight, at Sawyer's? "Rosen, of course,
will be the guest of honor and might like meeting you. He's probably read *Kiss-
ing Beethoven*, or at least heard of it. Oh, you know him! So why don't you take
him from the Old Capitol building over to Clapp Recital Hall? He'll be doing a
concert there. Then you could walk him up to the house. Thanks."

Well, I couldn't say no—but not because I, too, felt honored. Despite that
panic, I simply wanted to share the spotlight—as what mere scholar, with no pop-
ular audience, would not? So I put on my cha-cha heels, so to speak, and—after
teaching—headed over to the Old Capitol. Sawyer, even without such heels,
staggered there over to the podium. Clearly somewhat drunk, and also clearly
not knowing who Rosen is, he went on and on about his own alleged musician-
ship. When he finally managed to present the award, Rosen—not knowing who
Sawyer was—improvised a brief acceptance speech the transcript of which, un-
fortunately, seems to have been lost. I then congratulated Rosen, who—much to
my relief—seemed very glad to see me. So, I thought, he *hasn't* read my review.

The walk to Clapp was over a river—the Iowa River—and through some trees. Walking there together—*nous allons marcher ensemble*—I told Rosen what I knew about Sawyer. I also told him about Maximov, whom I'd finally worked up the courage to dump. (The lying—the meanness, in fact—got completely out of control. He'd told Warren, who told me, that I'd been sleeping with students. Maximov put this cleverly of course—a line I don't care to transcribe—but who cares. Slander is slander.) Then we both spoke of work—his books, my books. (He had heard of—but not yet read—*Beethoven's Kiss*. I'd send him a copy. He'd not heard of the one after that, on both Jean-Georges Noverre and Vaslav Nijinsky.) We spoke of his recordings, too, including one of the "Funeral March" Sonata. It felt great, catching up after all this time—eight years—and doing so, moreover— he was kind enough to let me think—as equals. It also felt great, one must confess, to be sharing this spotlight. For everyone in that hall—the entire workshop as well as many from both my own department and that of music—could now see the two of us entering, chatting away, and then sitting down together.

We were still chatting when, as lights dimmed, Rosen suddenly changed the subject and said: "You know, Kevin, you did a terrible thing to me in that book review." (He meant, of course, my having called his written work—unlike Koestenbaum's—"misogynist" and the man himself a "queen.") This, of course, felt horrible. In response, I may have spluttered something about either the return of the repressed or displaced aggression. Who knows. All I do know, all I did know was that Rosen was already walking away—alone. Walking over, that is, to the piano.

Needless to say, I couldn't focus on—and so nor do I recall—what he played. Clearly, I told myself, Rosen hasn't taken such behavior of mine—such a hatchet job—at all personally. (Rosen is not, in fact, effeminate. Nor is his work misogynist.) Clearly, he's known that someone—he in particular—had to make me stop it. (On the other hand, I now realize, Rosen's decision to shame me may have been a last minute decision. Maybe he, too, was playing it by ear.) Clearly, this had to be done both paternally and in person—or he himself would have called. Or sent a letter. Or—worse yet—e-mail. Clearly, too, he could see—or if not see, sense—that I'll never do such a thing again. Not to anyone—neither friend nor foe.

Nor have I ever, in line with that oath. ("I will publish nothing, favorable or unfavorable, about books or articles I have not read through at least once," writes Booth. "I will *try* to publish nothing about any book or article until I have *understood* it.") Or to be totally honest, I'll have only ever done so twice. No, three times—come to think of it. Make that four. First, when the LRB published something ignorant by Edward Said, the author of *Oriental-ism*, I dashed off—via e-mail—the following rant: "Said claims that illness prevented J.S. Bach from concluding the last piece in *The Art of Fugue*. If this literary critic knew as much about music as he pretends to, he'd know that you can't compose a quadruple fugue without writing the ending first, and that the 'missing' final page of Bach's final work, a self-inscribed musi-cal epitaph Busoni re-created in his *Fantasia Contrappuntistica*, must have been misplaced—probably by one of the composer's sons." This, too, was pub-lished—but with the *ad hominem* against Said removed by some editor. Ironi-cally enough, I was castigating him for not knowing something I myself had to be told by music theorist Thomas Christensen. I'd also had to be told by him about the Busoni.

I'll discuss the second time—a review of the book *Decadence and Catholi-cism*—in the chapter "Kiss and Tell."

The third time was that James Frey review.

The fourth, in yet another "performative," is what I'm now doing to—or showing about—myself.

At any rate, the walk to Sawyer's was up a very long hill. (Iowa, contrary to popular opinion, isn't all flat.) Rosen, of course, did not pick up where we'd left off. And so nor did I, despite the fact that an apology for that book review—clearly—was now in order. Instead, I described the house and also the scene we might find there: something intimate, no doubt, maybe even something interesting. I was mistaken. We found no one from the music department nor anyone else from English. We did, however, find workshop members, all of them, workshop students, all of them, even workshop administrators—all but the secretary who'd called. Also in attendance, for some reason, was United States Poet Laureate Robert Hass.

Sawyer, now thoroughly drunk, took a while to greet us. He invited Rosen alone, come dinnertime, to sit with him at the main table in the living room. A much smaller table—at which, presumably, I along with other nonentities would be placed—had been set in the dining room. Sawyer then handed us off to Thatcher, who, after introducing herself to Rosen, was still—I seem to recall—prattling about the Inquisition. Thatcher handed us off to Grangerford, who after not introducing herself said she had to leave now. Something more important had come up. Then she did leave. Hass came over, introducing him-self both to Rosen and to me.

Dinner, Sawyer announced, is served. Rosen, Hass, and I hung back as others rushed to the main table for what looked—but of course didn't sound—like a game of musical chairs.

Hass, clearly, would have liked to talk to Rosen. But he's too kind, too considerate to ignore students now clamoring—in the dining room—for his own attention. This, of course, left Rosen to me, which seemed fine by Rosen. I was the only one there he knew. And apart from Hass, I seemed to be the only one to know who he is. Unfortunately, though, it turned out that Grangerford *did* know, for—much like Alcibiades stalking Socrates at Agathon's—she then rushed back, burst into our room, and claimed that the "something more important" had just been cancelled.

I found this amusing. But now—and I swear this is true—she literally pushed me off my chair. This, of course, I found infuriating. I got another chair, shoved it between them, like some Proust quote, and sat there. Grangerford ignored me. Did he know, Grangerford began, addressing only Rosen, that tempo markings throughout Europe—prior to the invention of the metronome—used to be given *wildly* different interpretations? Rosen suggested this is nonsense. All professional musicians, no matter where, used to know exactly what an *andante* or *presto* meant. No, Grangerford insisted, it's like pitch. The A above middle C, back then, could be tuned to 450 hertz in, say, Beauvais but to 380 in *Torino*. (Grangerford—like Bob—does in fact say *Torino*, not Turin.) Or it's like pronunciation. Some word in French—I can't recall which one Grangerford used, but let's say *volupté*—would have been pronounced a certain way in southern France and another in the north. Rosen suggested various problems with this analogy. Well, then, did he know the late Beethoven piano sonata in B?

"There is no such sonata," I interjected, starting rather meanly to write a review I mean to cause a scene to which Hass—students be damned—was now particularly attentive. "There's opus 101 in A, opus 106 in B-flat (the 'Hammerklavier'), 109 in E, 110 in A-flat, and 111 in C."

C *minor*, I meant. Hopefully, though, Rosen's impressed. Hass too.

"No," Grangerford insists—now unable to ignore me. "There's one in B. I heard it last night—a recording I have by Richtman."

"That's *Richter*."

"Whatever."

"No, not 'whatever.' *Richter*. Sviatoslav *Richter*. There's no such pianist as 'Richtman.' And at any rate, there's no such sonata."

Grangerford turned to Rosen, hoping for confirmation.

"There *is* one," she insisted. "It ends with a fugue. In fact, I think the whole thing's called '*Big* Fugue.'"

"Oh, Emmeline," I crowed. "You're thinking of *Grosse Fuge*! And that's for string quartet, not piano. And anyway, it's not in B."

She was close, though. The key's B-flat.

"Kevin's right," said Rosen.

This, unfortunately, was too much for our seatmate—my poor tortured animal—to bear. So she got up, staggered over to the door, and once again, not glancing back, left—this time for good.

"Who," Rosen asked me, "was *that?*"

"That," I responded, "was 'Emmeline Grangerford.'"

As she'd won a Pulitzer, I assumed the name alone—unlike that of Tom Sawyer or even Becky Thatcher (unlike, that is, those of the people these represent)—must signify something to Rosen. She'd even appeared in the NYRB. Once again, though, I was mistaken.

"Who the *hell*," he asked, "is 'Emmeline Grangerford'?"

| | |

And that, I'm afraid, was the last time I saw either of them. Grangerford soon left for greener pastures. Rosen left the following morning for Manhattan, where I did send him *Beethoven's Kiss*. No response. I also sent "The Sonic Mirror," that essay of mine on *self*-audition: how pianists react to hearing themselves play. No response. I raved about *The Romantic Generation* in the LRB and then sent that as well. Still no response. Who knew why not, apart from my never having apologized—and also apart from Maximov's having perhaps lied to Rosen about me. Who knew, moreover, if he'd even read those things. Who, for that matter, knows if he'll ever read this one—this apology, in effect. Maximov might, of course—assuming Rosen hasn't dumped him. But even if Maximov does know—assuming I'd ever ask—who knows if he'd ever tell me the truth.

Why though, you may still be wondering, was I so mean to James Frey? He'd never, like Grangerford, failed to recognize me in person. Nor had he done so in print. Nor, like Rosen, had he ever paid attention to me. I now realize it's probably because—just as I'd trashed Rosen instead of Koestenbaum (both of them Callas fans, both of them Jewish)—I trashed the novelist instead of those nasty bloggers (all of them, like Frey, nearly illiterate, I thought, all of them idiots). And too, I thought, such a hatchet job—neither fair nor "square," to quote that editor again—was what the LRB must have wanted from me. Such journals, you see—and this is how any scholar thinks—are themselves celebrities. Or rather, they're the kind of celebrity who—like blurbers, supposedly—can make *us* famous. (Both Eve and Wayne, as you know, blurbed my first book, both Paul Reubens and David Hyde Pierce my last one.) So all we ever really want from them—and we'll do anything to get it—is attention. To get such attention, and to hold it.

Sometimes, though, journals do want—from us—what we think they want. The LRB, after all, had published what it called "Confessions of a Plagiarist"—which may or may not be good for me in the long run.

G712 (IDANT)

Then came adolescence—half my waking life spent locked behind the bathroom door, firing my wad down the toilet bowl, or into the soiled clothes in the laundry hamper, or *splat*, up against the medicine-chest mirror, before which I stood in my dropped drawers so I could see how it looked coming out. Or else I was doubled over my flying fist, eyes pressed closed but mouth wide open, to take that sticky sauce of buttermilk and Clorox on my own tongue and teeth.

—PHILIP ROTH, *Portnoy's Complaint*

The visual—barely even soft-core—pornography to which in youth I had access were ads, in the back of the magazine *Popular Science*, for bodybuilding. These, of course, showed white guys. And so despite having older brothers—three of them, at the time—to advise me if asked on technique, despite moreover my having already read hard-core verbal or at least literary porn—with *Fanny Hill*, as it's called—I had no idea, one must confess, how to masturbate. I never asked those brothers or my father. That novel's diction—or euphemism—I found confusing, and so its representations hard to picture. If only I had also already read *Portnoy's Complaint*. But that encounter—with adolescent Alexander Portnoy in his bathroom—didn't occur until my twenties. Or if only I'd also read *Lolita*. That encounter—with middle-aged Humbert Humbert on his sofa—didn't occur until my thirties. Or if only I'd read *Ulysses*, with Leopold Bloom on a beach. Or, with Jean in jail, if I had read *Our Lady of the Flowers*:

> Beneath the sheet, my right hand stops to caress the absent face, and then the
> whole body, of the outlaw I have chosen for that evening's delight. The left hand

closes, then arranges its fingers in the form of a hollow organ which tries to re-
sist, then offers itself, opens up, and a vigorous body, a wardrobe, emerges from
the wall, advances, and falls on me, crushes me against my straw mattress, which
has already been stained by more than a hundred prisoners, while I think of the
happiness into which I sink at a time when God and His angels exist.

I could have read even Rousseau's *Confessions*. I had no idea, rather, how *best* to
masturbate. (Louis Althusser, in *The Future Lasts Forever,* claims never to have
done such a thing at all until, as a prisoner of war in his twenties, the future
Marxist was advised or maybe shown how by other inmates. Even I, though, find
this dubious.) And so for years, to get off, I'd just hump some old tube sock I had,
which—truth be told—served mainly to keep the sheet clean. Neatness counts.

This sock method began, with brother Steve out of our room, in high school.
We hadn't had much privacy. It continued at college, Yale, where—even as
a sixteen-year-old freshman—I now had a room of my own. The building—
Welch Hall—had just been renovated. You can see it—circa 1950—in the film
All About Eve. As a sophomore-junior there—for just as I'd done three years in
two at junior high school I now did four years in three—I shared a room with
that "Waste Land" blender from the chapter "Hatchet Job." Not much privacy,
once again—with Bill often in—and so not much masturbation by me either. As
a senior, I again had my own room. And this room—thank God—was near that
of some guys on crew. Heavyweight crew. These guys I'd of course fantasize
about. (One, in fact, was like me a music major. Tom, too, took "Clapping for
Credit.") Still, though, I knew nothing really of any hard-core porn. And even if
I had known of it, I'm sure now that I'd have been too ashamed to buy let alone
borrow—maybe from Tom—magazines like, say, *Mandate.*

Soon after having had sex for the first time, at nineteen, I entered Columbia
Law School. My college friend Jesse and I, in an apartment near NYU Law,
now lived together. Brown-haired, brown-eyed Jesse Green is not the man I'd
had sex with. He's the first person I knew in person, to quote the chapter "My
Cortez," "who made me want to write." And both writing and masturbating, as
you may know—well, I'll come to that later. I soon, when he was out, found Jes-
se's *Mandates*—walnut dresser, bottom drawer, under some other stuff. I began
to use these, again when he was out, the way guys therein—some of them black,
but all of them sockless—would indicate I should. I began to give myself a hand.

After leaving Columbia, leaving that apartment to Jesse, getting my own
apartment, down by the World Trade Center, taking—and also passing—the

New York State Bar Exam, and starting full-time work, if you could call it that, at my first law firm, up in Rockefeller Center, I finally—*finally*—bought my own *Mandate*. And then another one. And then another one. And then, eventually, I bought videos like, say, *Score 10* (1991) by Falcon Studios. That one, in particular, my friend "Maximov" had told me about. (He's the liar from "Hatchet Job.") Eventually, I bought DVDs like, say, *Score 10*. Nowadays, of course, we have the Internet, with primarily white sites like—oh, I don't know—*Randy Blue*.

Back in 1991, though—when I first met Charles Rosen through Maximov—all we had were magazines and videos. (Plus texts like *Fanny Hill*—or as its properly called, *Memoirs of a Woman of Pleasure*. Yet who among us—what scholar, even—would choose verbal porn? What male one, at any rate. Women, I'm told, are not that visual.) This was fine by me. I needn't now—mentally—*animate* images. Also fine by me was the related idea of sperm donation. Such donation, I thought, such vendition, rather, could be an easy way to make a buck. Could be fun, too, I thought. Certainly more so than my other jobs at the time: part-time legal work, nanny work, etc. I did not, unfortunately, have a car anymore—turnpike, rainstorm—and so couldn't, for about two hundred bucks a pop, or quite a fortune to me back then, get to some sperm bank over in New Jersey. The most I could get here in Manhattan—at some East Side bank called IDANT—was fifty bucks, or somewhat more than just chickenfeed. So I shoved some *Mandate*, plus *Score 10*, in a book bag and then walked over there. Walked alone, of course, across Central Park. What, I wondered while doing so, might "IDANT" stand for? Indigent Dudes are . . . something something?

IDANT, turned out, is just south of the store Bloomingdale's. It's the only thing, I now realized, in the building's basement. And so everyone here—by ground-floor elevators—must know, I imagined, what I'm up to. Or literally down for—as if I were buying porn in some bookstore. And the name "IDANT"—now, in that basement, implied their brochure—doesn't stand for anything. That's odd, I thought. Made explicit here, though, is that no donee—nor even any child of hers by me—will ever know my name. It said, too, that my first of two hurdles, as a potential donor, will be to complete this form.

This form asked my age, of course. *Thirty-one*, I wrote in pen. It asked my race. *Caucasian*—although maybe less so, I now think, than I used to think. It asked my religion, which—being Jewish—I thought would make me pretty popular. This, after all—to quote Jesse Jackson—was "Hymietown." It asked my educational history, which—being Ivy League—I thought would make me even more so. It asked my medical history. It then, for some reason, asked my "complexion." Having as I do Gilbert's Syndrome, which although otherwise harmless turns me pretty green—in grade school through high school, then, friends said I look like Donny Osmond, whereas at Yale they said Bono, and then at Columbia they said Prince, and then at Brown, where after quitting my second law firm, south of Grand Central, I went to grad school, they said Bono again—I wrote down: *olive*. Friends these days say I look like Genet. Jean Genet, of *Our Lady of the Flowers*. Or one of them does: Elisabeth Ladenson, author of *Proust's Lesbianism* and *Dirt for Art's Sake: Books on Trial from Madame Bovary to Lolita*. David, my now husband, calls me "Gumby"—but not only because I'm green.

The form now, for some reason, asked my sexuality. Since IDANT, according to that brochure, screens all deposits for both CMV—or cytomegalovirus—and HIV, I inferred, from the question, that any self-identified homosexual like me will no matter what his either CMV or HIV status be shown, as it were, the door. Or, literally, that elevator door. We gay men, after all, are supposed to beget other gay men—when, that is, we're not seducing otherwise straight ones, or even just boys, into "choosing" our so-called lifestyle. (I myself, by the way, am HIV-negative.) So like Maximov I lied—by writing *heterosexual*—while telling myself that any boys of mine, if also already gay, will replace men now dying or even already dead of AIDS. Plus replace Steve, of course. I never yet thought of girls.

Having completed this form—this written exam—I now handed it over to the lab technician. Him I'll call, well, "Ishmael." He looked the thing over, then looked me over, and then for some reason, using pencil, turned my self-identified *olive* complexion to *fair*. So he, too, lied, hoping maybe to glamorize me. Think, here, of Zooey Glass—in J.D. Salinger—who, according to sister "Boo Boo," is "the blue-eyed Jewish-Irish Mohican scout who died in your arms at the roulette table at Monte Carlo." My own lie, though—*heterosexual*—didn't seem to faze the guy. Maybe I looked straight, to Ishmael, or he didn't care, or he too was gay. For I was now told by him about that second hurdle: a so to speak oral exam by IDANT's so to speak doctor.

"Is it right now?" I asked.

"Right now," he said.

Dr. "Svetlov," as I'll call her, was a middle-aged, somewhat fat Russian. Given that heavy accent, I thought, she's probably moved here recently—and so like me must be Jewish. Given, moreover, what I knew it meant—or did not mean—to be a "doctor" over there, she's probably, I thought, more adept at massaging people than curing them. Or maybe, more likely, she'd been a cabdriver.

Svetlov, having gotten the form from Ishmael, first reviewed my own medical history from it. This, back then, was nothing more than just a tonsillectomy-mastoidectomy at four and walking pneumonia at eighteen. Gilbert's Syndrome, being harmless, I had omitted. She then reviewed that of family. Yes, I confirmed, there's lots of heart disease: Grandpa Harry, Uncle Lou, Dad. But there's very little cancer. Grandma Sally had it. Neither Svetlov nor that form, for some reason, covered mental illness. If they had, though, I don't know what I would've either said to her or written there. As you'll see, in the chapter "Veritas," I've never quite understood Steve's personality. And it'd be years before I realized that Mom's is, I'm afraid, both borderline and narcissistic.

"No," I now replied. "I do not smoke. My father does."

No response to this, from Svetlov.

"No," I next replied. "I don't drink. We're Jewish."

I was reminded here of a cheer used—supposedly—at Yale's summer school in Norfolk, Connecticut: "We don't smoke. We don't drink. Norfolk, Norfolk, *Norfolk!*"

"So," asked Svetlov. "Are you married?"

"No," I said—meaning of course not legally. "Warren" and I, back in 1985, had had a so-called commitment ceremony at which the novelist David Leavitt—having wangled a plus-one invitation from us through Jesse—spent the whole time necking. And those two weren't even in the back of the church. Don't believe it? I've got very unsexy, non-pornographic pictures of them. See "Kiss and Tell," at any rate, for more on that ceremony; the chapter "Death to Gumby," for more on both Leavitt and another partner of his.

"Well then," she asked. "Have you ever had sex with a man?"

Technically, of course, I could've done so—in fact could still be doing so on a regular basis, which as you're about to read I wasn't at the time—without self-identifying as gay. But what, I wondered, might have prompted this question? Was I *that* effeminate? That, you know, *faggy*?

"No," I lied.

"Never?" asked Svetlov.

"No," I insisted.

"Never *ever*?" she asked—now straining for credulity.

"No."

"Never ever *ever*?"

Scratch cabdriver. The woman, clearly, was KGB. But given that I wasn't about to not stick with the lie and also given that IDANT didn't supply any of the devices "Grushenka," as I'll now call her, must have used back in Moscow—cattle prod, thumb screw—she then moved on and finally gave me the old, as it were, thumb's up.

"You may now," she said, "make an initial deposit."

"Right now?" I asked. "And then maybe three or four times a week?"

"No," said Grushenka. "It takes, for you to get enough sperm for us, three or four days of abstinence."

I couldn't imagine Warren would be thrilled by this, but—truth be told—we'd almost never have sex, if you could call it that, anyway. Neither he nor I, as you know, was the other's idea of a top. So I'd now, for the next four days, stay away from him—but also, no thrill there either, away from myself—and then once again walk over to IDANT.

This "initial deposit," though, wasn't much fun. Nor, despite a big, comfortable chair supplied, was it easy. First of all, this chair—in a closet—was just three feet from someone's desk out there. I could hear everything the woman was doing and so, presumably, could she hear me. Second of all, it's hard to jerk off with the one hand—I'm a righty, as a rule, yet like Genet's "Jean" a lefty when masturbating—but then come in a cup you're holding with the other. It's even harder when also somehow holding a *Mandate*. If only, I thought, I had true privacy here. Or had yet another hand. Or they had—for *Score 10*—a videotape player.

Eventually, though, I got the hang of it. But I got cocky, as it were, as well. I imagined, after a couple of weeks, that I had enough sperm to abstain from the requisite abstinence. I did not, said Ishmael to me next time, have enough. And so I'd now, being untrustworthy, have to use *two* cups: one for my first, most concentrated spurt, another, he said, for the rest of them. This, of course, was harder still. It was like juggling jello globs—only with my feet. And then after about a year of this, it was time for me—sans Warren—to move to Iowa. I walked over again—alone—to IDANT, took one last elevator ride to that basement, made my final deposit, which also happens to be what we here call turning in your dissertation, handed that over to Ishmael, as usual, and then must have told him, as you'll soon see, where I'd be going.

| | |

I have never, as an atheist Jew, considered spilling one's seed—or "onanism"—to be sinful. And nor even, to quote Rousseau, thought it "dangerous." He says— or writes—"dangerous *supplement*" in both those *Confessions* and the treatise *Émile*. Let's not, though, go much into what Onan either did or did not do, in Genesis, with Tamar. Jews, basically—although not in Latin—say *coitus inter-ruptus*, whereas for Christians it's masturbation. At IDANT, moreover, I hadn't spilled anything—neither literally, by some miracle, and nor figuratively and nor allegorically and nor—look it up—anagogically. That's why this chapter so far has—apart from the bit on Jesse—been pretty shameless. Yet several years af-ter I moved to Iowa, several before I met David, a divorced and childless woman asked for my help conceiving and then actually raising a kid with her. Thus began a chain of events that has made me think and write about what IDANT work, and you could call it that, has meant for other work I've done—writing, including this writing, and teaching. I've also thought what it's meant for any boys and or girls, sons and or daughters, of mine.

Black-haired, blue-eyed "Hester," as I'll call her, is an opera singer. She'd gotten pregnant, years before, by her husband but then much to her disap-pointment had to abort. As I myself, after Warren, couldn't yet foresee getting involved, seriously, with any other man, and as, despite that nanny work of mine in New York, I thought parenthood—like having a pet, maybe—might be fun, I said yes. We soon discovered, though, through testing, that where I was now CMV-positive, Hester was negative. This, unfortunately, risked hear-ing loss or even brain damage for the kid—a risk we couldn't take. I then re-membered that IDANT brochure and what it had said about screening. With all those maybe fifty or sixty deposits of mine, I thought, I too must have been negative *there*. So maybe, I thought, they'll send one to us. And so I telephoned IDANT, described our situation to some receptionist, and was transferred by her to the lab.

"I'm one of your donors, from a couple years back," I repeated to a man there, "but now I'm, like, in Iowa, and . . . "

"G712!" the man ejaculated. "This is *Ishmael*."

"G712," apparently, was my lot number—something, needless to say, I'm not supposed to know. And apparently I *had* been popular. Hence that ejaculation of his. I had been so popular, in fact, that there was now, said Ishmael, no such deposit left to send.

This, of course, was depressing—especially for Hester who to this day has never had children. And nor has she gotten involved with another man. And nor with a woman. I soon realized, though, that I had been much more excited, by this now aborted plan, on Hester's behalf than I'd been by it on my own. My desire, as is so often the case, was—to invoke Eve Kosofsky Sedgwick—imitative. To invoke *When Harry Met Sally* (1989), I'd have had what *Hester* was having—only not, as in that old film, because it both looked and sounded orgasmic.

| | |

And nor have I—until now—ever written about sperm donation. Not even in the abstract. I have, however, written about both masturbation and some of its equivalents: a type of speech, a type of writing, a theatre piece. My essay on the "orgasmics of truth," for instance—done for Robert Scholes—concerns how both Oscar Wilde and Roland Barthes found the verbal "utterance" of paradox to be like getting themselves off. Themselves alone, I should say. Or rather, as I did say there, they found it like "autoerotic asphyxiation." "The secret of telling a truth," I then claim in that essay, "of the 'third term' [to quote Barthes], of meaningful signification, [was], quite figuratively, for these men, the secret of such suicide." Or as Barthes himself, I also claim, might have put it: "to pronounce a perfect paradox [was for them] never to hear it deteriorate into a *doxa*." *Doxa*, you recall, means conventional wisdom, or what goes *without* saying. Or as Barthes did put it, in *The Pleasure of the Text*: this was "verbal pleasure [that both] chokes and reels into bliss." One infers, then, that it must have been, for them, like dying while—and in both senses of the word—ejaculating.

My book on Nijinsky, moreover, contains a Barthes-like analysis of an analysis by the composer and also writer Ned Rorem. That analysis, of his, is of himself, while home alone in youth, having—as he says, in ironic quotation marks—"danced" the de facto money shot from the ballet *Afternoon of a Faun*. Don't know it? It's of Nijinsky's faun humping—no, not a sock. Humping a scarf. The scarf belonged to a nymph. The nymph, the faun ignored. This shot, moreover, was purportedly non-pornographic—like those bodybuilding ads I used to use.

Rorem is of course gay. And so his analysis, I claim in that book, "indicates troublesome slippages from masturbation to narcissism and from narcissism to solipsism—troublesome insofar as they imply a lack of interest in nymph-like Others." This, more generally—I also claim—is the problem not with any such private performance as his but with any public one. For Nijinsky's faun itself—on stage—suggested such stereotypes, moving not just from the supposedly masturbatory, to the supposedly narcissistic, to the supposedly "solipsistic" or egocentric gay man, but also from the supposedly adolescent, to the supposedly effeminate, to the supposedly fetishistic, to the supposedly superficial, to the truly scandalous one. (Both faun and nymph, in fact, seemed literally frieze-like—or two-dimensional. Figuratively, then, they *were* superficial. That money shot, at the ballet's premiere, did cause a riot.) That then leaves us, if we too are gay, to transvalue such stereotypes. (To "transvalue" something—a term you may know from Nietzsche—means to reverse polarity: what's good is now bad, what's bad is now good.) This, in theory, is easy. In practice, though, it's hard. Just ask Svetlov, who'd have seen my own effeminacy—if any—as a problem no matter what I thought of it. Then again, ask Warren. Or just try it yourself, *kiddo.* Say that—like Rorem, only in public—you transvalue the supposedly *adolescent* gay man by thinking "I'm so *youthful.*" (Do not, however, masturbate there—in public—as Nijinsky on stage seemed to.) Others think, "You're *retarded.*" Or say you transvalue the supposedly *superficial* gay man by thinking "I'm so *stylish.*" Others—like those bloggers trashing my "My Cortez"—think, "You're *glib.*" Yet we really, I claim, have no other choice. We can't ever *be* gay, or at least act it, without negotiating some such stereotype—even if like Rorem's faun, or the faun the man himself using those quotation marks says he "danced," such negotiations are inept.

More to the point, though, as well as far more recently, I've done a limerick on not Rorem's imitative but Nijinsky's original faun. Why a limerick? To be not glib but *naughty*—as all such poems I think should be. And also to show—to tell, rather—how pornographic it in fact must have been. (Think, here, of those scandalized rioters.) How in fact—yes, I'll say or rather *write* it—"utterly" pornographic:

> Most audience members cried "Shame!"
> When Vaslav, Diaghilev's flame,
>   Defiled the veil
>   In a pastoral tale.
> But wankers were happy they came.

I have also, though, done one on Rorem himself:

> "Atonal is straight, tonal gay,"
> Claim students of Miss Boulanger.

Take little Ned:
Even in bed
He'd carry a tune all the way.

But that's about sex, really, not just masturbation. And I should explain, here, that "Miss [Nadia] Boulanger" taught music, in France, to Rorem as well as to such fellow American composers as Paul Bowles, Marc Blitzstein, Virgil Thomson, Aaron Copland, and even, late in his life, Leonard Bernstein—many of whom, like my "little Ned," were also gay.

Even more to the point, my next book—*Neatness Counts*—"uttered," in print, what that essay "Wilde, Barthes, and the Orgasmics of Truth," to use its full title, had itself come close to saying. Like masturbating, I now claim, *writing* for Barthes—and not just speech—was, despite his willingness to discuss the process, in writing, and then also publish such discussion, a "solitary, private, almost furtive pleasure." That's the basic reason why, like Proust, he worked in his bedroom. Or worked in *two* bedrooms: one in town, the other in the country. (The first use of the word *"recherche"* [meaning "search"] by Proust, in À *la recherche du temps perdu* [*In Search of Lost Time*], does in fact—in a draft of that novel—concern masturbation.) That's the *basic* reason why work done there, by Barthes, involved keeping purportedly unconventional truths to himself. It's the *secret* reason favorite writers of his, like Proust, were seen by Barthes as "nonconversational"—meaning for him that they never addressed anyone. It's why, too, he associated writing with an inept, probably Rorem-like amateurism, in that "dance" of his, or rather with Barthes' own no doubt bad piano playing while home alone—even while also, like Rorem there, fantasizing both a technical perfection to which Barthes admits in *Roland Barthes by Roland Barthes* and, I infer, an audience. (For more on that admission of his, see "Kiss and Tell.") As opposed, that is, to one's truly playing well—like some virtuoso pianist—in public, or to playing like Rosen. And yet just as with masturbation itself, I also claim, masturbatory writing, for Barthes, was as pleasures go pretty "sad and lonely"—although not as sad and lonely, paradoxically enough, as either cruising or cruisy writing were. See *Incidents*, by Barthes, for the man's literal cruising, and then A *Lover's Discourse*—written, Barthes himself claims there, in collaboration with students—for the man's figuratively cruisy writing. "To know that one does not write for the Other," Barthes tells both himself and those students, "to know that these things I am going to write will never cause me to be loved by the one I love (the Other), to know that writing compensates for nothing, sublimates nothing, that it is precisely *there where you are not*—this is the beginning of writing."

Bruce Chatwin, by the way, the author of *In Patagonia* and then other such travelogues, was both a pretty happy cruiser and a happily cruisy writer, either making connections or fantasizing communication whenever he wanted either intercourse or to reach some reader. "Kiss and Tell" will have more on this.

"Sad and lonely," I claim, but also pretty *neat*. (Recall, here, my old sock method.) This, I infer, made both writing and masturbating—for Barthes— both "weary and cheerful." And now comes the only passage that one reviewer, in trashing *Neatness Counts*, saw fit to quote there:

> When I play with myself, to be as exhibitionist as Barthes writing about writing, I never make the kind of mess sex with other people requires. Nor do I make one when I write. Barthes, I imagine, both worked and played the same way. I mean I *know* he worked that way. Among other activities there, Barthes adapted his desk to the pleasure of "sorting." So I suppose he played that way as well: arranging his desk, writing a bit, going back to bed, retrieving a favorite photograph [from a French *Mandate*?], one unaccountably eroticized by what [in *Camera Lucida*] he called some *punctum* (whereby the Other addressed *him*), undoing his belt, and then, well, you get the drift. Then cleaning up, rearranging himself, rearranging the bed, hiding the photo, going back to the desk, and getting back to the equally pen-ile work of sign extrusion. Now, in town, somewhat enervated by the somewhat egocentric interlude. Now, in the country, somewhat energized.

"But where are we, really, when we masturbate?" I add rhetorically. "And who are we? Who when we write? Who, rather, are we pretending to be?"

As for who that reviewer is, really: Paula Marantz Cohen, in the TLS. (This, then, explains the "autobiographical reference" in "Hatchet Job.") As for who "we" are—or who I myself have been—when if not masturbating then at least writing, see once again "Death to Gumby." Who when teaching? See the chapter "Bright One." As for to whom I've spoken, or written, in all these texts discussed plus others taken chronologically: "The Orgasmics of Truth" was of course primarily addressed to Robert Scholes. Both my dissertation and the book it became, *Love's Litany*, were—with Scholes as dissertation director—primarily addressed to him too. Plus to other committee members. Plus to Warren, to whom—with love—they're both dedicated. *Beethoven's Kiss*, my second book, was addressed—primarily—to Wayne Koestenbaum. *The Queer*

Afterlife of Vaslav Nijinsky was addressed—primarily—to its dedicatee: a heart-breaker I met shortly after that call to IDANT and who, as I must have known at the time on some level, would soon figure in my own life, ironically enough, pretty much the way Nijinsky had in Diaghilev's. And so I may neither name nor even call the guy anything here—not even "Vaslav." I will, however, confess that—to me, back then—he looked like the actor Matthew McConaughey, or some *German*-Irish Mohican scout. After that, though, and even throughout this book—with "My Cortez" an apology to brother Bob, primarily, "Hatchet Job" one to Rosen, and this chapter one to, well, I'll get to that—just whom I'll have wanted to reach gets complicated.

Yet before saying both how and why it does, I should mention that of course I haven't been the only scholar to write on both masturbation and its equivalents. There's Freud. There's Michel Foucault. There's Thomas Laqueur, in *Solitary Sex*. There's Jacques Derrida, in *Of Grammatology*, translated into English by someone in our Comparative Literature Department at the time: Gayatri Spivak. Here, with disrespect to Rousseau, both Derrida and Spivak claim:

> We read in *Émile* (Book IV): "If once he acquires this dangerous habit [*supplément*] he is ruined." In the same book, it is also a question of "mak[ing] up . . . by trading on . . . inexperience" [*suppléer en gagnant de vitesse sur l'experience*; literally "supplementing by out-distancing experience"], and of the "mind, which reinforces [*supplée*] . . . the bodily strength."
>
> The experience of auto-eroticism is lived in anguish. Masturbation reassures ("soon reassured") only through that culpability traditionally attached to the practice, obliging children to assume the fault and to interiorize the threat of castration that always accompanies it. Pleasure is thus lived as the irremediable loss of the vital substance, as exposure to madness and death. It is produced "at the expense of their health, strength, and, sometimes, their life." In the same way, the *Rêveries* will say, the man "who searches the entrails of earth . . . goes seeking to its center, at the risk of his life and at the expense of his health, for imaginary goods in place of the real good which the earth offers of herself if he knew how to enjoy it."
>
> And indeed it is a question of the imaginary. The supplement that "cheats" maternal "nature" operates as writing, and as writing it is dangerous to life. This danger is that of the image. Just as writing opens the crisis of the living speech in terms of its "image," its painting or its representation, so onanism announces the ruin of vitality in terms of imaginary seductions.

What does it mean, such I'd say nonconversational text? (For you know what the quotation per se means, of Rousseau by Derrida, just as—to some extent— you know what such quotation of Derrida by me does. But I'll *defer* for a bit—to use the man's own favorite word—just whom both that book and this translation I think should have addressed.) Let me just quote—extensively—the far more conversational hence readable *Columbia Dictionary of Modern Literary and Cultural Criticism*: "In the deconstructive philosophy of Jacques Derrida, the logic of the supplement is what undoes the metaphysical oppositions around which Western thought is organized. Derrida argues that all metaphysical systems, no matter what term they offer as embodying presence, have need of a supplementary term, which compensates for the absence of this source: for example, speech needs writing to stand for it when the face-to-face immediacy of the speech situation is lacking. As Derrida has shown, however, in each case the supplement actually can be seen to undermine [or perhaps 'transvalue'] this hierarchical relationship. Thus, in Derrida's own example from his reading of Rousseau, masturbation serves as a supplement to intercourse, just as writing serves as a supplement to the 'intercourse' of conversation. When the latter becomes unavailable, its supplement entices Rousseau with the mental illusion of a present partner. And yet at the same time that he condemns masturbation as a way of 'cheating Nature,' Rousseau is compelled to admit that it has its advantages over 'natural' relations, which are never so perfectly realized as the imaginary ones. In the same way, he observes that even though he has classified writing as a mere imitation of speech, it nevertheless allows him to express himself more perfectly than actual speech situations, which tend to make him nervous. In spite of their apparent artificiality, then, writing and masturbation both offer a reminder of the sense of presence that is lacking in their supposedly more 'natural' counterparts. Derrida's point is that even in those activities which are traditionally accorded priority, the loss of presence has already taken place, and that heterosexuality and speech are themselves nothing more than attempts to compensate for this sense of a fundamental absence. It is his contention that a similar 'supplementary logic' can be located in all such metaphysical oppositions."

Unlike Barthes, though, Derrida was straight. Plus he was Jewish.

| | |

I met David, a few years after the heartbreaker dumped me, in the spring of
2000. It was a mutual friend—the painter Bobbi McKibbin—who had offered
the introduction. Unlike the heartbreaker—who is of course younger than I—
David's my age. Unlike Svetlov, he's a real doctor—a surgeon, in fact. Unlike
me, he *is* "fair." And so other friends say David looks like a combination of
Ed Harris, the actor, and the pop singer Sting. To me, though, David—tauto-
logically—looks like David. Nor is there a difference between who he really
is—anywhere—and who in fantasy I'd have him be. Unlike me, he never lies,
maybe because David was raised here—in Iowa—on a farm. Nor, unlike either
Wilde or Barthes, does he consider truth "orgasmic." Unlike me, moreover—yet
like Hester—he has been both legally married before and then divorced. Unlike
her—and this is what matters most about him for this story—David's got three
kids.

Son Adam, when we met, was fourteen, Seth was thirteen, and Sam just ten.
All of them, I think, now look like David—Adam in particular. All, moreover,
are as bright, funny, and even musical as he. But after moving about two years
later from my own little home, an Iowa City bungalow, to their much bigger
one, in the town of Grinnell, I myself tried not to act too paternal. The boys, of
course, had David for that. Nor, despite such traditionally wifely duties of mine
here as cooking and cleaning, did I act too maternal. They had their mother,
Julie, for that. Instead, for the most part, I'd just—tautologically—be myself.
I'd act, that is, like their rather older friend. I have joked, though—often to
friends my own age, and sometimes to Adam, Seth, and Sam themselves—that
my role here has also always been some combination of Mary Poppins, Auntie
Mame, and, from the sitcom *My Three Sons* (1960–1972), Uncle Charley. Or,
alternately, of Uncle Charley and Peter Pan.

Such jokes, of course, mean several things. They mean I've always had fun
with "the boys," although probably not as much fun as either David or Julie has
and also a very different fun than I'd imagined back with Hester. They mean,
too, that I have in fact, from time to time, parented them—both paternally and
maternally. But only if need be, as when both David and Julie were out of town,
and so only, as Derrida might put it, supplementally. They mean too, of course,
that I love them.

Having moved, then, to Grinnell, eight things happened. First of all, I be-
gan not just cooking and cleaning but also—virtuosically—knitting sweaters:

ones for David, then Adam, then Seth, and then Sam; one for Seth's best friend, Keaton; and then ones for my own best friends Geeta Patel, who would in return send a sarong, and Doug Trevor, who in a story called "Girls I Know" had already published something I myself, by speaking to him of IDANT, inspired:

> Just a few months ago, Irena, a woman I know who works at the Victor Hugo Bookshop on Newbury Street, asked about my sperm. I don't know how she had learned about me whoring my DNA, but I had seen her more than once in the back row at the Grolier poetry readings with a woman I assumed was her girlfriend and I figured my part-time job was gossip that had bubbled up at one point. I told her that I was flattered by her interest and she quickly corrected me. "I don't want your seed," she replied. "I just want to know your lot number." It turned out, she explained, that some of the banks had a reputation for lying about the characteristics and backgrounds of their donors. I was intrigued and gave her my information. A week later I saw her in the bookstore, perched behind that enclosed counter they have, chopsticks sticking out of her hair. "They say you're a six-one Ivy Leaguer with blue eyes," she said. *Was there*, I thought, *nothing of me worth advertising?* "You should be thrilled," she went on, knowing—I inferred later—enough of my intellectual interests to see the irony of it all. "In twenty years, every adopted WASP in Boston will look like you."

Second of all, I began *Neatness Counts*. Or rather, I began turning my own unpublished fiction into criticism. (For more on that—note the quotation marks—"novel," see "Death to Gumby.") As such, it was now both dedicated and addressed, primarily, to David. As such, *Paula*, the thing clearly has a narrator: someone also named "Kevin Kopelson" but who—much as Nabokov's "Humbert" doesn't know that he's a child molester or Roth's "Portnoy" that he's misogynist—can't quite understand for quite a while what I'm doing there. That "Kevin," in other words, doesn't know throughout most of it that his book—despite the ostensible subject matter, or how writers' workspace relates to what they produce there—is really an elegy for Steve. So, too, was part of *Beethoven's Kiss*. So, too, is much of everything I've done. Nor, then, does "Kevin" know throughout most of it that the book is addressed to Steve as well, much as Humbert doesn't know *Lolita* is addressed not only to both that eponymous "nymphet" and the jury to decide if he murdered Quilty, but also of course to that—unlike Humbert—self-avowed such molester. Plus—again unlike Humbert—Quilty had made pornography.

Third of all, I began thinking about those IDANT boys—and girls—of mine. What, I now wondered, were *those* kids like? Were they bright? Were they funny? Were they even musical? Would any ever meet one another, but of course not know they're related? Would *we* ever meet and not know either?

And so—fourth of all—I decided to once again telephone IDANT. But no, said Svetlov now, they most certainly will *not* release my name—even with my permission—to any donee nor even any child of ours. So I sent a letter saying they should do so. No response, from IDANT. So I had lawyers send one, saying they should do so. No response, from IDANT. I then—in tiny, tiny print—put "G712 (IDANT)" on my professional website. I figured that Ishmael—if he still works there—might once again divulge if not my name then at least that lot number to such women and children. Or that maybe the women themselves will have remembered it. I also figured either they or, well, *you*—my sons and daughters—will now search for it. No response, yet, from anyone.

Now if like either Doug Trevor or Jesse Green I were a good novelist, I might write some metaphor—or simile, rather—for this last situation. As I'm not, though, all the ones I've thought of are rather off. For it has not been like placing a personal ad no one answers. Such ads, of course, demand sex, and they don't call on people to whom in some sense you're already connected. Nor has it been like that orphan Harry Potter, while alone in some empty classroom, gazing into the "Mirror of Erised" and seeing his parents—no longer dead, magically—reflected there. (An inscription across the mirror's top reads, "Erised stra ehru oyt ube cafru oyt on wohsi." ["I show not your face but your heart's desire."]) For I'm the parent, here, and my own kids—I trust—are in fact alive, and I can't quite picture them. So I'll just write that it's like what any writing was, he says, for Barthes. For that website cipher—"G712 (IDANT)"—demands not sex but love, of course, yet will never cause me to be loved.

I now began—fifth of all—to daydream encounters. I'd be playing the piano—the Schumann Fantasy, or maybe Chopin's *Berceuse* (meaning "lullaby")—when suddenly the doorbell would ring. And there—emerald eyes, auburn hair—would be little Franny. She, too, would play the piano. And then she'd chat about Proust. And then she'd ask all about me. And so I'd send her home with my own books—the ones I wrote, that is. And of course she'd love them. (This, of course, is like Barthes himself at the keyboard, fantasizing perfection. Or it's like Rorem "dancing." It's even—one must confess—a bit like masturbating, either with or without porn.)

Or I'd be washing dishes when the bell would ring. And there—same eyes, same hair as Franny—would be little Zooey. Or it'd be little Steve, more likely, who like his namesake—my brother—would take one look at me and be repulsed. (This, compared to masturbation, was like having sex—or at least *bad* sex. See "Kiss and Tell.")

In such daydreams, no kids—not even Franny—ever seem to care what I think of *them*. Nor are they more than about fourteen: Adam's age, when we first met. In reality, of course, they'd be older—just as Adam (as of this writing) is now twenty-four. (Steve's age, at death, was twenty-one—though perhaps you've already figured as much. And so for me, ever since, he's always been that.) The point, of course, is that I'd still have a chance to parent or rather to *father* them, if need be—*non*-supplementally.

I finished *Neatness Counts* at of all places Harvard. It was published in the fall of 2004. And then one day, while actually washing dishes, I was listening to both Sam and National Public Radio when—sixth of all—Terry Gross, the host of *Fresh Air*, asked Joni Mitchell about her having been on some ten-year hiatus. (Sam—as a high school freshman—was chatting about shenanigans there: something about a paint ball, I think.) Now as a "classical" musician, like Rosen, I knew almost nothing about Mitchell. Nor even much about any pop singer—other than Bono, Prince, and Sting. So I only sort of knew her famous song "Both Sides Now." ("Bows and flows of angel hair / and [something something] in the air.") Plus, for some reason, I knew Mitchell's "Songs to Aging Children Come." Plus her album "Hejira." For I'd just read a David Sedaris story—also called "Hejira"—that opens, circa 1979, with his playing it repeatedly:

> It wasn't anything I had planned on, but at the age of twenty-two, after dropping out of my second college and traveling across the country a few times, I found myself back in Raleigh, living in my parents' basement. After six months spent waking at noon, getting high, and listening to the same Joni Mitchell record over and over again, I was called by my father into his den and told to get out. He was sitting very formally in a big, comfortable chair behind his desk, and I felt as though he were firing me from the job of being his son.

He was "firing" Sedaris, it turned out, for being gay—which of course only a terrible parent would do. (When at eighteen—and somewhat maudlin—I came out to both of mine, Mom said: "Is *that* all? All your brothers went through that." "Did you, Dad?" I sniffed. "Well," she lied, "of course he did." Dad himself then stuck with the lie.) But at any rate, Mitchell told Gross, she could think of nothing "to raise her voice in song to at this particular time."

> "I wrote songs from the time that I lost my daughter until the time she came back, and since my family has returned to me I don't write anymore. It seemed like I mothered the world until I got my own family to—you know—mother or befriend."

What, I wondered, was she talking about? Turns out, Terry explained, that Joni—when twenty-two—had had a daughter she then gave up for adoption. She then never had other children. Those two—mother and daughter—finally found one another in 1997, when the daughter was thirty-two. Too old for her to be parented, of course, but at least, for the mother, there were now some grandchildren to spoil.

That publication, by the way, felt—but let's go back a bit. *Love's Litany*, upon release, had felt dead to me because Dad by then was literally dead but also because Warren, an addressee as well as dedicatee, had already dumped me. The Nijinsky book, upon release, felt that way because *its* dedicatee had just done so. *Neatness Counts* when published felt—oh, sorry, this is seventh of all—it felt, figuratively, like some child I alone had raised and then sent off to college. (Generally speaking, though, books are only truly alive—for authors—while being written. And of course my real, biological children, despite the fact that I still imagine them—alive—at about fourteen, are now, only without having been sent off by me, about to enter . . . well, not Harvard I hope.) So whatever happened to *Neatness Counts*—whether good reviews or bad, good sales or bad—would of course, I thought, be its own affair. But this thought, this emotion rather, must have been if not somewhat spurious then at least self-deceptive. For why else would I still keep mentioning, here, that hatchet job by Cohen?

I then started writing *Sedaris*. That book, I decided, would be unlike those others of mine. It would not be addressed to scholars, like Scholes or Koestenbaum, primarily. And nor would it be addressed at all to Steve—who, now that I'm so much older than he, fifty-one (as of this writing) to Steve's twenty-one, or about the difference between Rosen and me, I've begun to see less and less as a brother of mine and more and more as a son. And nor would it be to David, even. Instead, it would speak, primarily, to your average Sedaris fan. Short of or rather beyond that, it would speak primarily to your average student—one who, like those in my own classrooms, I think needs to learn something about both literary satire and confession. (Sedaris, I'm convinced, is not only the most famous but also both the funniest and most confessional—or autobiographical—satirist of today. That's why fans love him, much as—especially if unlike Barthes we find him conversational—we may love Proust as well. And *that* is why writers—or at least some of us—now if not imitate then at least emulate Sedaris. We ourselves want such love, plus such laughter, by fans. Plus, of course, the fame.) And it's just such a student to whom I think all scholars should now, primarily, be speaking. Should be writing, rather. Not to one another alone, primarily. And certainly not—both nonconversationally and solipsistically, as with Derrida and Spivak—to *themselves* alone.

Spivak, too, by the way—like Derrida—is straight. She is not, however, Jewish.

Now you'd think that, as a fan of his myself, I'd also address—if not quite cruise or even stalk—Sedaris. But the man—I won't say how I got his phone number—had already told me he'd never read my book. (This was years before we first met in person—at a Des Moines Starbucks where, as I said in "Hatchet Job," he seemed to want a friend.) In fact, Sedaris claimed, he doesn't read anything about himself. So scratch the notion, I thought, that I could ever compel this man I love to quote—or this man with whom I identify—to both read and write on me. I must confess, though, that I soon chose the title *Sedaris*, for the book, in order that—when browsing some bookstore—you might think his latest collection is for some reason called *Kevin Kopelson*.

Maris Callas, by the way, claimed pretty much the same thing—to never read reviews. But who believes her.

You'd think, too, that I'd also now quite deliberately address those biological children of mine—Franny, Zooey, Steve—especially after having just heard what Mitchell said about the hiatus. But I didn't, or at least not deliberately. Instead—eighth of all—I soon awoke at three o'clock one morning to realize that the one I really needed to address here, primarily, and even to father, was David's son Sam. (Sedaris, on the other hand, is a *mother*-like satirist. See *Sedaris*.) It's a realization that for some reason made now fully maudlin me burst into tears. This, of course, woke David up. And of course Sam, like me, is a youngest son. (Sedaris, with just the one brother, Paul, is an oldest.) As such, Sam's the one—of Adam, Seth, and Sam—with whom I most fully identify. And so by addressing him—one must confess—I'd also, solipsistically, be doing so to myself.

Mitchell, by the way—as I've also just learned from NPR—has begun to both write and compose again. To compose songs, that is, as well as to write lyrics—much like Cole Porter did. It's something Mitchell herself, she said, attributes to political concern—or renewed such concern. But she's no longer, Mitchell told Reese Erlich, "mothering the world"—nor even I'd say grand-mothering it—supplementally. What she's doing instead—by both quoting and revising an unlike Grangerford conversational poet with whom I suppose she must for some reason somewhat identify, just as I myself now identify with Mitchell—is *fathering* us.

Don't believe it? Read the transcript, which I myself—I'm afraid—must now both quote and revise. Or rather—like some, well, masculine schoolmarm—both quote and correct:

MITCHELL: One of the things that made me quit was I said I'm not going to write any more social commentary. I'm not going to write this. I just went, no. I just got stubborn with myself. No more, because, you know, I took a lot of flack and I just thought that I didn't want to go through the experience. I was mad at America. And I thought, you know, come on. Wake up, you know? Like wake them, shake them. But I didn't want to be the one.

ERLICH: But ultimately, she couldn't fight what was inside.

(Soundbite of song "Strong and Wrong")

MITCHELL: (Singing) Strong and wrong you win—/ Only because / That's the way it's always been. / Men love war! / That's what history's for. / History . . . / A mass-murder mystery . . . / His story // Strong and wrong / You lose everything.

ERLICH: Joni Mitchell wrote all of the lyrics for the songs on her new re-cording save one. It's called "If." Her musical setting of a poem by Rudyard Kipling.

MITCHELL: If you can keep your head / While all about you / People are losing theirs and blaming you / If you can trust yourself / When everybody doubts you . . .

(Soundbite of song "If")

MITCHELL: (Singing) When everybody doubts you / And make allowance for their doubting, too. // If you can wait / And not get tired of waiting / And when lied about / Stand tall / Don't deal in lies / And when hated / Don't give in to hating back / Don't need to look so good / Don't need to talk too wise.

ERLICH: Kipling's poem portrays a father giving advice to his son. Mitchell
            kept most of the poem but made some changes. She doesn't like
            Kipling's advice at the end.
MITCHELL: Basically, what he tells the boy in the last stanza is: If you can en-
            dure, you'll inherit the Earth. And I thought that's not what makes
            you inherit the Earth. So how *do* you inherit the Earth? By being
            awake.

Well, maybe you do—so *wake up, kiddo!* Kipling's original, though—and here's
my correction—really begins:

> If you can keep your head when all about you
> Are losing theirs and blaming it on you;
> If you can trust yourself when all men doubt you,
> But make allowance for their doubting too;
> If you can wait and not be tired by waiting,
> Or, being lied about, don't deal in lies,
> Or, being hated, don't give way to hating,
> And yet don't look too good, nor talk too wise;

It ends, moreover:

> If you can talk with crowds and keep your virtue,
> Or walk with kings—nor lose the common touch,
> If neither foes nor loving friends can hurt you;
> If all men count with you, but none too much;
> If you can fill the unforgiving minute
> With sixty seconds' worth of distance run—
> Yours is the Earth and everything that's in it,
> And—which is more—you'll be a Man, my son!

I don't think that's really telling anyone, as Mitchell claims, to just "endure."
But at any rate, my own sons and daughters: wake up, endure, whatever. Just as
long as you also accept this apology: not for my having helped conceive you,
of course, but for my not having helped raise you. And also for your not having
ever known me in person. And also, now, for my not knowing you at all.

Veritas

What illusion to believe that we can tell the truth, and to believe that each of us has an individual and autonomous existence. How can we think that in autobiography it is the lived life that produces the text, when it is the text that produces the life!

—PHILIPPE LEJEUNE, *On Autobiography*

Like many in academic life, I live for sabbaticals. It's not that I'm lazy, or just that I'm lazy. It's that I'd rather write than teach, plus that the two are incompatible. To write—or "produce text"—is to construct something. It's to design and build all at once. Or it's, as J.D. Salinger put it, to have "stars out." To teach, though, is to take something apart. It's to *deconstruct*.

I spent one sabbatical working on Marcel Proust at both the National Library in Paris and the Camargo Foundation in Cassis, France. This was quite a trick, by the way, with awful French. ("*Nous allons*," I'd say, "[*quelque chose quelque chose*].") I once waited for hours in that library, to see love letters from Proust to Reynaldo Hahn. Hahn was a composer. The letters I got finally were *to* Proust . . . from some Liane de Pougy. She, I later learned, was a prostitute. Or rather, a courtesan.

The sabbatical before that I spent as a "Mellon Fellow" working on Nijinsky—in Philadelphia—at the University of Pennsylvania. (That "Mellon," as you may know, refers to the Andrew W. Mellon Foundation. Andrew Mellon was Secretary of the Treasury, under Presidents Harding, Coolidge, and Hoover.) Meanwhile—back in Iowa City—the man I myself loved was falling for a graduate student of mine.

The sabbatical after that I spent working on "literary workspace"—for my book *Neatness Counts: Essays on the Writer's Desk*—at of all places Harvard University.

First, though, let me say a bit about "Philly." It's a hellhole. Or at least my living space there was. The regular occupant, a history professor on sabbatical, had left it a pigsty. So too is "Penn" hellish, or at least my workspace there was. That regular occupant, an English professor on sabbatical, had left it even messier. Plus I had to have an officemate: yet another Mellon Fellow who—having arrived there before me, to work on both Freud and Lacan's "death drive"—commandeered the one real desk. This left me to work, on Nijinsky, at what I think was an ironing board. To punish the man, named I'll say "Lane," I then repeatedly told him there is no such drive. Of course I could have worked alone, in sty number one. Of course, too, having such "stars out" is often best *done* alone.

Now about Harvard, where I wasn't even supposed to work. As a "Bunting Fellow," I was supposed to work at Radcliffe. By "Radcliffe," though, I don't mean the former women's college where "Jennifer Cavalieri," played by Ali MacGraw in the film *Love Story* (1970), plays the harpsichord. I mean what took that school's place: the Radcliffe Institute for Advanced Study, which had once been called—and so is still informally called—the Bunting Institute. (That "Bunting" refers to Radcliffe President Mary Bunting, 1910–1998.) But my office there—even with no officemate—was once again a hellhole. Not that it, too, was messy. It was, if anything, too neat for me. And so it was too tomblike: very dark, very cold, and empty but for a desk. Of course given not just that title of mine, *Neatness Counts*, that subject matter, or literary workspace, and an over-the-top orderliness in everything I do—when gardening, for instance, I'm only ever really cleaning the outdoors—but also given how if not quite death-driven then as you'll see elegiac my book now became, I soon found this ironic.

Instead, I worked at Harvard, in living space neither much too neat nor at all lonely. The move, from Radcliffe, was at David's suggestion. He's the man I now loved and who meanwhile—back in Grinnell, Iowa—was home with the boys: sons Adam, Seth, and Sam. The space was a single room in a—de facto—dormitory. The room, then, was a de facto bedroom—the type of space, coincidentally, in which, as you know from "G712," two figures central to *Neatness Counts* also wrote: Marcel Proust (1871–1922), most famously, and Roland Barthes (1915–1980). The de facto dorm was really a "residential college," Lowell

House. This is next to Kirkland House, where my older brother Bob—when at college—used to live. He's Harvard, Class of 1968. And there should be a Hoar House, too, after Harvard President Leonard Hoar (1630–1675). But of course—think whorehouse—there isn't one.

Why, though, did I choose to live at Lowell House, where technically speaking I was a so-called Visiting Scholar? First of all, I knew its so-called master. Diana Eck, that "master," is also a theology professor—at Harvard Divinity School. My former partner "Warren," having gotten a masters degree there just before we met, used to rave about her. "She's beautiful," he would say, "she's brilliant, plus very, very kind." I myself then, coincidentally, met Eck on yet another sabbatical. This one I'd spent in Italy, at work on "pianism" in a villa owned by the Rockefeller Foundation. Eck's maternal grandmother, I learned there, had lived near Grinnell—before getting fed up with farming and moving to the Pacific Northwest. Also at the villa—as a board member of that foundation, on a one-week board retreat—was Alan Alda. Alda had starred on the television show M*A*S*H (1972–1983). Before that, though—I also learned—he'd met his wife Arlene through my high school's orchestra conductor.

The rent at Lowell House—second of all—was cheap. Third of all, my so-called scholarship here came with a meal plan. (Like every such residential college, at both Yale and Harvard, the place has its own dining hall.) Fourth of all, I thought it might be fun living with students who were not my own students—just as with sons who weren't my own sons. And it *was* fun, especially at meals where pretty much every Lowell House kid—boy or girl—was nice to me. This included, to my surprise, Natalie Portman—that beautiful actress from the film *Beautiful Girls* (1996), who told me one night at dinner, lying beautifully, that I don't look a day over thirty. I was over forty.

Another "Visiting Scholar," at the time, was Livingston Taylor. He's the younger brother of James Taylor and, while less famous than James, is also a folk singer. Another such scholar was Paola Bacchetta, a beautiful, brilliant friend of both Diana Eck and—coincidentally—my own beautiful, brilliant best friend Geeta Patel. Paola, unfortunately, chain-smokes. But she did, when necessary, loan me her car. And another such scholar was Isaiah Jackson—a very handsome conductor. Isaiah, coincidentally, had been a college friend of Bob's—or as I now recalled his own best friend back then. For Isaiah—on breaks—often came to our house in Queens, New York. Isaiah himself, the man told me, now recalled both me and my brother Steve from such visits—at about ages six and eight respectively.

But the faculty! Apart from ones with Diana Eck and also a much younger woman whom I'll get to later, nearly every encounter with these self-important Pooh-Bahs made me, Mikado-like, imagine some delightful punishment, such as what—in reality—I did to Lane at Penn with that death-drive denial of mine or to the poet "Emmeline Grangerford" in that Iowa City bookstore ("You know," I'd said to her with the critic "Jessie Weston" there from Harvard, "we're in the same fucking department") or even such as what "Ishmael," with that two-cup, well, mandate of his, had inadvertently done to me at IDANT. And so, for your reading pleasure—one hopes—here are three of those encounters.

I myself, that fall, presented part of *Neatness Counts* at Radcliffe. Afterward, some English professor from Harvard, looking, I thought, like Ichabod Crane, attacked me for doing to the poet Elizabeth Bishop (1911–1979) "what Ike Turner did to Tina." ("His head was small," wrote Washington Irving on Ichabod, "with huge ears, large green glassy eyes, and a long snipe nose.") I was much too stunned—I'm afraid—to then respond to this, and upon reflection for a time still didn't know what the man was getting at. It now strikes me, though, that—like Grangerford today—Bishop used to teach at Harvard. And so unlike me, this Ichabod may have known the woman in person. It strikes me, too, that Bishop did so—teach at Harvard—only after some crazy lover of hers killed herself.

I then, that winter, presented more of *Neatness Counts* at Harvard—in its gorgeous Humanities Center. Afterward, the very same Ichabod attacked me for—I kid you not—doing to *Proust* "what Ike Turner did to Tina." What, I wondered, is *with* that guy? Or rather, what's with him and those *Turners*? This time, though, I could respond. "You know," I said to him:

> I do remember you from my Bishop talk. And *you're* the one like Ike. You keep beating me up for no reason at all, or at least none you care to articulate. And since you showed so much contempt there for both me and my work, since, moreover, I don't recall promising—in response to you—to reform, I'm really rather surprised to have to see or more to the point *listen* to you again.

That shut him up. But then some French professor—maybe a friend of Ichabod's—asked how I would *teach* Proust, to undergraduates. I said I'd probably have students read Barthes, or his *Lover's Discourse*, and then only after that Proust's "Swann in Love." "Well," the man snorted, "*I* wouldn't."

I should have known I'd be in for this. Not only are the faculty or at least the male faculty at Harvard notorious for such conduct—when clothed, that is, although when totally naked (huge ears, large eyes, long snipe nose, but no private parts of these men all that big) in locker rooms there, they'll also hit on you—I myself had already experienced it. One time, when applying to several doctoral programs, I telephoned—on Warren's advice—a young non-Jewish professor in that English department. As he did lesbian and gay studies, primarily, I'd have worked with the man—had I both gotten into and then entered this program. As you know, though—from "My Cortez"—I would not get in. "I can't talk now," he said to me, "but promise you I'll call back." He did not call back. We're friends now, as it happens, but I certainly haven't told him it was I who telephoned. Plus having not gotten tenure there, he's no longer at Harvard.

Another time, when at Brown University in a doctoral program that did accept me, I attended—with Warren—a Jewish such professor's all-male dinner party. Conversation there was so awkward that, figuring other guests—none of whom we'd ever met before—would respond in kind, I decided to mock myself. I told of the time I made ratatouille, for a coed party that Warren and I had had, with instead of two tablespoons two *cups* of olive oil in the dish! There'd been a typo in the first *Silver Palate Cookbook*. I'd then sent a letter to its publisher. "Dear Sir or Madam," this began. "As much as I love the unctuous . . ." No response, alas, from the press. Subsequent editions, though, did make the necessary correction. I told, too, of the time some garlic bread I made, for another such party, had suddenly burst into flames! I'd then hurled the bread— still flaming—over to Warren, who then tossed it out a window. Others guests, though, did not respond—to such self-deprecation—in kind. Nor did our host. And yet the next time I saw the man—at a lesbian and gay studies reading group—he blamed of all people *me* for having "ruined everything" that night. In response, one must confess, I told him such responsibility truly rests with those "awful, awful"—by which I meant just non-responsive to me—"friends of yours." We're now at least collegial, though, he and I—and he, too, having not gotten tenure there, is no longer at Harvard.

And then there was the time when, just finishing up or rather down at Brown, I actually interviewed for a job at Harvard. This would have been a tenure-track position, in English. The specialty called for, though, had been not lesbian and gay studies but "anglophone narrative." This, I figured, meant English-language novels and stories—only by "postcolonial" writers. And that, I figured, meant African or even Indian or even Caribbean writers—not American or even African-American or even Canadian ones. So I probably shouldn't have applied. And so, more to the point, they probably shouldn't have interviewed me. At any rate, there were about a dozen professors—including Weston—now present for the encounter. None, though, introduced himself to me when suddenly, right off the bat, I'm asked by someone—not Weston—about how I'd teach a graduate course on postcolonial theory. It's a question for which, in fact, I was totally prepared. Students would first read, I'd planned to say, work by Franz Fanon. (Born in Martinique, he then wandered off to Algeria.) They'd then read Gayatri Spivak. (Born in Calcutta, she wandered off to the United States.) They'd then read Homi Bhabha. (Born in Bombay, he too wandered to the United States.) But wanting to seem good at, well, extemporizing, I instead—stupidly—began my response with: "Well, I haven't yet *taught* graduate courses, nor even given much *thought* to one on such theory, but . . . " And at this point, I swear, someone else not Weston yelled: "Think about it *now*, goddammit!"

Why, then, did I apply to Radcliffe? I applied because with Brown, in Providence, Rhode Island, so close to both Cambridge and Boston, Massachusetts, Warren and I had often enjoyed much better times there than at that awful, awful dinner party: hearing art song—done first by Leontyne Price and then by Jessye Norman—in Symphony Hall; seeing dance—or the Boston Ballet—at the horribly named Wang Center. I applied because my friend Geeta—whom I'd first met in Iowa City—now worked nearby at Wellesley College while living in Dorchester. I applied so as to see Providence friends, including my dissertation director Robert Scholes. I applied to maybe make friends of fellow Bunting Fellows. And since, like those Lowell House kids, many of these I'd find were nice, I did make them. Some of these—although as old if not older than I—even behaved like kids: playing hooky with me from less than nice fellows' presentations; also gossiping about them. One such nice fellow, although much younger than I, was the novelist Zadie Smith—ostensibly there to work on "Morality in E.M. Forster" but also, one later learned, to secretly observe Harvard. She, too, in her novel *On Beauty*, would eventually satirize the school, in general, along with, in particular, by then Harvard English professor Homi Bhabha. Another such fellow was the visual artist and also architect Mark Robbins, né Rubinstein—also gay, and from Queens—who in a book called *Households* would eventually include some photographs he'd taken of me, posing half naked, in Lowell House. Check out, there, pages thirty-eight and thirty-nine. Know, though, that Mark "photoshopped" those images so as to make me look tall. I'm only, in reality, five foot ten—which is David's height as well. My weight, then: one-fifty.

How, though, you may be wondering, could I leave both David and the boys for an entire—academic—year? For the same three reasons, as far as David was concerned, I could leave that man who fell for my student. First of all, I'd have stayed home with him had I gotten some *non*residential fellowship—if, that is, something like, say, the MacArthur Foundation would just send me a god-damned check. Second of all, I knew—from having been told so by Warren—what it's like to live with a writer. Not fun. In fact as I write these lines—up here in our attic, while not on sabbatical—David's somewhere downstairs, maybe the basement, wondering no doubt when he'll ever see me today, if I'll talk to him at that point, and if so if it'll be about something other than this book. Third of all, I'd come home about once a month. Plus David, he promised, would come see me.

As far as the boys were concerned: both David and I thought, as did their mother Julie, that this would be a good opportunity for them to come see Harvard, and also Yale, and also Brown, plus maybe some other famous colleges with me. (Both Adam and Seth were by now high school students, with Sam still in junior high.) They eventually did do this, that year—thanks to Paola's stinky car. And though none, later on, would even apply to Harvard—which thanks to me they all hated—Sam liked Brown a lot, Seth liked Yale, and Adam, the Massachusetts Institute of Technology. It, too—like both Harvard and Radcliffe—is as you probably know in Cambridge. It's also, as you don't yet know, where Steve—when at college—used to go. MIT, he was, Class of 1979.

|||

I should have known, too, that I'd be haunted: in three cases by the still living, in only one case by the dead. With the first of these, I recalled, it all began the fall of 1967, at the beginning of third grade. This beginning, as you'll recall from "My Cortez," was at PS 135 with Mrs. Solomon. This memory, of mine, was what Proust—in translation—calls "involuntary." And the reason it didn't arise with Warren here with me, at Harvard, was probably that Warren was here.

Anyway, I had just moved up to the "IGC" class. This stood, as we weren't supposed to but did know, for "intellectually gifted children." Some black-haired, brown-eyed classmate, one morning at recess, asked if I'd be his "new best friend." His name, I'll say, was "Charles." And while there were now a couple of black girls in class, Charles—I recalled—was the only such boy. In fact, the whole school—as I've implied—was mostly white. It was not, though, mostly Jewish.

I hadn't yet—it struck me at the time—even met this kid before. I therefore had no idea why *me*. No other stranger, in my then seven-year-old experience, ever proposed such a thing. Nor had anyone already known to me. Still, I figured, I didn't yet have such a friend. Maybe this was how you got one. Plus my brother Bob's best friend, Isaiah, was black. So too was Dad's, from work—a man named Bob Sublett. Like the two of them, moreover, this Charles kid seemed nice. And so—I recalled—I said yes.

Charles, turns out, was very nice. Over the course of that year and then the rest of elementary school—grades four, five, and six, with Mrs. Froelich, Keaton, and Kelly—we were pretty much inseparable. We'd sit in class together. We'd eat together at lunch. We'd play at recess. We'd sing in choir. I recalled, in particular, having done the song "Maria," from *West Side Story*, with Charles there as a duet. (*Maria / I've just met a girl named Maria.*) We'd also pass novels back and forth, preferably ones with sex scenes. I recalled, in particular, his having shared *Johnny Got His Gun* by Dalton Trumbo. In return, I'd have shared *Fanny Hill*, but the mere existence of that sodomy scene there, or rather my already shameful interest in it, prevented me. So did the diction—the euphemism—or rather the related fact that this whole book, as I've already said in "G712," was hard for me to picture.

After school, not living close enough to each other to walk or even ride bicycles over, we'd almost always telephone. (His phone number, then: GR9–4731. My number: HO8–3661.) On weekends, though, having been driven over by a parent, we could visit in person. My own parents, I'm sure, loved Charles, as of course did I. But whereas I couldn't now recall him, specifically, in my house, I did recall being in his. That house, like Mr. and Mrs. Sublett's, seemed to me surprisingly lower-middle class: smaller, even, than ours and with not so nice furniture. I recalled, too, his family: Charles, Sr., who worked on subways for the Metropolitan Transit Authority; Juanita, a stay-at-home mom; plus Cassandra, a sister just two years older than Charles but already, she told me, pre-med. My own mother taught retarded kids. Sorry, Mom, "emotionally disturbed" ones.

Plus he *was* "gifted." Incredibly gifted, in fact—like Cassandra—and yet unlike me industrious. Charles, you see, aced every assignment, every exam—always scoring higher than I did—and yet also for some reason did "extra-credit." Upon elementary school graduation, then, he got awards for almost every subject. I got no such thing. No surprise there, I guess, but still it was depressing. It confirmed a message that my brother Steve, equally gifted, had always—rather meanly—conveyed: that I was a bit of a "tard." But it was a wake-up call, too. Thanks mostly to Charles, not Steve, I now felt—I recalled—that I should work harder than before, probably twice as hard, and so then maybe do as well as he would in junior high.

Charles and I, still together, were about the only kids from that IGC class to go to JHS 109. (While most such schools, in New York City, do have names—PS 135, for instance, is also the "Bellaire School," JHS 109 is also "Queens Village Junior High School"—people never use them.) Other classmates, for the most part, had been zoned elsewhere. And those who hadn't been chose JHS 109's three-year "SP"—or "Special Progress"—track. We two, instead, chose the accelerated *two*-year track, in which—once again—Charles was the only black boy. But whereas most of all of PS 135 had been white, most of the rest of JHS 109 was black: bused in, from Jamaica, Queens, under de jure desegregation. Unlike Charles, though, these kids were poor, and to me at least—along with other white boys—understandably mean. They'd even beat us up a lot, or at least threaten to, and only ostensibly for "lunch money." Charles protected me from such conduct, when he could. Steve—having already begun high school, or Bronx High School of Science—wasn't there anymore. But nor would he have been able to protect me. And nor—I thought—would he have even tried.

Charles and I—still inseparable—now did equally well in every subject. We had, I recalled, very cool, very pretty Miss Deutsch for English. Miss *Ava* Deutsch, that is, who at twenty-something must have been about thirty years younger than either Mrs. Solomon, Froelich, Keaton, and or Kelly. And while, with no choir at this school, we didn't sing together anymore, we did at least join band—Charles learning clarinet there and I the French horn. This, though—for me—had nothing to do with that predicate "French" nor for Charles to do with reeds. We'd been assigned those instruments by a Mr. Steier: very cool, as well, but also very sweaty. Charles already played piano—like both Steve and me. Plus like Bob, of course. As a lefty, though—like Steve alone of us three brothers—Charles was relatively hobbled at it.

And then like Steve and Cassandra we too went to Bronx Science. Although public, like PS 135 and JHS 109, the high school is "specialized." This meant you took a test to get in. It also meant: no zoning. It also meant: no busing. And so it also meant: geek nirvana. With a student body about one-third white, with most of us Jewish, one-third black, and one-third Asian, there was, I felt, no racial tension. With students living all over the city, including even Staten Island, and hence too far apart, for the most part, to visit each other after school, there was no class tension. It took Charles and me, for instance—like Steve and Cassandra, still—over an hour and a half to get there, by both bus and subway. And so we'd spend more than three hours a day commuting. Plus with all "Scienceites," even freshmen and sophomores like the two us, focused on admission to the same few famous colleges—Harvard and Yale in particular, with both of them having quotas on if not Jews anymore then Scienceites—there wasn't even sexual tension. (Yale, for instance, had never taken more than three Scienceites—out of about eight hundred—per year.) Who with all that studying not to mention commuting—I recalled—had any time to date? Who, for that matter, had energy for it?

Bronx Science, though, had neither choir nor band. It had, instead, an orchestra in which I played, the horn, but Charles—alas—did not. (I dreamt recently that our conductor there, Mrs. Rothenberg—Mrs. *Beatrice* Rothenberg, that is, who, I'd later learn in Italy, had already introduced Mr. and Mrs. Alda to each other—heard me play some Mozart, on piano, and then said to someone else present: "This guy *stinks.*" The comment, for some reason, made me giddy. Arlene Alda, née Weiss, is in reality a clarinetist, which must have been how she knew Rothenberg.) Charles and I did, however, once again have the same "homeroom"—like back in junior high. We also shared at least a few classes. As juniors, for instance, we both had that sexpot—Miss Florence Dragnet—for English. There, I recalled, papers we did on "desire" in the novel *Ethan Frome,* by Edith Wharton, got the exact same grade. As seniors, we both had a Mr. Harrison for advanced-placement or "AP" history. There, a paper Charles did on the so-called Gilded Age—so-called, that is, by both Mark Twain and Charles Dudley Warner—got a somewhat better grade than mine. No surprise there, as with those elementary school awards, yet now—at least after I, too, read the thing—no depression either. For both the argument and the writing by Charles were brilliant. Maybe as brilliant as what Twain could do.

We had different teachers, though, for AP English. I had Joseph Scavone—who was straight, clearly—whereas Charles had clearly gay Mark Rivkin. Those two, by the way, were friends. Best friends, it seemed—until Rivkin, as I'd also later learn, died of AIDS. (Not that Charles and I ever discussed those men's sexualities. Nor did we discuss our own.) We had different ones, too, for AP math, with Charles taking the upper-level and de facto all-male version called for some reason "AB Calculus" and I the coed, lower-level "BC Calculus."

And even there—I recalled—my grades were all over the place. (Nowadays, of course—like most people my age, maybe even including Charles—I can barely do arithmetic.)

Despite that math performance, as you'll recall from "My Cortez," I got into both Harvard and Yale. So did Charles. (Each school, for the first and maybe last time ever, took about ten Scienceites that year—pretty much the same ten.) But whereas I—so as not to go where Bob had—chose Yale, Charles chose Harvard. (He'd go on from there to get a journalism degree from Columbia University and then a law degree from Yale. His sister Cassandra, I've just learned from the Internet, did become a doctor.) Neither one of us thought things would change. And so when Charles signed my yearbook, he wrote:

> This is idiotic in 2 ways: 1st, this obviously is not the end of our friendship (or even a slowing down, etc., if you write); 2ndly, if it were, this short speil [sic] would not be anywhere near adequate. Good luck at Yale even though you made a *serious stupid error* in not choosing Harvard. (If you do not write, I will kill you.)

Not so brilliant, I know. But—workspace counts—we were on the subway at the time.

Things, though, did change—which I recalled having realized the one and only time, during our freshman year of college, that I ever saw Charles up here in Cambridge. I saw Steve then as well, in his Inman Street apartment over by MIT. But I was staying with Charles, in Matthews Hall on Harvard Yard. And so that was where—walking by the building one morning—this whole memory arose. Not only his roommate but also two "suite-mates," I saw to what was at last my surprise, were black. So too was some girlfriend of his, named Maria. And none of them, including Charles, was at all nice to me. So that was that, after which neither one of us ever telephoned the other. Nor did we even write letters. (This was many years before e-mail let alone text messaging let alone social network sites.) We did, however, see each other once more, a few years later, on Hillside Avenue in Queens. But it was by accident—on a bus. The Q43.

"We were friends and have become estranged," wrote Nietzsche, late in his own life, on what he called—in translation—"Star Friendship":

> But that was right, and we do not want to hide and obscure it from ourselves as if we had to be ashamed of it. We are two ships, each of which has its own goal and course; we may cross and have a feast together, as we did—and then the good ships lay so quietly in one harbor and in one sun that it may have seemed as if

they had already completed their course and had the same goal. But then the almighty force of our projects drove us apart once again, into different seas and sunny zones, and maybe we will never meet again—or maybe we will, but will not recognize each other: the different seas and suns have changed us!

And yet, I felt, this wasn't true here.

| | |

The second case, I recalled, began the fall of 1982. Brown-haired, brown-eyed "Vanessa," as I'll call her, had been to Princeton University for college and then up until a few months earlier Harvard for law school. I myself, at twenty-two, had just been to Columbia Law School. This memory, too, was involuntary. It arose one morning in the Harvard Law School library—or Langdell Hall—as I worked there both for a change of venue from Lowell House and as an experiment. (I was so to speak "doing" Bruce Chatwin [1940–1989], that literary cruiser—also central to *Neatness Counts*—who himself had claimed to use such public space to work in, though I'd later learn he was lying. He had really used friends' homes.)

Vanessa and I, at any rate, were at the same Manhattan law firm—that first firm mentioned in both "My Cortez" and "G712." Its offices, I should again say, were in Rockefeller Center—in what was then still called the RCA Building. It's the tallest one there—the building that, come Christmastime, dwarfs even that giant Christmas tree. Plus the two of us were officemates—as with Lane at Penn, later on, except the room here was neat and we both had real desks. The firm, though, was terrible. Whatever work we'd be given—as first-year associates—was boring yet difficult and just barely justifiable: stuff like defending tobacco companies in cancer litigation or oil companies in spill litigation. Don't believe it? Then ask David Hyde Pierce. He's the actor, from the television show *Frasier* (1993–2004), who at the time also worked—as a paralegal—at the firm. Unlike writing, by the way, such acting is rarely best done alone. (Acting, they say, is *re*acting.) Unless, of course, we're talking soliloquies—of which such sitcoms have none.

Worse yet, than that work, were those partners. (Partners, at law firms, have the equivalent of tenure; associates do not yet.) All of them were white. All but two, out of about a hundred, were male. Some hurled books at you, if you were a male associate, when they didn't like memoranda you'd either written or, as in my case, sometimes plagiarized: the kind of physical abuse to which as it happens that "Ichabod" of mine, at Radcliffe and then also Harvard, would later that year refer. Some said meet them at seven this Sunday morning in their office—and then never bother showing up themselves. Some literally screwed you on their desk, if you were a female associate, and then the next day have you fired. Or at least one of them did—at Christmastime. Another partner, named William Mathers—Yale Law School, Class of 1938—would at meals out with male associates tell what he called "nigger jokes." But when this happened with me there, I simply got up, told Mathers *I'm* black—which Vanessa, like both Charles and Isaiah, really is—and left the restaurant. It wasn't long after this that *I* was fired—for being gay, or as I now supposed for *also* being gay—which, while working in Lowell House, I (or rather my narrator "Kevin") would now finally confess in *Neatness Counts*.

The firm, then, was both misogynist and homophobic. Hence that desktop screw. Hence, too, those token female partners, one of whom, clearly, was lesbian, though you could also be fired, as at least one male associate was, for suggesting as much. Plus it was racist. Hence those "nigger jokes." Plus it was anti-Semitic. Hence, I recalled, our official summer "outing." This was held, one Saturday, at a Long Island country club that would never admit—as members—either blacks or Jews. Nor even knowingly admit gay men or lesbians. I therefore wore hot pants to the event, along with my "Star of David" tank top. And then a furtive, unofficial outing was held, the next Wednesday, at— you guessed it—Mathers' place. This, too, was on Long Island—probably "East Egg," Long Island. And while our few Jewish partners had been invited there, the likes of either Vanessa or me had not. Imagine, then, the two of us showing up for work that morning—but finding not one single partner in. Nor, we soon realized, was any non-Jewish white associate.

Thank God, then, for Vanessa. (There *are* no atheists in foxholes. But Vanessa is Catholic.) For not only, like Diana Eck, was she beautiful, brilliant, and kind, she was nurturing, protective, and funny as well. Like Jesse Green, my college friend and then apartment mate in law school, she'd try feeding me— while herself dieting unnecessarily. (I weighed one-thirty, at the time.) Like Warren, whom Vanessa liked a lot, she'd not only remember but also celebrate my birthday—with nice little surprise parties—in our office. (The day, in case you're interested, is January twenty-third—or one-two-three.) I, though, would stupidly, stupidly forget hers. Plus she'd warn me about who at the firm, whether partner or associate, was especially homophobic or anti-Semitic. I'd reciprocate, at least, with who there was especially racist or misogynist. She'd also tell very funny—but clearly false—stories. Most of these were about her having—in fantasy—shamed awful partners. "Are you *crazy?*" she might claim she asked such men—just as I really would tell that dinner party host, at Harvard, that his friends were awful or Ichabod that *he's* the one like Ike.

She also told not so funny true stories. Most of these were about Vanessa herself. Some, though, were about other black folk. I recalled, for instance, stories about her mother—a widow at thirty-four, with four children to raise. Three girls and a boy. I recalled, too, stories about some boy named Eddie. He and Vanessa—back in Roosevelt, Long Island—had grown up together. Unlike Vanessa, though, he'd never go to college. And yet he now worked—as did we—in the RCA Building. This "Eddie," you see, was Eddie Murphy—the actor, from 1980 to 1984, on *Saturday Night Live.* The television show got filmed there. And all such true stories were meant to show or rather *teach* me just what such lives, in reality, were like. They were meant, that is, to teach that—thanks to racism— African Americans have always had to work twice as hard as white folk . . . to get just half as far. But this, I thought—in Langdell Hall—didn't seem to be the case anymore. Not here in academia, at any rate, for the likes of Vanessa—and maybe not even law firms. It did, though—to judge not only from what Vanessa told me but also from what I myself saw with her at the firm, plus before that what I'd seen with Charles at our schools together—clearly *used* to be the case. Vanessa really *had* worked that hard: first at Princeton, as she said, and then at Harvard, and then at the firm. No reading Proust there for her and then calling it on timesheets—as I did—"professional development," nor any hanging out with that female associate whom I called—in "My Cortez," taking the name from Proust—"Albertine."

One day, though, and for the first time, Vanessa asked me to read some memo she wrote. To be honest, I'd forgotten by then—in Langdell Hall—what it was about. And the reason I forgot was that I wasn't just surprised but astonished by the writing. Here, as with Charles on the "Gilded Age" for Mr. Harrison and even as with Jesse on just about anything, was someone who could really work—and play—with both language and form, plus both thought and information; someone who had really done her homework and yet now wore such learning lightly; someone who devised long, periodic sentences—much like Proust—and yet unlike him never lost you in the process, who both held your attention and impressed you by simply—or not so simply—putting word after word after word, and then word after word after word, and also clause after clause after clause; someone, moreover, who devised short, epigrammatic

zingers; someone who to now quote Wayne Koestenbaum—later—on such al-
leged virtuosity in my first book, *Love's Litany*, really did move "with a litigator's
clean, panoptic brio" and yet without, as it were, breaking a sweat; plus some-
one who, more to the point, did these things just as well as if not better than I
myself could—or than I *thought* I could.

But then, I recalled, I was both astonished and ashamed I should be aston-
ished. I had not, after all, been surprised by Charles' paper—nor of course by
anything of Jesse's. So had I, too—like Mathers—now become racist? Or worse
yet, sexist *and* racist?

I next supposed, in that law library, that I had been stupid, idiotic, or maybe
even, yes, retarded enough to have confessed much of this to Vanessa at the
time, just as I'm now doing so—primarily—to her here. I'd forgotten that by
then as well, along with whatever her response to such a "speech act" might
have been. I did recall, though, that she'd never again show me memos. And
also that when a few months later I invited Vanessa to a piano duet recital, in
my apartment, she said she'd come but didn't. (The apartment, a very neat
one-bedroom, was—as I've already said in "G712"—down by the World Trade
Center. The duet partner—named Burkhard—was another male associate. Plus
he was my best friend, at the time. Plus I had a crush on him. He's straight,
though, like some Scavone to my Rivkin.) So that, once again, was that. And
then after—having been fired—I started working—really working—at my sec-
ond law firm, we never saw each another again. Not even, as with Charles, by
accident somewhere. I did, though, later get Christmas cards from Vanessa—
photographs included. These, at first, showed her married—to a black man
named Kevin. They also, eventually, showed their own three children. Two
girls and a boy.

| | |

The third case, I recalled, began the fall of 1993. Blond-haired, brown-eyed
"Carol," as I'll call her, had been to I'll say Vassar College and then Har-
vard for graduate school. Doug Trevor, too, a few years later, would get his
own doctorate—also in English—here. That department, as it happens, is in
the Humanities Center. But it wasn't the day of my allegedly abusive Proust
presentation when this memory arose. It was before then, in Harvard's art
museum—called the "Fogg Museum," after a William Hayes Fogg—as I was
studying "Caryatid II" by Constantin Brancusi (1876–1957). This sculpture

looks nothing like those white ladies of the Acropolis. It looks, rather, like a dark brown piano leg.

Carol had then joined our English department, as a first-year—hence not yet tenured—assistant professor. Plus, perhaps, as a token African American. For reasons not worth articulating, I'd neither done job interviews the year before—my own first year in the department—nor been otherwise involved in hiring. I myself, at any rate, may have been a token gay. For one thing, I'd been hired to teach—primarily—what we soon started calling not "lesbian and gay" studies but "sexuality" studies. And so I'd often joke that, unlike at law firm number one, I'd be fired if straight. I of course never joked Carol would be, if white.

Carol then became a friend of mine. An even better friend, in fact, than—before that memo reading—Vanessa had been. She, too—like Vanessa—was smart, funny, nurturing, protective, and kind. She, too—like Bunting Fellows here—would play hooky with me from both presentations and meetings. Plus, as friends, we'd compare—before any heartbreak—boyfriends. Mine, she liked, saying for instance: "You're so *lucky!*" Hers, though, I did not like—and not just because, like Carol, he was fat. Plus, as friends, we'd mock ourselves. I, for instance, told Carol about my Proust reading—on the job—at that law firm. She told me about having once—in some interdisciplinary class on "the gaze," at Harvard—kept naming the sculptor "Vancuzzi." The professor there, maybe Ichabod, finally asked: "Don't you mean *Brancusi?*" In a non-interdisciplinary class, Carol said, she once confused Pushkin, the poet, with—from the novel *The Idiot*, by Dostoevsky—"Prince Myshkin."

We would also read to each other. We'd read, that is, our work in progress. Or rather I myself—to impress Carol—did this a lot. (I now, of course, do so to David, as well as to the boys, as well as to some of their own friends.) Sometimes, I recalled, such soliloquy—such *rhapsody* rather, to invoke Plato—would be during telephone calls. (Soliloquy, on stage, is from memory; rhapsody, often from script.) And those calls, as with Charles in elementary school, happened almost daily. Mostly, though, such rhapsody would be—in Carol's quite messy office—during office hours.

There was, though, one rhapsody—in my own neat office—by Carol. She read, I recalled, a conference talk on let's say Sarah Vaughan, 1924–1990. The title—like Vaughan's nickname—was "Sassy." The thesis was that this pop but also jazz singer's—allegedly—"operatic" voice had made "race, gender, sexuality, and above all class indeterminate." This I thought—while listening—both silly and unwarranted. I thought it, as lawyers say, an *ipse dixit*. And yet unlike

Ichabod, because of or perhaps despite my friendship with her, I then said nothing of the kind—confession number one—to Carol. I also, as yet, then said nothing of the kind to other members of the department. I thought the writing bad, too, while listening, but—confession number two—then said nothing of that kind either, to either Carol or as yet other colleagues there. (To myself, though, I said that if this thing were a novel it'd be either *Love Story*, with awful, awful lines like the one by Jennifer on love being "never having to say you're sorry," or, closer to what was now for both of us home, *The Bridges of Madison County*. The author of *Love Story*, by the way, had taught Classics at both Harvard and Yale. Princeton, too, I think. The other author was basically a photographer.) I just—in response to this rhapsody—asked Carol *how* she worked. "Like a *crazy* lady," she laughed—beautifully. (She does, in fact, have a beautiful laugh, like either Colleen Dewhurst or Natalie Portman.) That "crazy," I guessed, meant very, very quickly. (I myself, as you can probably tell, write slowly: like the tortoise, in Aesop, to Carol's crazy hare.)

Three years went by. I got tenure. And then Carol, I recalled while "gazing" at that Brancusi sculpture, came up. Such promotion, to "associate" professorship at a research institution, requires there to have been—and rules are rules—not just acceptable teaching but also the presentation of various conference talks, the publication of various articles, and the publication of at least one book. "Sassy," I discovered upon reading the file, was my friend's only such talk. Plus she'd published no articles. Nor, as I already knew, had she published a book. There was, though, this book manuscript there—also called *Sassy*. It—allegedly—was under contract at some university press. I then read the thing, but—alas—found it pretty much the same as "Sassy." Same silly thesis. Same, I thought, bad writing. And so when, with the understanding that all such meetings, unlike those meals with Mathers, are of course confidential, we associate and also "full" professors discussed tenure for Carol . . . And this here, in this book, is no confession, for I didn't consider the following recalled "speech act" really trashing her, and nor did I consider it the equivalent of trying to fire her for no good reason, and nor even did I consider it the verbal equivalent of hurling books at Carol, because friend or no friend, goddammit, rules were rules . . . I finally had to tell others what I thought.

"The name 'Vaughan,' in *Sassy*," I began, "is often misspelled as 'Vaughn.'" No response, I recalled, from those tenured colleagues of mine. "Have you noticed that?" No response, once again—so I just guessed they had noticed. "Plus other names are totally misspelled," I continued. "'Beverly Sills,' for instance,

is 'Beverly Stills;' 'Franco Corelli' is 'Frank Coralli.'" "Those are *typos*, Kevin,"
someone barked. "No," I explained. "Such errors show either ignorance or neg-
ligence. Laziness, really. For it's bad enough for Carol not to know such names,"
as with Brancusi or even Pushkin, "but to *know* she doesn't know yet not bother
looking them up is, for a scholar, really inexcusable." No response. "Many dates,
moreover, are off, including, unbelievably enough, that of Vaughan's death."
No response. "So, too," I continued, "are many of Carol's song interpretations."
Though I didn't say it, back then, she's got even less musical intelligence than
I do. "She claims, for instance, that Gershwin's 'Summertime,' from the op-
era *Porgy and Bess*, is only really about gender [*Your daddy's rich / And your
mamma's good-lookin'*] and, worse yet, that the Nietzschean song 'Just Friends,'
by John Klenner, is about race [*Two friends / Drifting apart / Two friends / But
one broken heart*]." Still no response—so I stupidly guessed they're all with me.
"But maybe the most upsetting problem," I ended for now, "concerns this thesis
on 'indeterminacy.' Like a lot of work on both gender and sexuality, all vaguely
deconstructive and none of it even mentioned here, Carol presents no evidence
that anyone has ever really *heard* Vaughan this way. And the only such evidence
I can think of—George Kirby's impersonation of Vaughan on *The Kopykats*—is
missing." Still no response. "It's a television show"—broadcast from 1972 to,
once again, 1972. Just one season. Kirby (1923–1995), as you may know, was
black.

Carol would get tenure. For not only had I just been the only one in our
department to *argue* against such promotion, I'd be the only one there to *vote*
against it. That argument—or maybe that hatchet job on *Sassy*—was then dis-
missed—or maybe trashed—by one Jewish colleague as mere "projection" on
my part. (So despite what I'd later write in "My Cortez," they're not *all* nice
those colleagues of mine. To quote Proust, though, with reference to his nar-
rator's—Jewish—friend Bloch as well as to the non-Jewish narrator himself and
even, perhaps, to the half-Jewish author: "To the bad habit of speaking about
oneself and one's defects there must be added, as part of the same thing, that
habit of denouncing in other people defects precisely analogous to one's own.
For it is always of those defects that one speaks, as though it were a way of speak-
ing of oneself indirectly, and adding to the pleasure of absolving oneself the
pleasure of confession." This might apply, of course, to Professor "Projection"
denouncing me as well as to me denouncing Carol.) And then a Mormon col-
league—not "Becky Thatcher"—said Carol deserved extra "points" from us for
being black, much as the University of Michigan, he added, gives them to all

such applicants. (The United States Supreme Court, as you may know, would soon rule such practices unconstitutional.) None of this, I guessed in that art museum, should have surprised me. But it did surprise me, and so I myself— I recalled—then barked: "That's an *awful* analogy. Carol probably got these 'points,' from you, when you hired her, just as I—being gay—probably did. So the figurative question isn't whether we should *admit* Carol, which you already did, it's if she's now done enough to *graduate*."

After the vote a couple of things happened. But first let me say what did not happen. I did not resign in protest. For where else in the academy could I go? Nor did I complain to the dean. Doing so, I feared, might make me even more of a pariah—in the department—than I thought I'd become. And then—what did happen—two tenured female colleagues confessed to me, one by one in the privacy of their offices, that they, too, thought *Sassy* is silly. The second of these added: "Carol herself, though, is the best we'll get." This meant—I took it—that unlike women or even goddamned *faggots* like you in the academy, there aren't many, well, this woman must be thinking, *niggers* here. And so, *stupid*, even schools like ours—*public* research institutions IN THE MIDDLE OF FRIG-GIN' NOWHERE—have to take whomever we can get . No response, from me. Perhaps, though—I supposed in that museum—I should have responded to pro-fessor number two as I had to Mathers: by saying that *I'm* black and then leaving the room. Or, better yet, by saying that she probably should have said so—pub-licly—at our meeting. And then some other tenured colleague, I recalled, must have told Carol—both confidentiality and niceness be damned—everything I'd said there about her manuscript. So *that* was that. She never again spoke to me. Never again laughed with me. If only, I realized at the museum, I'd told Carol herself—in the privacy of my office—what I really thought about that talk she just read; and yet if only—in the office we shared—I had *not* told Vanessa what I thought about her memo; if only, that is, I'd been a better—non-"star"—friend to both women; not only might *Sassy*—in print, though it never has gotten published—be pretty good, but so, too—in person—might both Vanessa and I as well as Carol and I still be on good terms.

| | |

And then, that year, there was a white boy. He wasn't Warren, though, with whom I was still on good terms. Nor was he my brother Bob, despite memories of that Harvard graduation of his (nausea, vomit), and also of him doing both solo piano and chamber music recitals here, and also of him conducting opera: *Don Giovanni*, in Kirkland House. (Or was it, I now wonder, Isaiah who conducted?) I was haunted, too—most haunted, and in lots of places—by brother Steve. I'd see the *Harvard Lampoon* building, just outside Lowell House, and recall a photograph of it he took and then framed and then hung up in his Inman Street apartment. Or, having walked—alone—up Massachusetts Avenue past the Humanities Center, I'd see the fish place we once ate in and recall a confession to Steve I at least tried making there. Or, having walked further up "Mass Ave," I'd see Inman Square and recall even more stuff about the one and only time—during my senior year of college—I ever stayed with him in that apartment. Or—one time—I'd walk down Inman Street, to see if unlike Steve the apartment building still exists. (It does.) Or I'd be at MIT, with Adam, and see its so-called Building Seven—the importance of which for Steve I'll have Steve himself, in just a bit, once again show. And so I finally realized—at some point—that *Neatness Counts*, as had been true on some level of so much of if not all of my previous work, was really an elegy. And so "Kevin," its narrator, would soon also realize this.

It all began—for me—on a January the twenty-third. Others who share this birthday—one-two-three—include Muzio Clementi, the piano virtuoso, Django Reinhardt, the guitarist, and the actress Chita Rivera—or "Anita" in the stage version of *West Side Story* (1957). Anna Pavlova, the ballerina, died that day—in 1931. The year I was born was 1960. Steve was less than two at the time or not yet old enough to maybe appreciate such company. This, on the one hand, was ironic. I'd been conceived, according to Mom, to *keep* him company. Dad, though, said I was an accident—like all their kids. That's all I ever then really wanted to do: keep Steve company. On the other hand, it was unfortunate. Nearly two decades of both verbal and physical abuse by him—as by Ike of Tina—now began. He'd toss me out of the crib and onto the floor; chase me, at about age four, into the open, burning hot oven; stab me—quite painfully—in the leg with a pen. But mostly he'd just hit—hard—and if I told Dad on him he'd call it just a "love tap." It was as if he'd been dead set, from the outset, on literally beating such desire—such love—out of my system. The physical abuse, of course, happened less and less as we grew older. Even so, he did once nearly kill me, at age sixteen, by bashing my head against a wall. He then, while begging me not to tell, seemed stunned by what just happened. So I didn't tell. And yet the verbal abuse, the gist of which was always that I'm both ugly—because fat, very, very fat—and stupid, retarded even, never ever *ever* let up.

Structurally speaking, there's of course nothing that unusual about such rivalry. It's the oldest story in the world: Cain and Abel, Romulus and Remus, Frasier and Niles. *Post*structurally, here, what's unusual—I realized—was not just the level of violence but also how much I truly loved Steve. What's unusual, too, was how sorry for him I felt. And yet I must now invoke my—sibling-like, or rather brotherly-sister-like—friend Elisabeth Ladenson. In a recent conference talk—on Balzac—she described both structuralism and poststructuralism as "tendencies that appear to be at odds with each other until they're compared with anything else." It's now my favorite—serio-comic—line in criticism, after one by Monique Wittig. "For me," wrote Wittig in "The Straight Mind," "there is no doubt that Lacan found in the 'unconscious' the [language-like] structures that he claims to have found since he had previously put them there."

Yet—as with structuralism and poststructuralism—it can be hard to distinguish such emotions. Both love and or pity for Steve—I realized—always felt the same to me. Plus this was then also true—I realized—with Warren. Plus this was then also true with, well, let's just call that heartbreaker I was so "lucky" to have, "Matt." I'd both loved and or pitied Warren, who at age fourteen lost a twelve-year-old brother, named Allie, to leukemia. I'd both loved and or pitied Matt, who at age ten lost a dog. This was *not* now true, though—I also realized—with David. I love David, who at twelve lost a thirteen-year-old brother in a motorcycle accident. I do not also pity him.

Also unusual, I realized—while hoping that *I'm* not "putting structures" there—was how mentally off, or "emotionally disturbed," Steve was. For he wasn't just "gifted." He was also—like Charles and then Vanessa, or like Geeta, Doug, and David now—both brilliant and attractive: quite slim, as you know, although at five foot six, eventually, a bit on the short side; quite athletic, in both fencing and gymnastics; and with humor derived from both *Firesign Theatre*, that old radio show, and the Harvard Lampoon derived magazine *National Lampoon*, very, very funny. And yet—this being one reason for pity—he never to my knowledge had friends. Certainly no best friends, like Charles and then both Jesse Green and Bill Watson and then Burkhard and now both Doug and Geeta. (See "Kiss and Tell" and "Salome" for more on Bill.) He certainly had no girlfriends. And nor—to my knowledge—boyfriends.

Teachers, though, liked Steve. Mrs. Keaton—whom Steve had also had—once interrupted what she called our "class reading period" to announce: "You know, Kevin, your *brother* would have used this time to study *maps* up here." That was true, if also, as I *was* reading, goddammit, abusive of her. (So shame on *you*, Mrs. Keaton.) Steve loved maps. Foreign maps, in particular. In fact he loved all such insignia: foreign coins, which he collected; foreign stamps, which he also collected; plus tiny foreign flags. He bought those flags, maybe once a month, at the United Nations gift shop—in Manhattan. Steve displayed the flags by a model United Nations that, the summer before this reading period incident, both he and our oldest brother, named Eric but nicknamed "Ricky," had—"stars out"—designed and, using balsa wood, built. Its dome was a "spaldeen" ball—made of pink rubber—that they'd cut in half and then—using a silvery color—spray-painted.

"Ricky," as I still call him, is now a retired architect. At the time, though—1969—he was about to be drafted. During service in Colorado— blindness in one eye had kept him out of Vietnam—he'd get married, to another architect named Eileen, and then afterward wander off to California with her. Both he and twin sister Maureen—or "Micky"—are three years older than Bob. Both he and Bob are six feet tall—as was Dad.

Like Eric and also Eileen in California—Berkeley, California—Steve, too, was a lefty. All three, that is, were rather left-wing. Rather socialist. Rather "hippyish," I thought back then. Steve, though—unlike Bob and me and also Maureen—had pretty much always been that way. In Keaton's class, for instance, he refused to say the Pledge of Allegiance. And then, with Dad's approval, he once actually took *off* from school just to go to some stupid anti-war so-called moratorium march on Washington. The date was November 15, 1969, or nearly ten years to the day before he'd die: November 1, 1979. (For a long time thereafter, the date November first—or one-one-zero-one—was both my parents' security code as well as mine for anything. This began, for them, with a burglar alarm system; for me, with a briefcase.) And then Steve spent summers in Berkeley: building some communal playground with Eric, or running some "food coop" with Eileen, or even, for all I knew, nabbing Patty Hearst. He spent one summer, though, in Israel, on some kibbutz there that later seemed to me to have turned him into if not a Zionist, exactly, then at least a full-blown socialist. After that—with help from Dad—he taught himself Yiddish. (That's spelled *spiel*, Charles, not *speil*.) This took only, and quite typically for Steve, about a week. Like me, though—in after-school and also weekend classes from age six up until, at thirteen, one's bar mitzvah—he'd already learned Hebrew.

So, I told myself, Steve was gifted, brilliant, attractive, and funny. He was also—like me—obsessive. Plus manic, at times. Yet I still couldn't figure out—at Harvard—why there were no friends. Nor why he seemed—more than most such brothers—to truly hate me. (Don't believe it? Keep reading.) Maybe, I guessed as usual, I *was* hateful. If so, though, why—like some wife beater—did Steve also seem—once or twice, but come to think of it there were three times—to love me. Maybe, I then guessed for the first time, he too—like Mom—was "borderline."

| | |

It all began—for the two of us—in about 1964. And these memories, here, were *not* involuntary at Harvard. They are things I've recalled, obsessively, almost every day for the past thirty years. Steve and I—alone—were in our attic bedroom, maybe playing, when he said to me: "Let's touch tongues." Now, I had no idea why do this. I'd no idea why me. Still, though, I thought, why not. So I said yes. And then, giggling at first, we did it: tip to tip, for about a second. But then, this being an odd sensation, we burst out laughing.

Bob, about that time, took us—via subway—to our first ballet: *Swan Lake*, done at, I think, the Metropolitan Opera House by, I'm quite sure, the Bolshoi Ballet. I do know that I was just blown away by this. Once home, I told Mom everything. "Oh," she responded, "those women are *famous* for arm movement!" (She'd meant, in French, *port de bras*.) I then—stars out—made drawing after drawing, using crayons, of both Odette, dressed in white, and her "evil twin," Odile, in black. Steve had not been blown away. Nor was he now impressed by my artwork.

Eric, sometime thereafter, both designed and—with help from Dad—built a tree house for us. The tree was a tulip tree, out back. The house was A-frame. I never got to play up in it with Steve. He wouldn't let me.

Maureen, at about that time, took us to the Museum of Natural History—in Manhattan. Our first stop was the gift shop. Steve, she bought something I can't recall—maybe some foreign rock. Me, she got a Mexican "tree of life"—one of those beautiful but purely decorative candlesticks, sculpted from clay and after that painted many, many colors, that most often show Adam and Eve. Mine, though, had two hanging angels: just heads and wings there, with for some reason no bodies. Being—like all boys—pyromaniac, I then actually used the thing. And so candle wax dripped, then hardened, then obscured some of the paint. I used hot water to remove that wax. And so paint, too—watercolor paint, apparently—came off. Being—like any sissy—crybabyish, I now began howling. And yet Steve—stars out—fixed it all back up for me, in oil paint. Why, I wondered, would he *do* that?

We always bought our mom Mother's Day presents. One year, though, that day went badly. I'd gotten Mom a ring, with one black pearl. Steve, I recall, got her flowers. These, of course, Mom loved. But then the two of them, as often happened, got into some argument—I can't recall about what. Steve then demanded Mom repay him for those flowers. "And I mean every penny," he yelled as she, now crying, stormed off to her bedroom and both slammed and locked its door. Steve himself, seeming stunned by what just happened, burst into tears and—still crying—begged Mom to come out. No response, from her. "What did I *say?*" he asked me. I repeated, since he asked, that bit about the penny. And now he howled. I, for maybe the first time, felt sorry for him.

On my first day of high school, with Steve still a senior there, he would not let us go together. He would not, that is, share any of "his" subway cars with me. (He would, though—for some reason—share the bus.) Not that day, nor any day thereafter—until I happened, perhaps hatefully, to tell Dad about it. Not that it mattered much, by that point. I could always find Charles to go with.

Steve first came home from college, the next year, at Christmastime. I'd gotten him, as a Hanukkah present, just some book I can't recall. He got me, to my surprise, *The Damnation of Faust*. This not quite opera but "*légende dramatique*" is by Berlioz. That recording's conductor was Seiji Ozawa, with the Boston Symphony Orchestra. That label: Deutsche Grammophone. How, I wondered, would Steve know I'd *love* this? Or that I'd even *like* it? Did he *care?* I still wonder these things. I wonder, as well, at Steve's prescience. For like Faust, I too am now an old scholar—although not one, apart from still unknown IDANT kids of mine, to feel life has passed him by.

Nor were that paint job, on my once again beautiful tree of life, and this Hanukkah present Steve's only kindnesses to me. The next summer he came home for a bit. But with Mom and Dad themselves in Berkeley, visiting Eric, Eileen, and their own two sons, it was just we two—home alone together. And each of us there *was* pretty much alone, doing his own thing. One day, though, Steve suggested we go to the Bronx Botanical Gardens—not that far from our high school. Why *me?* I wondered. He'd never before proposed such a thing. But I said yes. He drove us there, using Mom's car. And then—*nous allons marcher ensemble*—we walked and walked, while also talking, all around that beautiful, beautiful park.

That fall, he came back for Thanksgiving. We were in Dad's car now, with Dad driving, when for no reason—as usual—Steve started in on how stupid I am. I, as usual, tried to ignore this. Dad, though, could not. "You know, Steve," he said, "by *objective* measures Kevin's smarter than you." Those "measures"—I supposed—were SAT (or Scholastic Aptitude Test) scores, plus grades we'd each gotten from the same teachers at Bronx Science. And now—seeming stunned— Steve once again burst into tears. "How can you *say* that?" he cried. Dad him- self seemed stunned. I just—once again—felt sorry for Steve. But then, shortly thereafter, I realized—for no doubt the first time—that I'm both damned here if I do, like either Faust or Don Giovanni, and unlike them damned if I don't. My being stupid—allegedly—Steve found hateful. But so, too—for him—was my not being stupid.

I must have invited myself, during not just my senior year of college but Steve's as well, to stay with him on Inman Street. (Where I did four years in three, at Yale, he—having double-majored in architecture and urban plan- ning—took five years to graduate.) For one thing, Steve—next fall—would be moving to that very same kibbutz. And so I didn't know how much more, af- ter then, I'd ever get to see him. For another thing, I wanted to come out to him—now—in person. I'd already, after all, just done so to our parents. And then Mom, in response, had claimed—as you'll recall from "G712"—that all my brothers "went through that." If so, I figured, Steve would understand. And even if not, he might feel sorry for *me*. But when, in that fish place—on Massachu- setts Avenue—I tried to say to him that I'm gay, he for some reason didn't want to hear it. Or to quote Steve: "I don't want to hear it." And so I didn't say it— didn't *confess* it, rather. We then just paid the bill and walked—alone together— back to his apartment. We then hung out there, for a bit, in his bedroom. That's both where and when I noticed the Lampoon Building photograph—hung—as well as one of a handsome young man with long, beautiful, non-Jewish hair and wire-rimmed glasses. "Just a friend," said Steve. Steve left the apartment, to go—he told me, maybe lying—to some fencing match. I went to bed, on a ply- wood board outside that bedroom. I could not fall asleep. The telephone rang. An apartment mate of Steve's picked up. He—I could hear—began talking to someone about Steve. "The guy is *gay*," he said.

My college graduation, at nineteen, took place just about a week before Steve's. Steve—along with the rest of the family: Mom, Dad, Eric, Eileen, their boys Evan and Eddie, Maureen, her husband Arthur, plus their two kids, Bob, his wife Reiko, plus their as of yet one kid—was able to attend this. (Maybe Dad made him; it's now impossible for me to know. I did, at any rate, graduate *cum laude*—with honors from Yale. Bob, at Harvard, had been *magna cum laude*—plus *Phi Beta Kappa*.) I'd be leaving, the very next day—Yale Russian

Chorus tour—for the Soviet Union: Leningrad, Novgorod, Moscow, Yerevan, and Tblisi. And after that—youth hostel tour—for Europe: a graduation present to me, from Mom and Dad. Come fall, I'd enter Columbia Law School. Steve, too—before moving to Israel that fall—would be in Europe. That was his present from them. Only—just like back on the subway and even further back up in the tree house—he'd never, he told me, be anywhere there *with* me. After packing up my room, loading up Dad's car, and dropping Steve off at the—New Haven, Connecticut—train station for his ride back to Massachusetts, I, too, got out of that car. I wanted, you see, a real goodbye. I wanted what I thought would be some kind of—provisional—closure. With Steve facing that station and me facing the car, in which both Mom and Dad sat watching this scene, I wished him well, saying, perhaps, "I wish you the very best of happiness," and then did say goodbye. And then—for the first time ever, maybe—I hugged Steve. Steve, though, did not hug back. He *hit* me—or rather hit my back, repeatedly, which of course our folks couldn't see. Not that he hit hard, anymore, or hard enough to hurt, physically. He hit just enough—and then some—to signal: "Stop *hugging* me." And so I did stop. And then Steve—alone—walked into that station. Walked away, that is, from me just standing there—alone. Walked away from the three of us. I got back into the car. Here, Mom said she'd waited nearly twenty years to see us two do such a nice thing. I myself, in response, said . . . nothing.

Shortly after law school began, I wrote Steve a letter. It was a long one, too, I recall, in which—if only in writing—I did finally come out to him. I did not, of course, mention I knew—from the apartment mate—that Steve himself was gay. That *he* would have to tell—or rather to write—me. I did, though, mention how much I just hated law. But what else—I asked rhetorically—was I supposed to do with my life? I asked—non-rhetorically—about Steve's own life, in general, as well as life there for him, in particular, on the kibbutz. And then I did not end, as Charles had senior year in high school: "If you do not write, I will kill you." But—and for more on this see "Salome"—I'd soon feel I might as well have.

I'm afraid I can't say, in detail, how eagerly—how anxiously, rather—I awaited some response from Steve. Some letter from him, in return. I may not have to. What I can—in fact, must—say is that I never got one. Here's what happened. About two months later, Dad and I were home, in Queens, sitting in the kitchen. He was reading some newspaper. I was reading a law book. Mom was out, grocery shopping.

The doorbell rings. I go get the door. There's some man here, with a telegram—from Israel. When Dad hears this, from me, he says to let *him* open the telegram. And then—like King Lear, with Cordelia's body—he just howls. ("Howl, howl, howl, howl! O, you are men of stones. / Had I your tongues and eyes, I'd use them so / That heaven's vault should crack.") I grab that thing from Dad, see two sentences, the word "suicide." Micky and Art, meanwhile, are on their way to Queens from New Jersey—where they live. They had been telephoned earlier, by someone at the kibbutz, with the same awful, awful news as well as details about Steve's having been found hanging there, in his bedroom, from a belt—Steve's body, that is—including two facts it'll take me years to understand: he hadn't any clothes on; there was no note.

This death, you see, wasn't really a suicide. And yet, unlike that of the original Grangerford's Steve—

Despised love struck not with woe
   That head of curly knots,
Nor stomach troubles laid him low,
   Young Stephen Dowling Bots.

O no. Then list with tearful eye,
   Whilst I his fate do tell.
His soul did from this cold world fly,
   By falling down a well.

—nor was it really an accident. What it was, really—as I've hinted before, in both "G712" and elsewhere, but, so ashamed have I been, so stupidly, stupidly ashamed, am only here and now, finally, able to "confess"—was autoerotic asphyxiation. Truth be told—my Steve hadn't really meant to kill himself, at least not consciously. He'd only meant—even knowing, one assumes, the stupid risk—to have a bit more, well, fun than usual while masturbating.

I'll spare you details—which I could supply—of when Mom got back from shopping, of when Maureen arrived, of the funeral a week later. This delay, due to an autopsy, was in violation of Jewish law. But at least the casket, in conformity with it, was closed. I'll spare you details, too, of my now half-craving, half-dreading some letter back from Steve. (What, I wondered, if he wrote me before killing himself? What if he then mailed the thing before that? What if it arrived *today*?) I'll spare you, too, details of my own new unnecessary "diet," self-starvation really, and then of my inadvertently abusive treatment by, his real name, Dr. George Train, now deceased, the homophobic (but of course Jewish) psychoanalyst who thought my problem not, as implied in both *Beethoven's Kiss* and "My Cortez," my being both grief-stricken and—needless, here, to say—guilt-ridden, but my being gay.

I'll spare you, too, details of Steve's "unveiling"—at the cemetery—a year later. Except to quote his epitaph, there: "Stephen Kopelson 1957–1979." That's all it says. I'll even spare you details of what it was like for me, at Dad's request, to now start going through the "effects" sent home from Israel and stashed down in the basement. Except to say just two things. First of all: not only did I not find any unmailed letter to me, I didn't even find my own letter to Steve. I did, however—second of all—find and then read a file marked "David." This contained, among other things, a paper Steve wrote for some college course on androgyny. Titled "Two Expositions and Four Extenuations from 1975," it began with the epigraph: "Whenever one loves another, which of the two becomes the friend of which, the lover of the loved one or the beloved of the loving one? Or does it not even make a difference? (Plato, *Lysis*)." And then—stars out—came this cruisy exposition:

When I first saw David it was in September of 1974 and he was sitting on top of the multi-leveled sitting area in the lobby of Building Seven, on the highest level. There was some sort of noontime entertainment going on, although I don't remember what it was. I was hurrying out toward the Student Center for a quick lunch before going back to classes, and I probably never would have noticed him then had he not been seated so prominently. His hair was longer then than it is today, and he seemed to be looking through his wire-rimmed glasses at nothing in particular, but in the general direction of the entertainers and the audience. I can remember stopping before I got to the doors, stepping aside out of the traffic, and staring at him (I think without him noticing me) for about forty-five seconds.

Actually, I spend quite a bit of time just staring at all the beautiful faces at MIT and lamenting the fact that because most of them belonged to other males, I would probably not be able to learn more about them than what one can learn from a distance of thirty feet and in only a few seconds. David's, however, seemed more important to me just then than the other faces, and not just for the reason that his was the only one I was studying at the time. He has a way of looking at you that makes you feel as though he is in some mode of communication with you higher and more piercing than the verbal-intellectual one. When other people try to affect this they give you only vacant stares. His hair was smooth, but not shapelessly straight, and it was dark and unselfconsciously

parted in the center; kempt enough to be attractive, but with a few wisps float-
ing in the breeze to indicate casualness. His look was lean, but not hungry. His
posture was unguarded and open, enough so that I didn't feel so lonely in staring
at him. In physique he was and remains slim, not to the point of frailty, but in
such a proportion to his body and stance as to make him as supple and yearning
in appearance as Michelangelo's Adam.

An awful lot of thoughts went through my mind in those forty-five seconds.
Everything about him suggested that he was my "type" but by this time I had
pretty well become convinced that anyone I ever found appealing would be
straight. Even though the statistics are more in my favor (about ten percent
of the American white male population between the age of sixteen and death
spend at least five years of their lives in a predominantly homosexual mode, and
this is even higher for urban college youth in an experimental phase of life), I
found that I was batting zero for finding anyone I really liked within that ten
percent. Friends who noticed this attributed it to a fear of success, and I seri-
ously wondered if they weren't right. The prospect of my never getting past this
psychological barrier frustrated me, and I felt particularly bad about this while I
was gazing at David. I also knew that I would never be able to forget him.

The file also contained an unmailed letter to—one assumes—this same "Da-
vid." Or maybe Steve did send such a letter, to him, with this thing just a draft.
Anyway, here's part of it:

> I won't wax romantic about you as the only one I could ever love because it
> simply isn't true, I hope. Conversely, I wish you the very best of happiness with
> whomever you choose to wake up beside for the rest of your life.

It also contained some notebook. So here's part of that:

> yes—because he touched me first—likes my writing—has the patience to sort
> through my pedantry—eyes that seem to say yes, but later—I have waited longer
> than I care to recall—we always get onto talking about my politics or his younger
> sister's rape or what a great place the Village is or his Fillmore West shirt—makes
> me think of all the places I'd like to visit with him—San Francisco is a great
> place to be alone with a friend or a lover—or just alone

And these—about twenty years later, at Harvard—are precisely what I'd have
my narrator, "Kevin," after realizing and also saying that *Neatness Counts* is an
elegy, then decide in conclusion to quote there.

But what, in reality—just after that basement reading in Queens—did *this* Kevin do? He grabbed Steve's address book from those "effects," found the only "David" in it, went back upstairs to their old bedroom in the attic, and then—I confess—wrote his own letter to him.

I had this stupid idea, you see, that if only that David had loved Steve—or if only *I* had even more than I did, or if only Steve ever loved *me* back—none of this, for I still thought Steve's death a suicide, would have happened. I was angry, too. Angry at Steve, of course, despite now also feeling even sorrier than ever for him. But there *was* no Steve, anymore, to be angry *at*. Nor could I, consciously, even acknowledge him—the poor thing—to myself (the poor thing) as such a target. And so, targeting this David instead—much as about fifteen years later I'd trash Charles Rosen instead of Wayne Koestenbaum and maybe Carol here (plus Professors "Projection" and "Points") instead of or in addition to myself—I told him, in writing—and I don't now think this mere *passive* aggression, as I probably did back then—that my brother, "as you may not have heard," has killed himself. But I just wanted to "thank you, on his behalf, for being such a good friend." No response came from him.

Why, though—in *Neatness Counts*—did I have "Kevin" quote those three passages? Why, moreover, have I myself just now *re*quoted them? For one thing, I'm—still—always trying to revive Steve. (Thanks, Dr. Train.) I also still think the writing in them, like that of both Charles and Vanessa, or both Jesse and Doug, is terrific—much better than my own writing, at any rate, or at least, as you can see, more visual than my own. And so you, my readers *as* readers should understand what, in part, you too have lost, or rather what part of Steve—maybe the best part, as Proust claimed—we've all lost. Plus—addressing myself alone, primarily, and neither IDANT kids nor anyone else—I've now twice forced Steve—in writing—to make the confession or rather the *involuntary* avowal of his own gay sexuality that—in person, but then also even just in writing—he'd more or less refused me. (Dr. Svetlov, *c'est moi*.) And that he had also refused if not Mom—or so she implied at my coming out to them—then at least Dad. And that he had also refused—as they all, like Dad, would later confirm to me—Ricky, Micky, and Bob. That letter—of Steve's—to David, though, contained another line I neither chose to have "Kevin" use in *Neatness Counts*—as I wasn't yet ready to show him being so mean, to any of us—nor now need see the original to quote. "I'm 'out' to pretty much everyone," he'd have told the man, or maybe did tell him, "except—those goddamned *kikes*—my family."

||||

Don't think, though, that this year at Harvard was all just gloom and doom for me. For it wasn't merely mulling over the absences in my life of first Charles, and then Steve, and then Vanessa, and then Dad, and then Carol—who is now a dean at Vassar. Nor, of course, was it all just mulling over the awful presence there now of men like Ichabod. I'd also, one must confess, *enjoyed* shaming Ichabod. Plus I'd had "stars out" while addressing both my own David and Steve—just as in this chapter I'm at least trying to have them out while addressing, primarily, Charles, Vanessa, and Carol. Plus—when not writing—I'd hung out with either Radcliffe fellows or Harvard kids, either Geeta Patel or Robert Scholes, either David or the boys. Plus, nearly forty years after that Bolshoi Ballet *Swan Lake*—with me, in fantasy, as both Odette and Odile—as well as five years after my work on Nijinsky—with me, in conscious fantasy, as Nijinsky, in unconscious fantasy as Serge Diaghilev—I took a dance class.

This, in fact, was my first such class—unless you count the one lesson I had, at about age seven, with Mom. She, for some reason, started this off with the jitterbug, and then claimed to have—at sixteen, in "Starlight Park" in the Bronx—won some dance contest with it. I'm pretty sure this was true. But Mom also claimed—more recently—to have gotten her trophy there from the actress Mitzi Gaynor, or "Nellie Forbush" in the film version of *South Pacific* (1958). If so, Gaynor herself would have been seven. And so probably, instead, that presenter was Mary Martin (1913–1990)—the original Nellie on stage. (Mom was born—on Bastille Day—in 1922. Martin became an "overnight sensation"—or star—in 1938, singing "My Heart Belongs to Daddy" in the Cole Porter show *Leave It to Me!*)

"Beginning Ballet," I should explain, was offered by Harvard. So I first registered, in person, at the dance department. I noticed a photograph there—both framed and hung above some desk—of Martha Graham (1894–1991). Of Martha Graham, that is, in black. I noticed, too, the dance involved: Graham's *Lamentation* (1930). I noticed, too, the photographer: my sister-in-law Reiko's father, Soichi Sunami. And then, in some store past Inman Square, I bought dance gear: black shoes, black leotard, black tank top or—as the boys called it—"wife-beater." (I'd long since lost that "Star of David" one.) The color black is slimming. Truth be told, though, I too—like Steve—was now slim. Post-starvation slim. (My weight, once again: one-fifty.)

The class met for the first time. We were in some second-floor room of yet another building outside Lowell House. I was the only male student there. I was also, I'm afraid—or rather am proud to say—the only slim one. Think of Disney's *Fantasia* (1940), with those alligator *danseurs* and hippo ballerinas. And then the—female—teacher arrived, looking rather more like Nijinsky, with big, muscular thighs, than some latter-day Pavlova. Jodi Allen, which is the woman's real name, was a five-foot-two, twenty-something year old with both short blond pigtails—but a big, booming voice to match those thighs—and her own awful French. *"Battement!"* she'd soon shout repeatedly, but only after having first had us *"clench the ass!"* This, however, came out as: *"Batman!" "Batman! Batman! Batman!"* Or she'd shout *"entrechat!"* This came out as: *"Enter, shah!" "Enter, shah! Enter, shah! Enter, shah!"* Or she'd shout *"rond de jambe!"* This came out: *"Ron, the jam!"* It was hard, for me, to not *un*clench the ass—and then burst out laughing.

Despite this—despite, too, the likelihood that she'd rather dance than teach, much as I'd rather write than do so—Jodi was terrific. For unlike me now—when grading papers though not in class discussion anymore—she didn't seem to mind how terrible at that *barre* we all were. She was, that is, the perfect combination—for any type of instruction—of drill sergeant and cheerleader. She'd correct, say, our posture or maybe our turnout or maybe our *port de bras*, but only after having first praised something about them. Plus—like some David Sedaris work, or like me throughout this book—she'd use confession to mask satire. She'd discuss, say, not our problems with technique ("shame on you") but *her* problems ("shame on *me*")—but then also how she managed to correct them. And so, of course, we loved her—I, it seemed, even more than any of those hippos.

David, one time, came to class. The boys, of course, would not when here. And although unlike me David is a great dancer, he'd only come to watch. To see the hippos, he'd said, and also this girl I've been raving to him about. But apart from Jodi, he'd later confess, he watched only me, or me—ass clenched—in that leotard. And even nowadays, at our local gym, he might recall that golden afternoon watching me *"Plih-YAY! Plih-YAY! Plih-YAY!"* and then suggest I do just a few more of what we call—it's an exercise—"ass-ups."

Another time—and I'll end now with this, provisionally—something terrific happened between me and . . . no, not Jodi. Between me and another woman. Jodi was shouting something at us, I forget what, when we suddenly heard even louder noise outside. Rushing to the room's floor-length windows, overlooking

Mount Auburn Street, we now saw the cause of it: about twenty male college students, all of them in drag, surrounded a red convertible and were walking it up the road toward us. A crowd of about two hundred—both "town" and "gown," it seemed—were watching this and cheering. As those—probably straight—drag queens got to just below our building, we now saw both who they were and who was in that car: a truly female passenger both waving at the crowd and blowing them all kisses. The queens were Harvard's Hasty Pudding Theatricals society. The passenger, I swear, was the actress Angelica Huston, here to receive its "Woman of the Year" award. (This award is given to people deemed by the group to have made a "lasting and impressive contribution to the world of entertainment." Past recipients, for example, include Liza Minnelli [1973], Beverly Sills [1978], and Mary Tyler Moore [1981]. They do not, however, include Mary Martin, Mitzi Gaynor, Colleen Dewhurst, or Natalie Portman.) When they all finally reached us, we too started cheering: I alone dressed in black surrounded by ballerinas all in, well, let's say white. They were my own "swan maidens," with me—in non-drag fantasy—as either Prince Siegfried or that "evil genius" von Rothbart. Angelica—Gretta Conroy in *The Dead* (1987), her own dad's last film, but also, more recently, Morticia in *The Addams Family* (1991) and Etheline in *The Royal Tenenbaums* (2001)—looked up at me. (Those "Tenenbaums," a student of mine just told me, are based on Salinger's "Glass" family.) Imagine this from her point of view: I alone in black, up there, resembling . . . well, not heartbroken Michael Furey, who haunts Gretta. I resembled either widowed, grief-stricken Chas Tenenbaum (played by half-Jewish Ben Stiller, born 1965) and or uxorious, tango-dancing Gomez Addams (played by Raul Julia, 1940–1994), and or maybe just an alligator. Or rather, she then looked *back* at me—this now Liza-like, Colleen-like, Natalie-like star—and then herself burst out laughing . . . and then blew me a kiss.

Kiss and Tell

Leave 'em laughing when you go.

—JONI MITCHELL, *Clouds*

I've "known" enough people, in the Biblical sense, to also know—as you your-
selves may—that most sex is, well, ridiculous. They've either no idea what they're
doing, or what I want done, or they know but don't care what I want, or the fan-
tasy they're enacting has nothing to do with mine, or they're fantasizing when
I'm not, or I am when they're not, or they look nothing like who I'd imagine, or,
for that matter, like who they must think they are, or they don't believe in de-
odorant, or douche bags, or they've propositioned both me and a friend, together,
but now it's he alone they want, or they talk too much, or that *hurts* goddammit,
or, along related lines, they seemed nice enough but turn out to be some kind
of rapist, or they seemed rapist but are nothing of the kind, or they don't like to
kiss, or they do but taste bad, or, look, I didn't want to do this in the first place.

One time, in Los Angeles, some surfer dude—now face to face on top of
me—began to sweat, and sweat, and sweat. It felt, to me, like snorkeling.

Another time, in a bathhouse there, some actor type—crotch to face—be-
gan, it seemed, to channel some porn video. "Oh, yeah," he commands, "suck
that cock, you know you want that big fat cock, suck my big fat cock, suck it you
bitch!" "What do you *think* I'm doing," I snapped, "flossing my teeth?"

Another time, some gym-coach type—standing face to face—grabbed my
hips, cartwheeled me to a handstand, and then, unusually demonstrative for a

coach, went down on me. This, though, was nothing to write home about. His tongue is not where it should be: on the frenulum, not the glans. My blood— rushing to my head—isn't there either. Nor, I'm afraid, was this anything to now say—or write—more on. I'm too much of a scholar, clearly, not to mention gentleman.

Of course, some sex is good. Some, even, is fantastic. Perhaps, at first, they conform to fantasy: farm boy, surgeon, swim coach. Or perhaps there's no need now for fantasy. That said, though, I both once again and as usual can't say—or write—more on it. For despite my not having been otherwise private, in print, or my having worked in what's now called sexuality studies, or my promiscuity in real life, I've never written a lot about intercourse per se: neither that which I myself have had, nor even that which I haven't. "Well, *why* not?" you yourselves command.

First, though, a word on "promiscuity." The Oxford English Dictionary defines this as: "the frequent, casual changing of sexual partners." I, though, would suggest: "having more sex than I do."

Also, a word on that "a lot." ("I've never written *a lot* about intercourse.") While I have on occasion analyzed gay sex—in novels by John Cleland (*Fanny Hill*) and maybe Oscar Wilde (*Teleny*), in nonfiction by André Gide (*If It Die*) and Roland Barthes (*Incidents*), in *Command Performance* (1992) by Falcon Studios—I haven't done such on non-gay or even lesbian sex. Write what you know, I guess, or maybe what you like.

And also a word on that "per se." ("I've never written a lot about intercourse *per se*.") Just as I've analyzed masturbation equivalents—"orgasmic" speech, "non-conversational" writing, a theater piece (*Afternoon of a Faun*, with Vaslav Nijinsky at first and then later on Ned Rorem)—I've also, on occasion, analyzed *sex* equivalents (or substitutes, sublimations, masturbatory "supplements"): "conversational" or better yet "cruisy" writing; Nijinsky's ballet *Jeux*, meaning "games;" "virtuoso" pianism. I have not, though, done such on "four-hand" pianism. Think, here, of Burkhard Bastuck—that lawyer and also duet partner I had a crush on. Think, too, of my brother Steve, who in proto-sexual duets with me—assigned by our piano teacher Mrs. Graa—would of course play top. It's the easier if less rewarding part—much as in bed. (No pedaling, for such tops, but then no getting to just enjoy those melodies either; no rectal pain, for sodomy tops, but then no prostate stimulation either.) Brother Bob, in duets with me, played bottom—as would Charles Rosen. ("Charles" from elementary school and I never played them.) A Juilliard friend, though, named Beth—Beth

Sussman—now claims she had a crush on me back then. She also claims, correctly, that being "versatile," we'd *alternate* duet parts: *primo*, for top; *secondo*, for bottom. Plus, she says, we'd sometimes *improvise* duets—with one such piece called "Slide-Upon" and another "Euthanasia."

At any rate—to quote not Mary Martin, the actress, but Julie Andrews as the real live governess Maria von Trapp, née Kutschera—let's start at the very beginning. The beginning is a dream I had. The year, I think, was 1965—same as that film: *The Sound of Music*. So I'm five years old. I'm up in our tulip tree—before the tree house got built—standing up there, in fact, at the very top. This of course is thrilling. But now it's just terrifying, as—I realize—there's no way back down. Just then, though, looking down, I see some handsome, possibly shirtless man. He's on the ground, standing up, and also looking up here. So he sees me, sees that I'm terrified, and then, holding out his arms, says to me to just "let go." I do let go, and then float down and down and down into these big beefy arms.

So that's my primal fantasy. My primal *reality*—of sex—happened down in the subway. The year was 1973. I'm thirteen years old. It's my first day of high school. The morning commute there, sans Steve, had been without incident. I'm not allowed, he'd said, to share any of "his" subway cars. Coming back home, though, is—to quote the actress Edith Evans as "Lady Bracknell"—crowded with incident. Like most of us here in this car, I'm standing up—while hanging on to some strap. I see some ugly, drunk-looking man, also standing—but not hanging on. Now he's coming toward me. And now—clearly drunk—he's, well . . .

In *The Swimming-Pool Library*, a novel by Allan Hollinghurst, "William Beckwith" is annoyed, merely, by such an encounter. "One of the strap-hangers," he narrates, "a man whom I spotted eyeing the erection which even the shortest journey on the tube or bus always gives me, inclined to swing or jolt towards me as the train lost or gained speed, and the pressure of his knee on mine, and of his eyes in my lap, irritated me." Joe Brainard, the painter, had in real life been thrilled. "I remember 'Korea,'" he writes in a memoir:

I remember rainbows that didn't live up to my expectations.

I remember big puzzles on card tables that never got finished.

I remember my first sexual experience in a subway. Some guy (I was afraid to look at him) got a hard-on and was rubbing it back and forth against my arm. I got very excited and when my stop came I hurried out and home where I tried to do an oil painting using my dick as a brush.

But neither Brainard nor Beckwith at the time—not to mention Hollinghurst while writing—was as young and innocent as I. Beckwith, in fact, was promiscuous. And nor—I'd imagine—were their subway men ugly. Those encounters with them, then, were not—for Brainard and Beckwith—"primal realities." And so nor were the encounters—for Brainard and Beckwith—"rainbows that didn't live up to expectations." This is also to say, nor were they Proustian. (Think of Proust's narrator—named "Marcel," maybe—when thirteen. He's disappointed, at first audition, by the actress "Berma"—invented by Proust— as Racine's "Phaedra." He's then disappointed, at first sight, by a supposedly Persian-looking church—invented by Proust—in Normandy.) And so, unlike Brainard and Beckwith, I myself at the time was neither "excited" nor "irritated" by this subway man. I was repulsed by him. Now, though, to quote the actor Mr. T as "B.A. Baracus"—on the television show *The A-Team*—I pity the fool.

My first enjoyable not to mention recumbent such encounter happened just before college graduation. The year, as you may recall, was 1979. I was nineteen years old. David Abell, a brown-haired, brown-eyed violist I'd met—in the audience—at a performance of the G.B. Shaw play *Saint Joan* and who—while the two of us rehearsed the Haydn oratorio *The Creation*—then flirted with me over the next couple of days, also then offered to walk me "back home" after our concert. (I'd sung in the choir—the Yale Concert Choir—for this *Creation*. David Abell, appropriately enough, played in its pickup orchestra.) I said "fine," in effect. (*Nous allons marcher ensemble.*) I now felt, as we walked together, overcome by both love and lust. Not yet knowing, though, what to try doing with or even say to this lovely, sexy guy, I was terrified as well. And so when we reached my residential college and then de facto dorm room in it—sans roommate—all I managed to ask, rather sheepishly, was: "Would you like to stay, or what?" David's response: "Let's stop playing games." I didn't think I was playing anything. I didn't yet know how to flirt, and nor how to seduce, and nor of course how to "make love." (See "G712," on my belated introduction to both visual porn and, hence, onanistic dexterity. Well, not *dexterity* per se—sinisterity.) He then moved over to where I was standing and kissed me. When I opened my eyes—as, come to think of it, I've already written elsewhere—I saw, past David's face, head on, my own face reflected in a mirror above a dresser by the closet. And even after, still in concert garb, we lay down on a twin-size bed next to that dresser, I imagined a movie camera—up on the ceiling—filming my own gay debut there. I therefore saw—in fantasy—only what that camera would have.

The morning after this "debut," as I've also written elsewhere, David Abell announced: "You've just slept with someone who slept with someone who slept with someone who slept with someone who slept with *Liszt!*" "So what?" I replied, "I *study* with someone who studied with someone who studied with someone who studied with Liszt." It was an odd thing for him to say. He'd traced his sexual competence, as well as his "homosexual" predilection, to a musical master known to be a ladies' man. It was also an odd—not to mention competitive—thing for me to say. I'd equated "sleeping with" and "studying with," but also discriminated between the two. I'd won, I imagined, by having fewer of the same kind of intermediaries, but also won by having engaged in a better kind of intercourse.

David Abell then dumped me—in a telephone call—saying, among other things, that I was just too "mysterious" for him. This, unfortunately, was the day before Steve died. One year after that, my next boyfriend—blond-haired, blue-eyed Paul Friedman—also played viola. Paul, though, I've never written about personally nor about the sex we had. This may be because, among other reasons, no one who mattered much to me at the time—apart from Jesse Green and Bill Watson, my other best friend from college, and also a law school friend named Ken—would ever let me *talk* about him: neither Dr. Train, my inadvertently abusive therapist, who thought I should be straight; nor Dad, who paid Train for such treatment; nor even Mom. ("Ken," by the way, was also my father's name.) "Look," she snapped once— upon my mentioning some minor non-sexual problem Paul and I had. "I am *not* your friend, I'm not your *therapist*—and I don't want to hear about it!" (So much, then, for "Is *that* all?"—Mom's reaction, two years earlier, to my having come out to them. So much, then—one must confess—for my ever wanting anything more to do with the woman. I'd later learn, though, that her personality is both borderline and narcissistic.) And so at least two reasons for no such writing yet—on Paul—have been: habitual silence and residual shame.

I then—just before law school graduation—dumped both Train and Paul. That therapist, I told: "I don't want to pay you." This was true, no doubt. For while I was about to start earning even more money than Dad said he did and so would no longer have to "let" the man cover such expenses of mine as college tuition, room, and board, travel abroad, law school tuition, head-shrinking by Train, and rent for that apartment I shared with Jesse, I was both too cheap in general—still—and too irritated in particular—at last—by this awful,

awful therapy to now care to *take* care of this one expense myself. In response, Train just sighed. That lovely, sexy boyfriend, I don't know—I'm afraid—what I told. But whatever it was—true or false, and probably false—Paul just laughed, kindly, in response.

I lost track of them both. Train, though—as I've learned from the Internet—is dead. And this—one must confess—makes me happy. But so too, I've learned there, is Paul: of AIDS, at age thirty-seven, in the year 1994. All I have of him now, sadly, are relics—two of them. The first, dashed off at a piano, are song lyrics he wrote: funny, corrective ones—with deliberately awful German—for "The Trout" by Schubert. That original fish, in poetry by Christian Schubart, got caught—seduced, really. Paul's, though, gets away:

> The trout is in the water, boy can that fish swim.
> Perhaps it is a mother or maybe the fish, she's a him,
> But that fact doesn't change a thing, that I have to say,
> Because this song isn't about anything but the fish his-self.
>
> *Mein Gott* the day is gorgeous. Water blue as sky,
> The trout is with another, perhaps a girlfriend on the sly.
> They're jumping, splashing, swimming, frolicking like mad.
> One thing is certain—trouts are seldom sad.
>
> I've got *mein* rod and tackle (*auf Deutsch ist Rod und Reel*)
> And with that fish I'll grapple, land him on the keel.
> The bait I use *ist* worm, pink and oh so small.
> Maybe it's getting too late to catch that trout at all?
>
> *Nein, ja*—the sun *ist* shining, still, I'm heartened to say.
> Besides, the trout is swimming—he would be anyway.
> I throw the line into the lake, or *Loch* as we say in Bonn,
> With heightened hopes of catching a big fat trout upon.
>
> *Mein Gott* I think I've got him, the trout is almost mine.
> And soon my friends will gather to eat this fish so fine.
> But wait—no, *ja*—the line is broken. The lousy trout has got away.
> I take my rod and break it, tonight I'm eating eggs.

The second relic, taken in the Berkshire Mountains—up in some woods there—is a photograph. He looks, in the picture, like Paul Newman. He's holding a pomegranate.

After Paul came blond-haired, blue-eyed let's call him "Mitch," someone from my apartment building—the then new Battery Park City by the nowadays missing World Trade Center. Like me, Mitch was Jewish. (Paul Friedman, like Paul Newman, was only half Jewish; David Abell is Anglican.) Like me, Mitch played piano. Plus we had near identical ones: seven-foot Mason & Hamlins, both of them made about 1920. Our first real time together, come to think of it, consisted of playing duets on his: the Schubert Fantasy, and then some Mozart, and then some Debussy.

Most of us, of course, are attracted by opposites. We then—as Edmund White, the novelist, writes somewhere—try to make them twins. If we can't, he says, we're furious. If we can, we lose interest in them, and then find people even more "outrageously unsuitable." I think it's in a memoir of his. That memoir, called *Our Paris*, is illustrated by White's lover at the time: Hubert Sorin, who—at thirty-two in 1994—would also soon die of AIDS. (Brown-haired, brown-eyed "Warren" and I had them both over for dinner once, when White taught writing at Brown University. Hubert said little there, as his English was awful. Edmund, being very chatty, was charming and yet—I thought—also misogynist. He claimed, for instance, that "there's no such thing as 'lesbian fiction,' or no *good* such fiction." My friend Elisabeth Landenson—the author of *Proust's Lesbianism*—now says she agrees with White about this.) Here, though, with Mitch, I'd been attracted by a twin—not an opposite. This meant I'd no real interest—in sex with him—to begin with. Nor had Mitch interest in sex with me. Think: Romulus and Remus or rather Tweedledum and Tweedledee getting it on. And so what little sex we did have—unlike with Paul—was, well, repulsive. Plus his bedroom furniture—which, like that of Proust, was stuff he'd had since infancy—irritated me, the bed in particular, which appropriately enough was twin-size. Plus I was very annoyed, in the end, by his having telephoned one night when I had some friends over—to say he might have given me herpes. (Luckily, he hadn't. Those friends, by the way, included David Hyde Pierce—with whom, come to think of it, I'd also play duets.) "Okay," I said rather meanly. "We're done now."

Between that experience, plus residual shame, plus law-firm-number-one homophobia, I thought maybe I should try *not* being gay. And so I contacted brown-haired, green-eyed "Naomi," a lovely, very funny, and also Jewish woman. Prior to college, she'd met Jesse Green in Michigan. She then went to the University of Michigan, studying both jewelry design and metalsmithing. The soon-to-be pop star Madonna, née Ciccone—while studying dance there—then stole a boyfriend of hers. I myself, while at Yale, had met Naomi through Jesse. She'd been visiting him. And now—just below that law firm, in the so-called Diamond District, she both designed and—"stars out"—made jewelry.

Naomi, of course, knew that I'm gay. So, too, is Jesse. But when I suggested sexual, possibly romantic involvement, she—who, like Madonna, I'd imagine, certainly did know how to flirt, seduce, make love—said, in effect, "fine." Maybe she wanted to help me. Maybe—unlike Steve—she felt sorry for me. I've never asked. Yet what sex we had—and there was a lot of it—was itself fine, I thought. But—one must confess—I never used condoms. The year was 1983, the season early spring. Plus I didn't feel desire—unlike with Paul—only lots and lots of pleasure. Plus when Naomi suggested, well, cunnilingus—that irritating word—I did what I could, or what she told me to do, only to realize I couldn't possibly not be gay. I couldn't, that is, now fantasize men—Paul in particular. In fact, nowadays, I tell any guy questioning his homosexuality to imagine or better yet—I mean worse yet—attempt such heterosexual intercourse and then ask himself if he really, truly finds it appealing. If so, he's straight. If not, he's gay—period. It's something, I also realized, which that friggin' therapist of mine should have known. At any rate, when Naomi and I, shortly thereafter, went to the Pocono Mountains—for a stay at Buck Hill Inn—one of the things we did there, other than non-cunnilingual sex, was read to each other. I don't know—I'm afraid—what she read to me. I, though, read her both *Franny* and *Zooey*—all of them—by "stars-out" J.D. Salinger. This, of course, took a while. And something about that reading, that "rhapsody," rather, perhaps an all too clear preference on my part for Zooey, made her realize, kindly, that *we* were done now—as lovers at any rate. For we stayed friends. And I've now any number of relics—mementos, rather. These include a photograph taken up in woods there. She looks, in it, like the actress Natalie Portman—although not quite as tiny. They include a hand-carved angel, from Mexico, which she later gave me: it's male, I think, and, unlike those now missing "tree of life" ones that Steve fixed up for me, has a body. And it's usually in my stepson Seth's old room, hung up on a wall. Come Christmastime, though, it's always on our Christmas tree, up on top, kind of like me—come to think of it—in that dream. Those mementos also include a beautiful little heart, in bronze, that Naomi made for me. Here, I'll trace it:

I fell for Warren—sight unseen—that fall. And so for me—as for Charles
Rosen with the opera singer Maria Callas—it was love at first audition. Here,
though—with us two actually trying out, at age twenty-three, for the New York
Choral Society—I'd have "audition" mean more than just hearing.

Some high tenor, singing the "Kyrie" from Bach's *Mass in B Minor* while
hidden from me by a curtain up there, was on the stage of that group's rehearsal
space: CAMI Hall—for Columbia Artists Management, Inc.—across the street
from Carnegie Hall. This mass, I realized, was music I'd never heard before.
This voice type—both lovely and angelic—was sound I'd never heard: a com-
bination of Julie Andrews and the pop singer Rex Smith. The guy will get in, I
thought. And then he himself—*looking* angelic, or at least the choirboy type—
emerged. To be specific, he looked like a combination of Gene Kelly as "Danny
McGuire" in *Cover Girl* (1944), although not that hunky, and Farley Granger
as "Phillip Morgan"—a murderer (plus concert pianist) based on either Nathan
Leopold or Richard Loeb, those real live killers. That Granger performance is
in the 1948 Alfred Hitchcock film about which, to his credit, hunky D.A. Miller
has written:

> *Rope* has in fact been famous for two things: not just its [apparently seamless]
> technique, but also the fact that it seems to be about [to quote François Truf-
> faut] "two young homosexuals." Yet these two things have stimulated criticism
> in quite opposite, if equally unfruitful ways. On one hand, *Rope* criticism (in-
> cluding Hitchcock's own) indulges the appeal and propagates the repulsiveness
> of the film's technique with a loquacity as little embarrassed by hermeneutic
> obligation as by fear of monotony. Concerning the narrative homosexuality, on
> the other hand, it affects a bored indifference that seldom goes beyond a brief
> banalizing acknowledgment à la Truffaut, as though to suggest that the idea and
> image of men kissing, sucking, fucking one another, were altogether devoid of
> the fascination that, on the contrary, the problems of the mobile camera may be
> taken for granted to hold in abundance.

Miller, by the way, was an accordionist in childhood—like my Uncle Lou—and
not a pianist. (See *Place for Us*, by Miller.) At any rate, my own Farley Morgan
/ Gene McGuire / Rex Andrews now left the building. It was my turn, then, to
sing or rather to *sight*-sing the same music—as a bass. If I too get in, I thought,
I'll ask the guy out.

I did get in. While on break at our first rehearsal, I chatted the guy up—and also memorized his nametag. *Warren D. Wingfield, Warren D. Wingfield, Warren D. Wingfield.* Two nights later, I telephoned directory assistance and then Warren himself. But—apart from Naomi—I'd never asked anyone out before. That proto-proposition of mine to David Abell—"Would you like to stay, or what?"—didn't really count. At any rate, he'd already offered to walk me home. So, too, had both Paul and Mitch asked me out. So I was very, very nervous here, saying I hoped this doesn't sound too "preposterous" but "might we have lunch together?" Like Naomi, Warren said, in effect, "fine." I'd later learn, though, that he had no memory of me talking to him at rehearsal and so no idea who I was.

Warren really was—or at least had been—a choirboy. He'd grown up in Roanoke, Virginia—among Bible-thumping Baptists. He'd just graduated from Harvard Divinity School—as an atheist. "It happens a lot there," he told me at lunch. And so he now worked as a fundraiser for St. Thomas Church, which, being Anglican, "doesn't really need more money." St. Thomas, by the way, is just three blocks north of St. Patrick's Cathedral. The Diamond District, where Naomi worked, is three blocks south. I worked up in Rockefeller Center, or its RCA Building there—just one block west.

We first "got it together" as they say, or the soul singer Barry White did, on our second date—coffee at Warren's place. And it was I, thinking shock tactics might work, who pounced. But kissing was, well, not so hot. And then—well, you can't possibly want me to be graphic. Or *I* don't want to be: it's one thing to describe, if only minimally, sex with someone you don't otherwise know, like that "surfer dude;" it's quite another to describe sex with someone you do. So I'll just say what I've said—or written—before, in jest: that neither Warren nor I was the other's idea of a top. But I really was, alas, in love. And so too, eventually, was he. And both of us, I assumed, were perfectly content to fantasize not only other men, Paul in particular, but also other maneuvers during the basically soft-core couplings we'd now started having every couple of days.

Such fantasizing, though, wasn't enough. Not for me, at least, or not for long. But before I say what happened, as a result, I have to take you back—*way* back— to something at Rockefeller Center other than that law firm job of mine. Every now and then, throughout childhood, both Steve and I, with Mom, would get on the "tube," the subway rather, and go to its Radio City Music Hall. (Mom, said Dad, looked like Lena Horne. That's why—as a nickname for Ida—he'd call her "Inky.") We'd never know show times—we'd get there when we'd get there—and so usually arrived mid-movie. (*Were* there show times, back then? Probably not.) If we liked what we saw, or were sufficiently confused by it, we'd wait for the next show and then watch the whole thing. If we liked that, we'd watch it again. One such film, in 1967, was *Thoroughly Modern Millie*, with Julie Andrews and Mary Tyler Moore. Another, one year later, was *The Horse in the Gray Flannel Suit*, with Dean Jones, a very young but already sexy Kurt Russell, and some horse, of course, named "Aspercel"—gender indeterminate, to me, at the time. That name, "Aspercel," was the brand name—in the film—of a stomach pill.

One year after meeting Warren and then having him move in with me—still at Battery Park City—I met brown-haired, brown-eyed Evan Wolfson. Evan, unbeknownst to me there, had also been at Yale for college. He'd then gone, like my now former law firm officemate Vanessa, to Harvard Law School. But there was nothing sexual—for me—about this encounter. Both Evan and I had volunteered for *pro bono publico* work at Lambda Legal Defense and Education Fund, Inc.—a gay rights organization run by blond-haired, blue-eyed Abby Rubenfeld. (Having just seen *Another Country* [1984], a film with sexy brown-haired, brown-eyed Rupert Everett as the real live spy Guy Burgess and sexy blond-haired, blue-eyed Cary Elwes as his otherwise-straight boyfriend "James Harcourt," I now—at last—completely loathed homophobia. Evan volunteered, in part, so as to meet other men. Abby, incidentally, is the sister of Paul Reubens, né Rubenfeld—better known as "Pee-wee Herman.") We'd been asked by her to write Lambda's *amicus curiae* brief in *The Board of Education of Oklahoma City vs. The National Gay Task Force*. This was a United States Supreme Court case about a state law that said that any teacher who "advocates, promotes, or encourages homosexual activity" in elementary through high school classrooms—meaning, of course, any gay or lesbian teacher—will be fired. Ironically, such advocacy, promotion, and encouragement was precisely what—if only indirectly, or *supplementally*—I myself, after going to Brown for a doctorate, would do in both undergraduate and graduate classrooms as well as in print.

Evan—who, unlike me, is brilliant at law—did most of this work. (Just one year later, he alone wrote Lambda's *amicus* brief in *Bowers vs. Hardwick*—the Supreme Court's first sodomy case. He then, as a reward, got to kiss sexy Michael Hardwick [1954–1991]. This sounds like but was not the guy's porn name. My own such name, using the formula first-pet-name plus first-street-name, would be "Oedipus Pompeii." That "Pompeii"—Pompeii Avenue—is in Queens, New

York. That "Oedipus"—a parakeet—was blue. Wayne Koestenbaum, in porn, would be "Jocasta Doyle;" Elisabeth Ladenson, "Scuffy West Sixty-Fifth;" Evan himself, "Boots Beechwood.") I alone, though, wrote the part:

> Clearly, speech about homosexuality does not necessarily, or indeed ordinar-
> ily, fall within any category of speech held by this Court to be excluded from
> the protection of the First Amendment. When speech about homosexuality
> constitutes defamation, obscenity, or "fighting words," such expression may be
> prohibited because these categories of speech fall outside the protection of the
> First Amendment. Any fortuitous content involving homosexuality, however, is
> irrelevant.

Rather "lofty," don't you think? ("In any life," writes Wayne, "as in any inven-
tion or any work of literature, however lofty or pedestrian, there exist a fixed set
of dominating themes.") Of course, neither Evan nor I—as mere *amici curiae*,
or "friends of the court"—was to do the oral argument. That would be done
by Laurence Tribe, of Harvard Law School, lead attorney for the Task Force.
We would, though, go hear that argument in Washington, D.C.—with Warren
staying home.

Evan took one train there, from Pennsylvania Station. I took another on
which, like Emmeline Grangerford on that flight with me from Chicago, I spent
most of the time telling some woman—my poor tortured seatmate—about my
educational background and professional life. Or *bragging* about them. She
did a good job pretending to be both interested and impressed, but must have
wanted to kill me. My friend Bill Watson picked me up—in his car—at Union
Station. I'd be staying at his place, over by Dupont Circle. Tomorrow, we'd both
meet Evan by the courthouse.

Laurence Tribe, that day, did a great job. And so we all—with Abby here,
too—felt elated. I suggested dancing to celebrate. Evan, unfortunately, had
other plans. As did Abby, she said. Bill, though, did not. He chose the place—a
bar, he said, called the Phoenix. We'd go back to his place to eat dinner. We'd
then, he said, have to take a "disco nap." We'd drink coffee. Then off we'd go!

Was I hoping, that night, for some as we now say "hook-up"? I'm not sure,
anymore. It is true, though, that—unlike Bill—I wasn't much of a dancer. (Nor,
as I mentioned at the end of "Veritas," am I one these days, compared to Da-
vid. David Coster, that is—father of Adam, Seth, and Sam—whom I'll come
to again at the end of this chapter.) But neither, probably, was this sexy-looking
gray-haired man—ten years older than I? twenty maybe?—just standing over

there, by some fatso, while tapping his foot to the beat of a different drummer from the one I heard. I tried getting Gray-Hair's attention by staring at him—but couldn't seem to. But then Fatso, somewhat tipsy, came over to us, said he'd noticed me noticing his friend and would I like an introduction? Bill wandered off somewhere.

"Dean," as I'll call him, was shy—or not at all chatty. Still, though, he seemed interested. We "danced" together. But this was ridiculous. And so—shock tactics—I kissed him. Well, I thought, he's not much of a kisser. Worse, even, than Warren. Or maybe *I'm* the problem. Maybe *I'm* bad at kissing, as bad at it, and maybe even at sex, as I clearly am at dancing. Still, though, the guy *is* sexy. I'd still like to celebrate. And now he at least knows how interested, nay determined *I* am. But no, I said, I'm afraid I don't have a place we can use. Bill's was just a "studio" apartment. And sure, I said, I'll go to your place—wherever it is. It's somewhere, said Dean, out in the countryside. So I found Bill—who was dancing beautifully with some not so beautiful black man—and told him what no good I was up to. In response, Bill just smiled—kindly. Dean found his own friend. And then the three of us left that bar—to go jump in some car outside. Fatso's car.

Off we went: with Fatso in front, driving, and Dean and me in back—groping. This, of course, was a very stupid thing for me to do. These guys could have been maniacs, like Leopold and Loeb—which luckily they weren't. But it was stupid, too, for all of us. Fatso, I'm afraid, was now very drunk. (Dean, he himself said, didn't know how to drive. And Fatso wouldn't let me.) He was also quite resentful about—unlike us—having not hooked up. Plus he had considerable time to express this. The trip, to me, seemed endless. Where'd they live, I wondered—Roanoke?

They did live in rural Virginia, or in what I later learned is called "Horse Country." They did not—thank God—live together. Fatso, finally, dropped us off somewhere. It being so dark, though, I couldn't see a thing. No—literal—stars out here. No moon, even. Dean's home, though—lights on—was a kind of shack. His bed in it—even smaller than Mitch's, or for that matter than mine back in college—was a kind of cot. His technique there—lights off—was, well, from what I later learned about that emperor, Napoleonic. Dean made love, as they say in France, *à la hussarde*. (The complete expression is: *faire l'amour*, or *prendre une femme*, *à la hussarde*, meaning to make love, or take a woman, like a soldier.) This, at the time, wasn't much to my liking. (He seemed nice enough, Dean did, but—that *hurts* goddammit—turned out to be some kind of rapist.) Judging, though, from what my friend Ken, who was the one to say back in law school that I looked like the pop singer Prince, had also told me there about his own such liking—at least in fantasy—I thought it might still be—even in reality—to his.

So off Dean went, in me, but—as back with Naomi—without his having used a condom. Or even any lubricant. This was worse than stupid of me. It was idiotic. Retarded, even. Everyone, by now, knew about AIDS. Dean, I for some reason only just then realized, might be HIV-positive. So maybe *I'm* infected now, I thought. And so now maybe Warren will be. Who, after all, really knew how this virus transmission worked.

I somehow fell asleep, with Dean—face to face—still pretty much on top of me. Come morning, I woke up first. For the life of me, though, I couldn't think of the guy's name. Was it Doug? Was it Dan? But nor could he recall mine, as I inferred when Dean, too, woke up and, suddenly shy again, said "Hey . . . you."

Dean, I was told over awful, awful coffee, is a horse trainer. ("So *what?*" I thought. "Who *cares?* Get me some *good* coffee. Make me some *eggs!*") He'd even, many years ago, trained the one in that Kurt Russell film. Now this, to me, was interesting. Did he mean *Aspercel?* "Yup," he said. "She's over there across the road." "Let's go see her," I said—because this, to me, was *incredible.* Did horses live that long? "Some do," said Dean, "some of them." And here, sure enough, stood Aspercel, looking pretty much like what I remembered, from back in that "music hall," only female, clearly, plus a bit long in the tooth.

Back in the shack, I telephoned Bill, who, apparently, with that unbeautiful black man, had been up to no good of his own. Could Bill, I asked, come get me? He could. And although I don't know—I'm afraid—how Dean and I spent the next couple of hours, I do know that I told him all about lovely, sexy Ken. I know, too, that I gave Dean my telephone number—above which, as a gentleman, I also wrote my name—making it abundantly clear, I thought, that if he's ever in New York City he'll have to meet the guy.

Evan and I took the same train back to Penn Station, on which I spent some of the time telling him about Dean. (In response, to his credit, Evan just read me the riot act.) Needless to say, I would not tell Warren. Yet a few weeks later, when he and I were in our queen-size bed together—reading—the telephone rang. Warren answered, had a brief exchange with this caller, and then, with an odd look on his face, handed him over to me. It was Dean, now here in town. And when could we get together? "We?" I asked. "What about Ken?" "Who's 'Ken'?" asked Dean. There was, of course, more to this conversation—but I'm sure you can imagine it. And when it was over, as I'm also sure you can imagine, Warren himself had a few questions. My answers, all of them truthful, provoked grief, and then rage, and then, a couple of weeks later, the question: Will I marry Warren? Or rather: Might we have a "commitment ceremony"? That, he must have figured, should keep me faithful.

I said yes, partly out of guilt, but mostly—truly—out of love. (Plus pity, as you know from "Veritas.") We found some church for this—Walt Whitman's old church, in Brooklyn Heights—and also a woman minister: Orlanda Brugnola. We registered, for silverware, at Bloomingdale's. Warren, there, was listed as the groom; I, in the harder part, was listed as "bride." Naomi would both design and make rings for us—from three kinds of gold—as well as be my, no, not "maid of honor." She'd be my "best woman." A female friend of Warren's, from Roanoke, would be his. Two other friends of his, also women, would host a reception. It was all very nice, very exciting—very feminist, we thought. The only problems in planning arose: (1) when my brother Bob, not knowing Naomi's role, offered to be my best man, just as he'd been brother Eric's, but then, even knowing her role, wouldn't take no for an answer; and (2) when Jesse, for personal reasons, meaning, here, professional ones, asked if we'd also invite David Leavitt, the novelist, whom neither Warren nor I ever met before—oh, and could Leavitt also bring a date? But the morning of the ceremony, I felt both *un*excited and very, very sick to my stomach—maybe in need of the drug "Aspercel." So I telephoned Carey—yet another friend of mine—to tell her about it. (This brown-haired, brown-eyed woman was my officemate at law firm number two, just one block south of Grand Central Station. Plus she herself had just gotten married—to a blond-haired, blue-eyed architect.) "Every groom," she told me in response, "gets butterflies." "But Carey," I joked, "I'm the *bride*!"

Maybe she's right, though, I now told myself. Maybe these butterflies don't mean a thing. I'd eventually realize, of course, what I should have known that morning: that not just my stomach but my entire body—with reason—was yelling at me to "run!" But I stayed and went through with the ceremony anyway, which, in addition to both cheating on Warren and maybe, I thought, putting us both at risk for AIDS, is something else I should now confess. I also confess, that is, to having been both oblivious and weak. I was oblivious of what both of us really needed, which was not to figuratively speaking *marry* one another, nor even to stay involved—except, perhaps, as friends. And so I was weak enough to not leave him, as they say, at the altar. Or rather, I was weak enough to have given him, as groom, the chance to leave *me* there. Or to quote the final words, to his wife, of the narrator in Marguerite Yourcenar's novel *Alexis*—simply *brilliant* lesbian fiction, Edmund and Elisabeth: "I undertook imprudent obligations toward you to which life refused to subscribe. With the utmost humility, I ask you now to forgive me, not for leaving you, but for having stayed so long." (It's even better, I imagine, in French: *J'avais pris envers vous d'imprudents engagements que devait protester la vie: je vous demande pardon, le plus humblement possible, non pas de vous quitter, mais d'être resté si longtemps.*) Only—at age thirty-two, after almost ten years spent then following me to Providence, Rhode Island, for my graduate work at Brown, and then back to New York City, for among other things my sperm donation work at IDANT, but not, at last, to Iowa City—it was Warren who'd dump me. His own non-final words, then:

> I won't wax romantic about you as the only one I could ever love because it simply isn't true, I hope. Conversely, I wish you the very best of happiness with whomever you choose to wake up beside for the rest of your life.

Or they were something like that. And then I became promiscuous.

| | |

I became—to use celebratory words for men—a rake, roué, libertine, lothario. To use derogatory ones, for women: whore, hussy, trollop, tramp. David's son Sam, though, would say I was a "man-whore."

When, exactly, did this happen? In 1993, or several years before Internet dating—hook-ups, really—took off. How often, for me, did such encounters now occur? Every couple of days, depending on both horniness and happiness. The hornier I was, or happier, the more times per week. (No need, as back at IDANT, for three or four days of abstinence.) The sadder I was, the fewer times per week. And where, exactly, did they happen? At a dirty, nowadays missing Iowa City bookstore—not Prairie Lights—that with all due respect to Roland Barthes I'll call the Dragon. Technically, though, it was in the adjacent town of Coralville— next to a nowadays missing truck stop. In it you'd find several rows of cubicles, each with a lockable, plywood door, a plank therein, for sitting, some porn video, usually straight, and a "glory hole" or two. They were about three-foot square, those cubicles—big enough for masturbation, while either sitting or standing and watching the video, or for sucking someone else, who'd be either sitting or standing, with you either kneeling or squatting, or for being sucked that way yourself, or for fucking someone else, also standing, or for being fucked that way yourself.

("Rise, sir," says Lady Bracknell to Ernest Worthing, "from this semi-recumbent posture. It is most indecorous.") There'd be kissing, too, to invoke D.A. Miller on *Rope*—though not with men, often married, who either didn't know they're really gay or for all I know really weren't. Hence the straightness of the porn: it gave such men the excuse or maybe the ability, while fantasizing women, to either do whatever they were doing to you or have done to them what you were doing. So you'd hear, here, all those videos, both gay and straight, along with real live slurping, moaning, groaning, growling, commands like "suck that cock," "suck it, you bitch," or even "*take* it, you bitch," and then, at last, orgasmic sounds.

But mostly you'd sit, sometimes hours, waiting for someone sexy to walk by—and also wishing you'd brought a book to read, or even papers to grade, or, better yet, cleaning supplies. Ideally, of course, he'd be your type, this Mr. Sexy, or at least one of them: farm boy, surgeon, swim coach. Or maybe he'd be close to one: choirboy, tree surgeon, gym coach. Ideally, then, he'd stop, look you in the eye, the crotch, the eye. You might nod. He'd enter your cubicle, close the door, lock it.

Or you'd just walk around, stop somewhere, look in some cubicle at someone else, who might nod.

Glory holes per se didn't interest me much, unless too many sexless hours went by—or what was now emerging through this one looked just huge.

With whom, though, in reality, did such encounters occur—or more likely not occur? Dragonites, as I'll call them, included not so much surgeons or even tree surgeons as truckers, probably; plus teachers for sure, as I'd know them from work; plus men I'd know either from their own work at, say, Prairie Lights or just socially; plus unknown men who did who knows what—professionally— who knows where, maybe Iowa City, maybe other so-called cities like Cedar Rapids, or maybe towns like Coralville, Swisher, and Tingley. (These last two come to mind because a non-gay, married colleague here—in our French Department—and also good friend of mine named some cats of his that.) For you couldn't ask such Swisherites, say, what their jobs were. You couldn't even ask his name, or at least last name, or even if that first one was a fake. ("'Dorian'? *Really*?") You couldn't, in fact, do lots of things: seem to recognize let alone talk to let alone cruise anyone otherwise known to you; or cruise anyone already cruised there before by you, unsuccessfully; or murmur to anyone there, with all due apologies to Barthes: "I love you."

Of course, most such bookstore sex—for me—was ridiculous. They'd either have no idea, those men, married or not, what they were doing, or what I wanted done, or they'd know but didn't care what I wanted, or the fantasy they'd be enacting had nothing to do with mine—and so on. (Or maybe, once again, *I* was the problem, as when kissing either Warren or Dean. Maybe I seemed nice enough, to him, but turned out to be some kind of rapist, or, more likely, I seemed rapist but was nothing of the kind, or I didn't want to kiss, or I did but tasted bad.) Saying so, to anyone there, was another thing you couldn't do. Such were the protocols, pre-Internet, of homosexual whoredom. Sorry, Sam—of homosexual *man*-whoredom.

One time, some Dragonite—from Spain, originally, he said—also said he's forty-three years old, to my then thirty-three, and please call him "Paris." This name—"Paris"—sounded doubtful to me, especially for a Spaniard. Unless, I thought, he's one of those *Greek* Spaniards. Or maybe he's Trojan. But—screw it. I don't care. That cock, being huge, was fun to suck.

Just two months later, though, he's a fifty-something *Mexican*, the same guy said, and please call him "Carlos." Like Warren, then, he had no memory of our first encounter. Plus he now made love, standing up, "like a soldier"—which I'm pretty sure he wasn't. If I had to guess, I'd say he *taught* Spanish—although not in that department of ours.

It was my brother Bob, by the way, who at age twenty-three had first revealed to me, at ten, the facts of life. I didn't believe him, yet. For the only two sex-related questions I had ever asked our father, at ages eight and nine respectively, were: (1) "Dad, what's a 'blow job'?"—which was something I'd heard at elementary school; and (2) "Dad, what's 'hung like a horse'?"—something I'd read in one of brother Steve's *National Lampoon* magazines. Response number one, from Dad, was: "oral sex," which I now thought meant just *talking* about it. Response number two: maybe not so kind laughter, and then—ba-*dum*-bum— "Ask your mother."

Another time, at the Dragon, some choirboy—brown hair, brown eyes— nodded me into his cubicle and then afterward, breaching protocol, asked to know my last name. And so—being a gentleman—I told him. "Are you," he now asked, "*Bob's* brother?"—which is all I'll say about that.

It was Bob, by the way, who, shortly after revealing the facts of life to me, also, if inadvertently, revealed *himself* to me—in a primal scene—having "missionary position" sex. This is all I'll say—or write—about that. It's all I really *can* say—except that the scene was very late at night on some hotel room balcony in Spain with some Asian-American woman and also that the sight of it, for me, was just a very quick glance. The glance, moreover, is something of which

neither sex partner, to my knowledge, has—until now, perhaps, if they're read-
ing this book—ever been aware. Afterward, I asked him—somewhat knowingly,
maybe Socratically—what the two of them were doing out there. "Talking" said
Bob. "Just talking." I once again, of course, didn't believe him. But at least I did
now believe those facts.

Another time, at the Dragon, some gym coach nodded me in. He had blue
eyes and what looked like thick, beautiful hair: very glossy, and very, very black.
So I touched it, then ran fingers through it—or tried to. The hair was fake; the
poor man himself, embarrassed now.

And then some heartbreaker nodded me in. He, too, had great hair—real
hair. The man himself was very sweet, if somewhat tipsy, and very, very nervous.
"First time here," he said. "That's okay," I joked. "I'll just tell you the protocol."
"Actually," he said, "it's my second time. But nothing happened before. No one
looked, well, nice." "Well," I joked, "I *am* nice." "Actually," he said, "it's my first
time—period." "You mean with a guy?" I asked. "Nope," he now confessed.
"It's my first time with anyone." Yet he was thirty-two years old, to my then
thirty-four.

This, for me, was love at first both sight and audition. For where Warren
had looked, in reality, like just Farley Granger in *Rope*, Mr. Heartbreaker—
or "Matt"—looked, in both fantasy and reality, like—as I've already said in
"G712"—that hunk and also "movie star" Matthew McConaughey. Plus where
Warren's voice, in song, was just lovely and angelic, Matt's, in both speech and
song, was lovely, angelic, and sexy. And so where Warren, in both fantasy and
reality, had been just a choirboy, Matt—in both fantasy and reality—was both
choirboy and farm boy. David Coster—in both fantasy and reality—is choirboy,
farm boy, and surgeon.

Sex, then, with Matt, was fantastic. We enjoyed both lots of pleasure and
lots and lots of desire. For not only was each of us—no joke—the other's idea
of a top, each was also his of a bottom. And so neither of us would now have to
fantasize other men, other maneuvers. Not even—in my case—ones with Paul.
Not even after I'd had Matt—a friend, coincidentally, of my friend "Swisher-
Tingley"—move into that bungalow with me. (No so-called lesbian bed death
for us!) Not even when, as a "Mellon Fellow" at the University of Pennsylvania,
I'd be in Philadelphia for the year—with Matt staying home. Or so it all seemed
to me. Plus, you know, I both loved and felt sorry for the guy. All those wasted,
lonely years—as a virgin. All those lonely, *shameful* years as a so-called closet
case. And then there was that dog he said he'd lost at age ten—a beagle. Plus I

was more and more convinced—when in bed with Matt, or just by our having sex there—that true communication was happening. I fell deeper and deeper in love, as well as deeper and deeper and deeper in lust.

Out of bed—or when using actual words—communication wasn't so hot. We were opposites, you see, not twins, with each of us "outrageously" unsuited to the other. Matt, for instance, didn't "believe" in the unconscious. Otherwise, though, he's very, very smart. I myself didn't believe in exercise—or not as much as he did. Plus what I really was to him, both in and out of bed, was a kind of teacher—or cheerleader but not drill sergeant. I even had to know—subconsciously—that I was. For I'd both show and tell him what to do in bed. (Sensual instruction.) I'd tell him—rather loftily—what love is: "a form of attention *always* paid, Matt, even in public, and only ever to the 'loved one.'" (Sentimental instruction.) I'd even tell him—one must confess—not only what literature to read, first Salinger and then Proust, but also what music to hear: first Mozart and then Schubert. (Cultural instruction.) But of course—to my credit—I'd also tell Matt to come out. And so having *admitted* Matt to my own private proto-academy—as Socrates had with Alcibiades—I really should have known, too, what I would have known—quite consciously—had I not been so desperately and hence hopefully in both love and lust. And this, of course, was—when leaving him for Penn—to just let the guy *graduate*. "Okay," I'd have said nicely: "You're done now."

Six months later, Matt fell for that graduate student of mine. Let's call the kid "Brad." Matt then—a few weeks after this—had Brad move in with him. Let me both clarify and—like Wilde in *De Profundis*—confess on "Bosie's" I mean Matt's behalf: my own "loved one," unbeknownst to me, had a new beloved; this new beloved of his, unbeknownst to me, was my own student; and they were both, unbeknownst to me, living in my own house. This all became "beknownst" to me only when that fellowship ended and I returned from Penn.

Matt, for some reason, couldn't pick me up at the Cedar Rapids airport. I therefore took a taxi back home. I arrived there, of course, expecting a very, very romantic nay *rainbow*-like reunion with Matt. Instead, I found some as of yet unidentified other guy's stuff—some books, some cigarettes, a hooded sweatshirt—strewn about the living room. I then found, in the bedroom—on the dresser next to that same old queen-size bed of mine—some new diary of Matt's. This I took to be a subconscious command—by him—for me to read it. "I am *not* in love with Kevin," Matt wrote there. "I *am* in love with Brad."

(Ironically, though, or tragically, or farcically, Brad himself wasn't in love with Matt. He was in love, he'd later confess, with me.) When Matt himself arrived, I confessed to having read that diary. This provoked—from him—possibly fake rage. As I'm sure you can imagine, though, I now had a few questions. Matt's answers, all of them truthful, provoked—from me—just grief.

And so, I now sensed, there *is*—to quote Jacques Lacan, on at least non-gay love—"no such thing as a sexual relationship." Of course, this wasn't what I thought back then. I was thinking, or quoting, a poem by Heine—who unlike Lacan was Jewish:

> A youth loved a maiden
> who chose another.
> The other loved another girl,
> and married her.
>
> The maiden married from spite
> the first and best man
> that she met with;
> the youth was sickened at it.
>
> It's the old story,
> and it's always new;
> and the one who she turns aside,
> she breaks his heart in two.

It's better in German, says Burkhard—"Peter Rhine," in porn. (That pet "Peter," too, was a parakeet—like my own "Oedipus.") And although "old," it's not the oldest story in the world, which, for me, as you know from "Veritas," would be Cain and Abel, Romulus and Remus, Frasier and Niles Crane. (The oldest profession is—ba-*dum*-bum—whoredom.) Or, as I knew this Heine only from its jaunty, almost laughable setting in the *Dichterliebe* cycle by Schumann, much as I'd know that Baudelaire line ("*Luxe, calme, et volupté*") only from a song by Duparc, I wasn't so much quoting as singing it, to myself, and doing so, in fact, or rather in fantasy, while imagining Matt's or maybe even Warren's voice— much as Barthes or even Gide, as amateur pianists, might "hallucinate perfection," to quote Barthes, at the keyboard. (*Roland Barthes by Roland Barthes*: "the piece, in the perfection attributed to it but never really attained, functions as a bit of a hallucination.") But I was also, and far more frequently, playing—as

badly, in reality, as those two Frenchmen—the grief-stricken, almost unbear-
able accompaniment to the next song:

> On a sunny summer morning
> I went out into the garden;
> the flowers were talking and whispering
> but I was silent.

> The flowers were talking and whispering
> and then looked at me with pity:
> Don't be cruel to our sister,
> you sad, death-pale man.

Matt then dumped me—on the day before my thirty-seventh birthday—saying,
among other things, that I'm just too "complicated" for him.

| | |

For revenge, among other motives, I wrote a novel—an autobiographical and
of course Proustian one. I mean by "revenge" that it was very mean, where Matt
was concerned, because I myself—at last—was both grief-stricken and enraged
by him. (Hell, to misquote William Congreve in his play *The Mourning Bride*,
hath no fury like a *sodomite* scorned. The actual line there is: "Heaven has no
rage like love to hatred turned, nor hell a fury like a woman scorned." Con-
greve's own birthday, by the way, is the day after mine.) This novel of mine,
luckily, has never been published. Let me just say that in it . . .

First, though, I'll say more on some for the most part *non*fiction of mine:
those analyses I did of either gay sex or equivalents, like virtuoso pianism, plus
omissions there like duets. I'll concentrate, in doing so, on connections: links,
if any, between that writing and whatever sex I had; links, as throughout this
book, between professional work and personal life.

So, once again, let's start at the very beginning. The first such analysis—
done, as a high-school virgin, for Miss Dragnet—was "*Ethan Frome* and De-
sire." I can't now quote the thing, of course, and nor do I really remember it. I
do know, though, which scene—from that novel—both my best friend Charles
and I handled: the one where Ethan and Mattie, as lovers, eat pickles with
donuts together. I myself, no doubt, found this repulsive—the meal, that is, if
not the non-gay metaphor, the food if not the fucking—and so maybe said so.

At Yale, studying music, I said no such thing—in writing. This, of course, was just as well. I was still a virgin there, still ignorant, too, of porn—of visual porn, that is, or just such magazines.

At Columbia University, studying law, I said no such thing as well—in writing. As a lawyer, after this, all I ever wrote on sex was part of that Supreme Court brief: "Clearly, speech about homosexuality does not necessarily, or indeed ordinarily, fall within any category of speech held by this Court to be excluded from the protection of the First Amendment"—and so on.

At Brown, I wrote that thing—eventually published—on *Fanny Hill*. It's a novel that, as you know, I first read in elementary school, and yet couldn't share with my friend Charles. (Like the very old encyclopedia from which—in a primal larceny—I took the entry "Cortez," it, too, came with the house.) I read it, in fact, shortly after, unobserved by them, I saw Bob and, well, Reiko Sunami, my then future sister-in-law, on that hotel room balcony—neither talking nor eating. The scene from this novel, now handled by me alone for some graduate course, is one where Fanny—likewise unobserved — sees, to quote Miller quoting Truffaut, "two young homosexuals."

For presently the eldest unbuttoned the other's breeches, and removing the linen barrier, brought out to view a white shaft, middle-sized and scarce fledged, when after handling, and playing with it a little, with other dalliance, all received by the boy without other opposition, than certain wayward coynesses, ten times more alluring than repulsive, he got him to turn round with his face from him, to a chair that stood hard by, when knowing, I suppose, his office, the Ganymede now obsequiously leaned his head against the back of it, and projecting his body, made a fair mark, still covered with his shirt, as he thus stood in a side-view to me but fronting his companion, who presently unmasking his battery, produced an engine, that certainly deserved to be put to a better use, and very fit to confirm me in my disbelief of the possibility of things being pushed to odious extremities, which I had built upon the disproportion of parts; but this disbelief I was now to be cured of, as by my consent all young men should likewise be, that their innocence may not be betrayed into such snares, for want of knowing the extent of their danger, for nothing is more certain than, that ignorance of a vice, is by no means a guard against it.

Slipping then aside the young lad's shirt, and tucking it up under his clothes behind, he showed to the open air, those globular, fleshy eminences that compose the mount-pleasants of Rome, and which now, with all the narrow vale that intersects them, stood displayed, and exposed to his attack: nor could I, without a shudder, behold the dispositions he made for it. First then, moistening well with spittle his instrument, obviously to render it glib, he pointed, he introduced it, as I could plainly discern, not only from its direction, and my losing sight of it; but by the writhing, twisting, and soft murmured complaints of the young sufferer; but, at length, the first straits of entrance being pretty well got through, everything seemed to move, and go pretty currently on, as in a carpet-road, without much rub, or resistance: and now passing one hand round his min-ion's hips, he got hold of his red-topped ivory toy, that stood perfectly stiff, and showed, that if he was like his mother behind, he was like his father before; this he diverted himself with, whilst with the other, he wantoned with his hair, and leaning forward over his back, drew his face, from which the boy shook the loose curls that fell over it, in the posture he stood him in, and brought him towards his, so as to receive a long-breathed kiss, after which, renewing his driving, and thus continuing to harass his rear, the height of the fit came on with its usual symptoms, and dismissed the action.

Clearly, they've fucked—or not so clearly. As you also know, I couldn't quite picture—or mentally "animate"—any of this at age ten. Still, though, it stayed with me. Or rather, it *did* something to me, which "something" I'd now—at age thirty—try or at least pretend to try to articulate.

Fanny, in what we're to think of as her real life, was of course a prostitute. But she's also, now, an author. She's the author, in fact, or rather in fantasy—*our* fantasy—of the book "she" herself, or Cleland, actually called not *Fanny Hill* but *Memoirs of a Woman of Pleasure*. In reality, though—*our* reality—she's its narrator, and as such is both mask and mouthpiece for Cleland. (So, too, in a similar sex change, does "Alexis" both speak for and disguise Yourcenar; so too, perhaps, does "Lady Bracknell" speak for Wilde, although both "Ernest Worthing"—her future son-in-law—and his friend "Algernon Moncrieff"—her nephew—are better at it. "Marcel," of course, speaks for Proust—no sex change there, as with both Ernest and Algernon. There is, though, a sexuality change. Plus change of religion. "William Beckwith" does not speak for Hollinghurst. If anyone, his doctor friend—"James Brook"—does.) At any rate, this so-called sodomy scene, by Cleland as Fanny, is of course—despite the euphemism I'd found, in youth, so confusing ("an engine, that certainly deserved to be put to a better use"), despite, even, the fake homophobia ("all young men should like-wise be [cured of this disbelief], that their innocence may not be betrayed into such snares")—pornography. Or rather, it's *verbal* porn. And yet in glossing it, at Brown, I was far less dirty than deconstructive, less prurient than poststructural, less physical than metaphysical, more lofty, in fact, as in that law brief, than, as both Cleland and Fanny themselves were, simply down to earth—or lusty. Unlike Fanny, for instance, I claim that some of us "get to see homosexual sodomy, if not all the time, at least often enough."

> But even for us, there will always have been that first sighting in which it was not so much we who discovered a new kind of sex, as a new kind of sex that saw, and showed us, who and what we had been, who and what we could no longer be. Because to envision sodomy turned out to mean our revision by sodomy. Alienated from our sense of who we were, alienated from "sense" in its larger sense, we suddenly became the Other we were not, our own significant Other—which is to say, insignificant. At least, that is, until we discovered the other Others who we, as "gays," were not.

"Is it too bourgeois, too sentimental," I conclude, "to regret the lapsing of that senseless moment when, cast adrift from sexual significance, we felt we were everything, anything, and nothing?"

Well, I don't know about "bourgeois" or "sentimental," but it's certainly ridiculous: the false bravado plus wishful thinking here, or bragging plus denial—as ridiculous, no doubt, if not "repulsive," as pickles with donuts. For—to repeat myself—when first reading the scene at age ten, I couldn't quite "envision" sodomy. I could, though—and did—now see myself as if not "gay" yet then at least "homosexual." And when first seeing sodomy in some magazine, or *visual* porn, the very last thing I felt—having by then *become* gay—was "alienation" from any sense of who I am, let alone from "'sense' in its larger sense." I was just trying to see if I'll be a "top" or "bottom" perhaps. Bottom, probably. And then when first seeing sodomy in some video, the pain now clearly shown there—and also heard by me—probably, if provisionally, helped me decide: top, for sure. (But was it real, that pain? Was the "porn star," I now wonder, faking? If so, then why?) And then when first actually *having* sodomy—at twenty, with Paul on bottom—well, I'm not even sure my eyes were open. They weren't—at first—when kissing David Abell. I am, though, sure—once again—that the very last thing I felt, with Paul, was "alienation." Finally, as you also know, I wasn't having such sex at *all*—let alone "often enough"—with Warren at the time of composition. I was only ever seeing it on video or in magazines, or for that matter still reading about it—no longer that confused—in both Cleland and Wilde.

And so *yes*, I guess: this certainly was "sentimental" of me, only not in the sense intended. For I wasn't really regretting the loss, at some point in time, but only for a second, of deconstructive insignificance, the loss, that is, of some allegedly "queer" sense of being. I was regretting a more conventional loss: the loss of innocence—in that hotel room, perhaps, or then maybe on that subway, or then maybe at Yale with David Abell. Or, more likely, I was regretting the next one who got away. I was regretting, that is, the loss—and not yet the death—of Paul. And *that's* what I should have said at the time—or written, even, for class. I should have done something *truthful*, some "articulation" like this one here: primal fantasy (tulip tree, at age five); primal scene number one (hotel room balcony, at ten), primal scene number two (*Fanny Hill*, also at ten); primal reality (subway, at thirteen); first kiss (with David Abell, at nineteen); first blow job (also David Abell); first porn magazine (Jesse's); first porn video (Ken's); first sodomy, on top (with Paul, at twenty); first sodomy, on bottom (with Dean, at twenty-four), which of course wasn't just ridiculous, but—in that lubeless reality—painful. Fanny's "young sufferer," *c'est moi*. Or *c'etait moi*.

After this, I thought of doing—under Robert Scholes—a whole dissertation on sodomy. But—it turns out—there's not a whole lot of *literary* sodomy. Not even in French. (For exceptions to this, see work by Genet. For analysis of that work, see *Homos* by Leo Bersani.) And even if there were, I now worried, would I ever get a job with such a thing? Well, maybe a *blow* job, by some reader, but probably not a teaching job. Not even for a position, as it were, in sexuality studies. So instead—inspired by both Proust and Barthes—I chose a rather less sexual topic. I chose, that is, love. Or *romantic* love, as seen in twentieth-century work by both gay men and lesbians—including Yourcenar. Plus Gertrude Stein and Virginia Woolf. And by "romantic love," I mean everything from the happy notion that opposites attract, as in Gide, to the unhappy one, in Barthes, that they do not.

Love's Litany: The Writing of Modern Homoerotics was a dissertation—and eventually a book—that one might, in all honesty, call *anti*-homosexual. Homophobic, even. (That title, by the way, comes from Wilde. "Do you wish to love?" he once asked. "Use Love's Litany, and the words will create the yearning from which the world fancies that they spring.") Male writers discussed there do not, in general, much care for kissing, sucking, or especially fucking. (I restrict female ones there to fantasy—as if all lesbians do with one another, in real life, is *dream* of each other. Up in *cherry* trees, maybe.) Take Gide, who no matter what the position—I claim—found sodomy "repulsive." My evidence for this? The memoir *If It Die*—deliberately published autobiography—where he reports having seen, while also being observed by them, two other men doing it. The top there, writes Gide, seemed like "a huge vampire feeding upon a corpse." The bottom: "horrifying." Why? Because Gide himself, he now brags, only understands pleasure "face to face, reciprocal and without violence"—which pretty much describes all Warren and I ever did—and "am often satisfied, just like Whitman, by the most furtive of contacts." And the few men—in my book—who might enjoy such activity, never quite manage it. Or having managed it, they find it very, very sad. Take Barthes, whose own experience with cruising (*la drague*)—I claim—fails to warrant his own linkage, in deliberately published *non*-autobiography, of such activity to the "blissfully insignificant"—or queer—"commingling" of both sexuality and love. My evidence? The posthumous memoir *Incidents*, where—in a passage not meant by Barthes for publication—he reports:

> I hang around at home (I have some toast and feta cheese), then, telling myself that I have to break the habit of *planning* my pleasures (or my distractions), I go out again and go to see the new porno flic at the Dragon: as always—and perhaps even more than usual—deplorable. I don't dare cruise my neighbor, although he seems available (idiotic fear of being turned down). Descent to the back room [*la chambre noire*]; afterward, I always regret this sordid episode where I invariably expose my loneliness.

Here, I explain, Barthes himself indicates some problems that—as he knows—stem from that *non*-cruise, at the Dragon, having begun an all too conventional search for sex when what he really—or also—wanted there—or *even* there, where he couldn't possibly find it—was all too conventional love. For there is no "glamorous *coup de foudre*," I also claim, where that "available" neighbor is concerned. And there's "certainly no *coup de foudre* in *la chambre noire*—no love at first sight when you can't see a thing." (Americans call such a place the "back room," although a literal translation from French would be "*black* room.") Barthes, I explain, "could hardly have turned to some strange man"—or boy, even, as Gide might do—"in some dimly lit porn palace and murmured 'I love you.'"

> He would have been out of line. And even if he had, the utterance would not have escaped stereotypology. It would have been a premeditated, prescribed attempt to say something unpremeditated, unprescribed. ("Telling myself that I

have to break the habit of *planning* my pleasures. . . . ") The declaration would have been *studiedly* spontaneous, which is as unstereotypical as stereotypes ever get. Finally, when Barthes cruises the back room rather than his neighbor, he is left desolate. He "exposes his loneliness," but not because he doesn't get what he wants (unadulterated sex—why else is the episode "sordid"?).

"Every back room habitué," I conclude, "can get what he wants." And so for Barthes, in general, "even cruisers who get lucky are unhappy."

Once again, though, this is ridiculous—even apart from that word "stereoty-pology." First of all, not every back room habitué can get what he wants. I was still relatively young, hence attractive, when I wrote that. More to the point, I was completely inexperienced. I had not yet been to any "Dragon" of my own. (It would more than two years before I first went to the one in Coralville.) Second of all, and beyond such fantasy on my part, I was bragging—yet again. I was pretending to possess a relatively insouciant, hopefully sophisticated attitude toward anonymous, or at least near-anonymous, or at least loveless, sex that I most certainly did not indeed *could* not yet have had when I wrote that, and also that—as of *this* writing—I'm not sure I've ever had. It may be, though, that I thought I'd develop such an attitude not by going out and cheating on Warren some more, which by the way I did, but by simply—or not so simply—saying such a thing in public. ("Do you wish to *boff*? Use Boff's Litany and the words will create"—and so on.) Third of all, you most certainly *can* fall in love—even at first sight—at some dimly lit porn palace. Or at least I could, in another two years—with Matt. Fourth of all, it may be that all Barthes really wanted there was—not love—but company. Fifth of all, maybe that *cheese* was the problem. I mean, come on—*feta*? At least brush your teeth, Roland. And then gargle.

For motives I now consider both mean and competitive, I began my next book with an abortive and—as you'll see—all too prescient encounter between both Gide and Barthes. The book is *Beethoven's Kiss*, which I also began, one should confess, while otherwise occupied at my own "Dragon" and then fin-ished while still with Matt. Why here confess? Because I claim there—to help make a point on sublimation—that "I, for example, haven't had sex with anyone since I began this book." It's a lie, of course—a *false* confession. And as such, it's mostly meant for me. "You're not doing anything in that dirty bookstore," I'm now saying to myself—primarily—in public. "You're not even *going* there." You are not, that is, becoming Barthes—in real life. It's also pretty shameful, that lie. For I simply couldn't imagine, at that point, telling anyone the truth in print:

"I, however, when doing this book am also doing any number of strangers—or having them do me." Nor, back then, could I say it to anyone in person. At any rate, here's the encounter:

Roland Barthes, a writer I can't but love, never met André Gide, a writer I can. But imagine what might have happened if he had. September 1932. Gide, out for a late afternoon stroll, notices a young *lycéen* reading *Le Temps retrouvé* and, emboldened by the concurrence of fine weather and good health, decides to cruise the boy. He takes an adjacent seat, sighs, pretends to notice the book's title, and mentions that he'd known the author personally. Barthes, who recognizes Gide but thinks better of saying so, asks whether, in light of that intimacy, he has reason to believe "Marcel" has been less than honest about his sexuality. Gide, impressed by the boldness and cunning of the question, as well as by the charm of the feigned ignorance (for it's clear the boy *must* know who he is), suggests they continue this discussion at his home, over tea and cookies. Barthes accepts the invitation, of course—in large part because, oddly enough, he finds the old man somewhat attractive.

Gide's rooms are cozy and his refreshments are tasty, but despite the structural implications of the rendezvous, neither party manages a sexual overture. Intercourse, to their mutual frustration, remains literary. Consequently, when Barthes asks his host to play something on the piano, Gide, thinking that music making, which will allow him to reveal hidden talent, passion, and sensitivity, might do the trick, obliges. He makes an unwise selection, however—the Chopin Barcarolle. His performance, as is so often the case when he plays for someone, is completely inept. Barthes, unintentionally cruel, asks whether the piece is harder than it sounds. Gide, intentionally cruel, suggests Barthes play something as well. Hoping to rekindle the erotic interest Gide's poor performance has extinguished, Barthes attempts the last movement of the Schumann Fantasy but, even though the piece isn't very difficult, fails to do it justice—a failure of which he, like Gide, who considers both the rendition and the taste evidenced by the selection to be far worse than his own, is well aware. The rendezvous is now irreparable. Barthes says he must be going, and Gide has no choice but to let him go. Before he does so, however, Gide calls Schumann "unbearable," offers Barthes a copy of his essay on Chopin, and suggests they get together again soon. After Barthes leaves, Gide eats dinner, practices the Barcarolle for two hours, and writes in his journal that he's "perfected" it. Barthes walks home, eats dinner, climbs into bed, reads a few more pages of Proust, masturbates, and waits for his mother to come kiss him goodnight.

So it's fiction, this encounter—the only fiction, in fact, that I'd ever yet published. (This is why I wrote, above: "I'll say more on some for the most part *non*fiction of mine.") But despite what you yourselves may expect now—some "rainbow," perhaps—I'll not call this "ridiculous." What I will do, though— reading myself symptomatically—is say that I seem, there, to be projecting my own sense of inadequacy, or *sexual* inadequacy, onto Gide. I'll also say that as a writer I'm trying to *top* Barthes. (This, by the way, is something I'd not only refuse to do with David Sedaris, in my book *Sedaris*, but say there that I won't do. "It's time for me to stop showing off," I confess. "It's time, that is, to renounce a certain style—a certain selfish virtuosity.") I'll also say, here, that with this non-sodomy scene—actually, with Gide, it'd have to be non-*frottage*—sex per se, or rather any writing of mine on it was now—I thought—a thing of the past.

And so on to sex equivalents. Like dreams, I figured—or like me for boy-friends one and four—these should be if not more interesting then at least more mysterious and complicated than whatever desires or fears they express. Take, for instance, my treatment in *Beethoven's Kiss* of the novel *Teleny*. When discussing this verbal porn—allegedly written or at least edited by the man who, at his trial for "gross indecency," famously, if inadvertently, incriminated himself by declaring some boy "too ugly" to kiss, not to mention suck or fuck—I am far more concerned with the narrator's reaction, which is a hand-job fantasy, to his both seeing and hearing some sexy concert pianist, or virtuoso, than I am with anything hard-core these two guys—post-concert—then "really" do together. "My lips were parched," he says, "I gasped for breath; my joints were stiff, my veins were swollen, yet I sat still, like all the crowd around me."

> But suddenly a heavy hand seemed to be laid upon my lap, something was hent and clasped and grasped, which made me faint with lust. The hand was moved up and down, slowly at first, then faster and faster it went in rhythm with the song. My brain began to reel as throughout every vein a burning lava coursed, and then, some drops even gushed out—I panted—

I am even more concerned, there, with that "song" performed: a Liszt-like and therefore perfectly appropriate "rhapsody." So when going on from there to discuss *Command Performance*—visual porn in which "B.J. Slater," both seeing and hearing "Chuck Hunter" play Rachmaninov, the Prelude in C-sharp Minor, now imagines fucking him—I'm most concerned with the rest of that concert program. Chuck, you see—or hear, rather—may have begun with Rachmaninov, but, while still in B.J.'s mind being sodomized, then moves on to both

Debussy and Satie: *Clair de lune* and then the first *Gymnopédie*. Such music, in such a context, is—I claim—inappropriate. Unlike what one can only imagine or perhaps "hallucinate" in the Wilde—that Liszt-like rhapsody—it neither grows with intensity nor, sodomy-like, increases in excitement. It's "lis[z]tless," I pun. Plus it's Chuck himself—a sexy in fact lovely bottom but an amateur nay horrible pianist—who does the actual playing. And so unless you press "mute"— which, one must confess, I still do while using this on DVD—it's almost impossible to keep if not your eyes on the screen, then your own mind on sex.

If you do mute, though, he's perfect. He's far more perfect, in both fact and fantasy, than any such bottom, or top, you'd ever see—or smell, or taste, or feel—in real life. This is true of pornography in general, whether visual or even just verbal. It creates false, rainbow-like expectations of sex: no stench, no soreness. No excess body hair. No body fat at all. And this, once again, is something Rousseau said long ago: that no "natural" relation—assuming, against what Lacan would later claim, there ever is such a thing—is so well realized as an imaginary one. Likewise, no amateurism—whether at some Mason & Hamlin concert grand or some, as here up in our attic, Macintosh computer—is ever virtuosity. And against what Barthes said ("the piece functions as a bit of a hallucination"), we know it's not.

In my next book, on Vaslav Nijinsky, I discuss both choreographed masturbation, with *Afternoon of a Faun*, and choreographed orgy. *Jeux*, I reveal, only *seems* to show some tennis game. It really—if only for Nijinsky—shows Diaghilev, his lover at the time, sandwiched between Nijinsky himself and some other guy. My evidence? His diary:

> The *Faun* is me, and *Jeux* is the life of which Diaghilev dreamed. He wanted to have two boys as lovers. He often told me so, but I refused. Diaghilev wanted to make love to two boys at the same time, and wanted these boys to make love to him. In the ballet, the two girls [Tamara Karsavina and Ludmilla Schollar] represent the two boys and the young man [Nijinsky] is Diaghilev. I changed the characters, as love between three men could not be represented on the stage.

I also reveal, there, this choreography. These dancers, I say—and note the insouciance, the celebratory words—"flirt, embrace, couple, regroup, pose, observe, and caress themselves." I do not, though, reveal—nor even suggest—that I myself, by then, had "had" one such three-way in real life. Just the one. Nor, then, do I say that the thing—beyond ridiculous—was just awful. Warren and I, at Brown, had some classmate of mine—also friend of ours—cast in the Diaghilev role. But the friend cast Warren that way. And so—to say the least—there was no such flirting, embracing, coupling, posing, observing, or caressing ourselves. (A subsequent such three-way, in that Los Angeles bathhouse, fared no better. And so for me, anonymity was no solution. Nor, after that—and also a few martinis— did a real live four-way go well. And so alcohol was no solution. I now guessed, at bottom, that I'm just a one-man man. Or one man at a time.)

After the Nijinsky book came *Finishing Proust*—that mean, unpublished novel of mine. Its narrator, though, isn't much like me. He's neither mask nor mouthpiece—I thought—for me. In fact, he's "Stephen Kopelson"—still alive and, late in his own life, now trying to understand why younger brother "Kevin," a *famous* literary critic, couldn't finish some nonfiction book of his, also called *Finishing Proust*, on why that Frenchman couldn't finish his own novel, and also to understand why Kevin hanged himself. Maybe, Stephen realizes, not-so-sweet, not-so-smart "Mike" could help—if, that is, the guy hadn't just gotten drunk, as usual, and then died—horribly—in some car accident he caused. As you can see, then, I punished Matt—in furious fantasy—for having broken my heart. ("Confession is an *art*," I now keep telling myself. "But it's not a *martial* art.") Worse yet—in furious reality—I sent Matt the manuscript. (His response to this: no response. In fact, he stopped speaking to me.) As you can see, too, I forced brother Steve—in self-pitiful fantasy—to pay me the same kind of atten-tion I'd paid him. And so there's no sex, here, nor even very many equivalents. (At one point, late in the novel, Stephen does recall piano duets with Kevin.) There is, however, a kiss—just the one—between Stephen and "Wayne Koesten-baum," an old friend of Kevin's whom Stephen has only just met for the first time and who then, unlike Mike, does help him. Mystery solved.

So I'm not a great novelist. That plot, clearly, is both punitive and pedan-tic—and also, mostly, self-therapeutic. ("One writes," said Michel Foucault, "in order to become other than what one is.") In these confessions—I think—it's only partly that. (Not that there's *plot* per se, here.) I've other limitations as a fiction writer—ones I imagine you yourselves, if only from having read that Gide-meets-Barthes encounter quoted above, can imagine. ("Roland Barthes, a writer I can't but love, never met André Gide, a writer I can"—and so on.) And yet I'll tell them to you anyway . . .

First, though, I'll discuss my poetry—by which of course I mean limericks. I wrote these, initially, not for publication but rather to amuse myself, impress friends, and either celebrate or trash certain sexuality-studies "stars." The first one, done soon after I moved to Iowa City, concerned Eve Kosofsky Sedgwick.

It refers, primarily, to her work—in *Epistemology of the Closet*—on sodomy. It refers, too, to what the woman herself—admittedly—would rather do in bed:

> A spankable critic named Eve
> Wrote books that made homophobes heave.
> > She'd give them depictions
> > Of anal addictions
> That showed them how *not* to conceive.

Another, much less elegant one—

> There once was a diva named Judy,
> A vengeful and paranoid beauty.
> > With gender she fucked
> > In prose that just sucked
> But tickled the queer-hypersnooty.

—concerned Judith Butler.

The limerick form, as you must know, is basically *hyper*sexual: "There once was a man from Nantucket"—and so on. And yet my own limericks were not. They were, that is, no more about sex per se—in graphic terms—or even sex equivalents than my own allegedly non-sucky prose had been. (You think my prose does suck? Sue me.) Instead, they were about—in non-graphic terms—books like *Epistemology of the Closet* and, by Judith Butler, *Gender Trouble*. They were also about that form itself. Or rather, about how allegedly clever I am at if not turning something naughty—the limerick per se—into something nasty, then turning something lusty into something lofty. Or at least *pseudo*-lofty.

But then two things happened. First, I turned—as you may recall from "G712"—to "real-world" stars like Vaslav Nijinsky and Ned Rorem:

> Most audience members cried "Shame!"
> When Vaslav, Diaghilev's flame,
> > Defiled the veil
> > In a pastoral tale.
> But wankers were happy they came.

> "Atonal is straight, tonal gay,"
> Claim students of Miss Boulanger.
> > Take little Ned:

Even in bed
He'd carry a tune all the way.

Second, I decided—perhaps delusionally—that some of this work was just too good not to publish. I also worried, though, that such self-exposure, by making one seem at least somewhat ridiculous, might undermine even my own—non-star—position within sexuality studies. I therefore created: "'Gumby' Louis Boots." He's the totally ridiculous but more to the point also rather naughty—make that rather lusty—scholar who, apart from a couple of serious books in sexuality studies, or "queer theory" as it was still then called, also wrote—I'd have Gumby himself claim in print—those limericks of mine. (In other words, he's a "Fanny Hill" of my own—only without the sex change.) Friends of mine, of course—plus a couple of colleagues—would know this to be a lie. They'd still know that *I'm* the poet here. But if they'd also know what's *good* for them, goddammit, they'll keep it to themselves.

I then wrote, as Gumby:

While posing above an abyss,
Poor Oscar said something amiss—
    A damnably glib
    Sodomitical fib:
"The boy was too ugly to kiss."

But this wasn't yet very graphic. So I now wrote, as him:

A power-crazed prof who knew Greek,
Apparently phallicly weak,
    Told an old Brahman
    With insight uncommon:
"I can't make my subaltern shriek."

And this, I thought, was really *porno*graphic.

This "prof," I'm afraid, is Michel Foucault. ("A power-crazed prof who knew Greek"—and so on.) I'll explain the "Brahman" joke—or in-joke—later, in "Death to Gumby." I'll say more there, as well, on "Gumby" Louis Boots. *Much* more, in fact, as well as on a—note the sex change now—female counterpart of his. I will say here, though, that the last name *Boots* had nothing to do with "Boots Beechwood"—Evan Wolfson's porn name. It's a nickname of David Coster's for me—as are, for that matter, both *Gumby* and *Louis*. "Gumby," because I'm both flexible and—from the Gilbert's Syndrome mentioned in "G712"—somewhat green. "Louis," because—like "Louis Ironson," the "word processor" in the play *Angels in America*—I'm both Jewish and neurotic. "Boots," finally, after a hand-sewn pair of shitkickers I wear. (They're alligator skin—dyed burgundy.) David, you see, rather fancies them. And so maybe *he's* into cowboys.

You know, though, it's not *that* odd for someone like me—*in propria persona*—to not write graphically about sex. (See, for instance, the rest of that D.A. Miller essay on the film *Rope*—"Anal *Rope*." Or see almost anything by Sedgwick—apart from her own self-therapeutic book, A *Dialogue on Love*. Or see anything by Foucault. For an exception to this, see *Unlimited Intimacy* by Tim Dean. He's an ex-lover of my officemate at Penn. Plus the book—being Lacanian—is horrible, *telling* readers as it does that gay men actually want to be killed and *showing* or rather bragging to them that Dean is an exclusive top. For another such exception, see, once again, *Homos* by Leo Bersani.) Nor am I the first such scholar to have observed—if not quite complained—as much. (David Halperin, the author of *Saint Foucault*, began his brilliant book *What Do Gay Men Want?* by asking, appropriately enough: "What do gay men want?" His answer, initially, is: "According to a number of recent novels, gay men just want to be held. According to some current writing about HIV/AIDS [such as by Tim Dean], gay men actually want to be killed. According to most critical work in queer studies—well, most critical work in queer studies has nothing to say on the subject." There are, of course, Halperin adds in a footnote, "some distinguished exceptions to this generalization: principally, D.A. Miller, *Place for Us*. See also"—he writes there—"Ellis Hanson, 'Wilde's Exquisite Pain;' Wayne Koestenbaum, *The Queen's Throat: Opera, Homosexuality, and the Mystery of Desire*; [and] Kevin Kopelson, *Beethoven's Kiss: Pianism, Perversion, and the Mastery of Desire*." But that's another story.) Like lawyers, you see, we scholars—even if in sexuality studies—are not supposed to produce smut. As with lawyers, in other words—or as with doctors when they're not so to speak "*playing* doctor," or as with those psychiatrist brothers on the sitcom *Frasier*—there's a generic, or disciplinary, or rather impersonal limitation at work. And in *other* other—more discipline-specific—words: we're not really pornographers. Nor are we really limericists. And nor, especially, are we novelists—as not only both Cleland and Wilde but also Proust, Gide, Genet, Yourcenar, and Woolf used to be. Or, to cite a more recent and also more clearly straight plus both Jewish and neurotic example, as Philip Roth—at least as of this writing—still is. All we scholars, or critics, are supposed to do, instead, is analyze—and maybe even *psycho*analyze, using if not Lacan then Freud—such texts. Say, for instance, that Roth, in his novel *Sabbath's Theater*, writes:

> Lately, when Sabbath suckled at Drenka's uberous breasts—uberous, the root word of *exuberant*, which is itself *ex* plus *uberare*, to be fruitful, to overflow like Juno lying prone in Tintoretto's painting where the Milky Way is coming out of her tit—suckled with an unrelenting frenzy that caused Drenka to roll her head ecstatically back and to groan "I feel it deep down in my cunt," he was pierced by the sharpest of longings for his late little mother.

All some critic—true to form—might write is: *What an amazingly blasphemous little mélange that is. This sentence is really dirty, and partly because it conforms to the well-known definition of dirt—matter out of place, which is itself a defini-tion of the mixing of high and low dictions. Since the comedy of the subject matter involves moving from one register to another—from a lover's breast to a mother's— it is fitting that the style of the sentence mimics this scandalous shift.* In fact, some critic *has* written this. He's James Wood, in the book *How Fiction Works*.

Of course one reason, probably the main reason, we're not novelists—or even pornographers—is personal. It's that we can't think *visually*. Or rather, that we can't write that way. Another such reason, or limitation, is that—unlike both Proust and Cleland, in particular—we can't think *metaphorically*. Yet another one is that, to invoke the novelist Henry James, we simply prefer *telling* stuff to *showing* it—or "diegesis" to "mimesis." All three of these, of course, are what I'd imagined, above, that you yourselves could imagine—about me, at least—not only from having read that Gide-meets-Barthes encounter quoted earlier but even from having read any of the rest of this here *nonfiction* book. If not, then you'd certainly do so from reading that novel of mine.

Plus there's always the possibility—even for some of us in sexuality studies, or maybe especially us—that an even more personal reason why we've got, to quote Halperin, "nothing [graphic] to say [in print] on the subject" of sex, or why, like me, we may prefer treating sex "equivalents" there, is—even or maybe especially now we're no longer, in real life, so "inexperienced"—that we've also never much liked *talking* about sex. Not to strangers, anyway. And nor even to friends. And nor—sorry, David—even to lovers and then husbands or wives. And nor—sorry, Adam, Seth, and Sam—especially to children. ("Dad, what's a 'blow job'?" "It's oral sex.") "Well, *why* not?" you command. Who knows.

Worse yet, there's also the possibility that, as Leo Bersani, the author of *Homos*, has confessed on behalf of if not himself then at least the rest of us: "There is a big secret about sex: most people don't like it." By "sex," though, he means just sodomy. The line begins his essay "Is the Rectum a Grave?"—written before *Homos*. The essay theorizes homophobia as a fantasy of men participating, principally if not exclusively through anal intercourse, in what is presumed by them to be the terrifying—not to mention suicidal—phenomenon of female sexuality.

Speaking for myself, though—along, that is, with David, Matt, or even Paul, and *not* with soldierly Dean or "Carlos"—I find the claim dubious. I've even said so before, in print. This was about ten years ago, in a hatchet job—called "Critical Assholes"—that, for revenge, I did on *Decadence and Catholicism* by Ellis Hanson. About twenty years ago, you see, he'd trashed *Love's Litany* in a book review. (Sorry, Ellis. Sorry, for that matter, Judith, Leo, and Tim.) That review of mine—not to brag—begins:

> Fifteen years ago, Leo Bersani began "Is the Rectum a Grave?" with the dubious claim that most of us hate sex—sodomy in particular. Five years ago, and shortly after taking a whack at Bersani in a very mean, very funny review of *Homos*, Ellis Hanson qualified the claim. *Many* gay men, we learn in *Decadence and Catholicism*, hate sex, including, unbelievably enough, every single author Hanson considers—Baudelaire, Verlaine, and Huysmans, to name a few of the French, Pater, Wilde, and Firbank, to name a few of the English. Blame the false promise of both scriptural and hagiographic porn, Hanson suggests: "Anyone who has learned about sexuality from the Bible or the lives of the saints must surely be in for a grave disappointment upon encountering the real thing." Rousseau, of course, faced a secular version of the problem. Blame, too, he suggests, the superior pleasure of writing one's own porn.

It ends by saying that although sex can, in fact, "suck," it doesn't really *have* to—even for Baudelaire and company. "So isn't Hanson, like Bersani, speaking for himself here?" I ask. "Shouldn't what he presents as indirect discourse be read as self-revelation—or confession?" (Such discourse, by Hanson, includes lines like: "The ecstasies of art and religion are infinitely superior to the physical spasm of sex;" and "Those of us with a morbid inclination to romance would rather read about [Wilde's] Salome.") "After all," I add, "some of us—call us 'shameless,' which Hanson does—some of us who've read the Bible (if only the Hebrew one) and even a hagiography or two (*Saint Foucault*, at any rate) and who really do enjoy [what he calls] 'the highly erotic pleasures of writing' still prefer sodomy to sentence structure."

| | |

About a year after Matt dumped me, something called the "International Society for the Study of European Ideas" (ISSEI) asked me to speak at a conference. The venue, it wrote, would be Haifa University in Israel. The theme would be "twentieth-century narrative." There'd be guided tours of both Haifa and Jerusalem. There'd also be such "site-specific seminars" as *Bahá'í Architecture* and *Druze Hospitality*. Most of this, I thought, sounded pretty sketchy. Weren't the Druze, like Palestinians, more or less *homeless*? Weren't the Bahá'í *Persian*? Wasn't Haifa some kind of *beach resort*? As for "twentieth-century narrative," what—other than haiku and epigrams—could it possibly *not* cover?

ISSEI, though, I soon learned from my friend "Swisher-Tingley," was a rather odd if not quite bogus group. Its *raison d'être*, apparently, was to meet once a year at some vacation spot where—boondoggle-wise—all you need do would be to present work and then go sunbathe. Tours were optional, he said, as were seminars. As perhaps were "ideas," even—whether or not European. Well, I thought, I've never *been* to Israel—Jerusalem in particular. Plus I could also see that kibbutz, named Nachshon, where Steve hanged himself. See his old room there, where this happened. I'd get closure, then. *Final* closure, unlike the mere "provisional" kind I sought pre-mortem.

So I said "fine," in effect, to the invitation. I then quickly wrote a talk, for that conference, on being influenced by *Remembrance of Things Past* even when—pornography-wise—you've never really read it. "Jean Cocteau," it began, "once wondered whether 'Proustians' read line by line or skip."

André Gide, of course, was one such Proustian when he skimmed the first few pages of À *la recherche du temps perdu* and decided not to publish it. But he was another kind of Proustian after his change of heart: the kind that can't finish the novel. So was Virginia Woolf, and it's instructive to compare the two. Their analogous failures suggest the extent to which we should look beyond literary misreadings toward *non*readings—supplementing Harold Bloom's notion of the anxiety of influence with a Barthesian concept of the *fantasy* of influence. The failures suggest, in other words, that Proustian writers—if not Proustian readers—who, to a certain extent, merely *imagine* Proust feel both constrained and liberated. And they suggest ways in which any writer, to quote Barthes, can afford to be "indifferent to his own stupidity." Or if not stupidity, ignorance.

I then wrote to the married couple, named Mermelstein, who apparently *still* ran Kibbutz Nachshon. "Please do come," they wrote back.

But I couldn't come. The morning I'd have made this pilgrimage, it was suddenly all too clear what would happen there—to me. The Mermelsteins, in their fifties or sixties by now, would meet me at some bus stop. Or maybe their son would—the one who at age thirteen, my sister had been told, found Steve's body. We'd either walk or drive to Nachshon. I'd be fed, and also given coffee. I'd be shown around. I'd be shown that room of Steve's. But with nothing of him in it, anymore, I'd feel awful. No closure at all. In fact, an awful old wound— only somewhat healed not by Dr. Train, of course, but by my having written *Finishing Proust*—would now reopen. (So, too, might another such wound have opened for my hosts. Having become and then stayed slim, by then, I looked even more like Steve—I think—than like Prince. Or more like what Steve *would* have: dark brown eyes, curly brown hair, and—thanks, I imagine, to rapist old Mongols, or that so-called Golden Horde—almost no body hair. Steve, though, had very long eyelashes, whereas I've got almost none.) So I telephoned with an excuse: "boils," I think I told some kibbutznik in English. My Hebrew, like my math skills, was by now almost nonexistent. Or maybe I said "frogs."

There I was, then: sitting in my hotel room with nothing to do. I'd toured Haifa yesterday: Mount Carmel, Bahá'í Shrine. I'd done Jerusalem the day before: Wailing Wall, Temple Mount. I'd presented my talk the day before that. Plus the conference was over. So I called my panel's moderator—also somewhere in that hotel—to ask if he'd go to the beach with me. Brown-eyed "Woody," as I'll call him, is another gay Jew about my age—also American—although unlike me, at the time, he had a lover back home. "Sure," he said. "And I know the bus to take."

Woody, I'd say, looks like Howie Mandel, the comedian turned actor turned self-confessed "germophobe" and game show host: bald, now, and a little scary. But he's both amusing and readily amused. He told me, en route, what that lover back home had told him—in jest: "Watch out for your heart!" Most Israeli Jews, you see, aren't like American Jews—the men there, at any rate. They are not physically weak. They are not neurotic, even. They are not, that is, Alexander Portnoy. ("Portnoy's Complaint," according to Roth, is "a disorder in which strongly-felt ethical and altruistic impulses are perpetually warring with extreme sexual longings, often of a perverse nature.") For whereas men like Woody and I—he'd imagine—spend the best years of our lives eating bonbons and either reading *Remembrance of Things Past*, in its entirety, or practicing Schumann, which, although physical activity, isn't really exercise, these guys, with mandatory military service and all, spend them either doing push-ups in the desert or making love *à la hus-sarde*—to women. (Steve, though, would have had to serve there as well.) And so a lot of the young ones at the beach, nearly nude, would look almost pornographi-cally unreal to us. Or they'd look, to me, like either Doug Trevor at the gym— "Aussie Humboldt," in porn—and or, more to the point, Jesse Matz there—"Max Holder"—and or, even more to the point, "B.J. Slater" and "Chuck Hunter," only both hairier and more clearly straight than these last two.

Woody was right. The scene where we hit the beach and then dumped our clothes was—if you can imagine it—like the calm before some Israeli *Command Performance*. Wayne can, funnily, in "Best-selling Jewish Porn Films." "*Jewish Gold*," this poem begins. "*Jews Between Themselves / Wet Jew Stories / Jewish Jocks*." There were just so many hunks, here. Too many of them—and not just nude, nearly, but also of course speaking Hebrew. None, though—I imagined—were attracted to me. Any "opposites," for them, must be female. And even if gay, like Steve, they'd be *much* more attracted to each other—or to at least *physical* twins. "We have *got* to leave," I said to Woody. But he just chuckled. "No kidding," I said. "Let's *leave*."

He then suggested, as a gentleman, that the two of us "take a little stroll." So we walked south—water on our right, sand on our left, fewer and fewer men anywhere. (*Nous allons marcher ensemble.*) He told Jewish jokes. ("We don't go *there*.") I told Jewish jokes. ("So look who thinks he's nothing.") We both trashed ISSEI. We then noticed some dark brown young man—slim, too, but with straight black hair—sitting about fifty feet ahead. He, too, seemed to see us, took off his swimsuit, and then ran into the water.

The guy was now about fifty feet out there, in the water, bobbing up and down and also—it seemed—waving at us. Woody stopped strolling, took off his own suit, and then ran to join him. I, too, stopped, watched them some—chat-ting, maybe cruising each another—and then, thinking "oh, what the hell," did likewise. Desire, after all, is imitative.

Now all three of us were chatting. The guy's English, I noticed, was aw-ful. Worse, even, than that of Hubert Sorin. So it was hard to tell which of us—if either—he preferred. Woody, though, in an aside, said "It's you he wants, Kevin"—and then swam back to shore, put his suit back on, and left. Back to base, I figured. Back to *Wet Jew Stories*.

Now the two of us, still nude, were sitting where I'd left my own suit. Or rather, *he* was nude. I was just *naked*. (The nude body—whether male or female—is always beautiful. It is an ideal one. It does not return the viewer's gaze. It is a mere passive *object* of that viewer's gaze and also of his or her desire. And so it invites—indicatively phallic—penetration. The naked body, though, may or may not be beautiful. He or she is real. He or she does return the viewer's gaze. He or she is an active *subject* of desire—as well as of everything else, to quote Nietzsche, "human, all too human." And so he or she invites not penetration but—indicatively maternal—protection.) I guessed, correctly, that the guy was thirty years old. I was thirty-eight. His name was let's say "Razi." He was Druze, he said—not Jewish. His eyes—thanks, I then imagined, to rapist old Frenchmen—were blue. "Crusader blue," I thought. But, like me, he had almost no body hair. And he'd lived, he said, in Berlin for a couple of years. Now, though, having "termulated" some job he had there—having been fired from it, I thought—he was home, at his parents' house, for a "very long visit." He just hated Maria Callas—as did I! He just loved Montserrat Caballé—as did I! I then went on and on about Caballé's recording of the opera *Salome*, by Richard Strauss, but can't be sure Razi understood. It does seem, though, that by doing so I may have indicated to him, to quote Ellis Hanson, some "inclination to romance"—possibly "morbid." He then went on and on about her recording of *Norma*. This guy is sweet, I thought, and not so nervous. Not so *soldierly*. Plus, as he eventually said, he's also got a place—some friend's apartment—that is "not so very far from your . . . *Gasthof.*" He did not, though, say it's one we can use.

We'd rendezvous, we agreed, at four o'clock at some outdoor café. My plan, lest some problem arise, was—like "Gide" in that encounter I made up, though without his distaste for *all* sodomy—to then either get Razi up to the hotel room with me or—like "Barthes" there—myself over to the apartment with him. So I put my suit back on, then also headed for base. ("*Three Jewish Brothers / Jewish Room Service / Jewish Sexual Healing / Jews Beg for Mercy.*") I did find Woody there, told him what no good I'd now be up to, put my clothes back on, and walked—alone—back to the bus. Once back in the room, alone, I got into bed, re-read some Proust, considered masturbating but didn't, tried to nap but couldn't, and started sprucing up for what I hoped would be not ridiculous but simply meaningless sex. By "meaningless," though, I don't mean what I'd once claimed, deconstructively, the first sight of *any* sodomy could be. I meant *anonymous*. Correction: *nearly* anonymous. This, after all, wasn't the Dragon. It was more like the Phoenix.

I arrived for coffee a bit early—wearing jeans and a nice tee shirt. Razi was late—in slacks and a dress shirt. His hair, I noticed, now looked greasy—grooming I disliked. His odor, I noticed, was now feminine—a smell I disliked. (*L'eau d'Issey? Emmeline?*) We talked some more about what work— selling clothes—he did in Berlin. "What now, then?" I asked. But he didn't understand the question, or at least pretended not to. I asked, then, about the Druze, which question Razi did understand. Like Laurence of Harvard, I took it from the response, they're a tribe. (Actually, to quote Wikipedia: "The Druze are a religious community whose traditional religion is said to have begun as an offshoot of the Ismaili sect of Islam, but is unique in its incorporation of Gnostic, neo-Platonic and other philosophies. Because of such incorporation most Islamic scholars label the Druze as non-Muslims or at least as an 'unorthodox' Islamic sect. Theologically, Druze consider themselves a 'reformatory sect.'" I'd have known this, perhaps, if I'd gone to that seminar.) I then asked about Razi's family and where they lived. Some town, he said, just outside Haifa. (His voice, I noticed, was girlish—a sound I disliked.) I told him I'm now from Iowa City, which of course he'd never heard of. I also said I'm Jewish, but of course he'd figured as much.

At this point, the hook-up was going to plan. No problem, apart from that greasy-looking hair, feminine odor, and girlish voice. But when I now suggested going somewhere inside, Razi, instead, proposed something "very special." Have I ever heard, he asked, of Druze hospitality? Well, here's what we should do. Razi will telephone his parents, telling them we'd both be at the house in a couple of hours. Meanwhile, he'll show me a "very special" part of Haifa that I didn't get to see on tour. And then we'll get *more* coffee. And then we'll take some bus.

Here's what I thought about *his* plan: Clearly, it seemed, Razi is interested. He wants sex, that is—not just yet, maybe, but later, no doubt, upon return from that town. Clearly, too, he'll be either insulted or hurt if I reject the plan— which might prevent sex. At any rate, when else, not to mention where else, would I ever experience such hospitality? So I said "fine," in effect. He made the call, excitedly—from a telephone booth at the café. And off we went.

I'm not normally much of a coffee drinker. I have a cup or two in the morning and then none after that. So by the time our bus came—at seven o'clock—I was *wired*. The bus, I assumed, went all the way to the town. But it "termulated," instead, at Haifa University. We got off of the thing. "And so *now* what?" I asked Razi, who in response just stuck out his thumb. "RUN!" yelled the not so stupid part of me to the stupid one. "You are not hitchhiking God knows where with this . . . *Arab*." (Wikipedia: "In Israel, the majority of the approximately 120,000

Druze consider themselves a distinct ethnic group and do not identify them-
selves as Arab.") Or at least, it said, make some excuse—boils, frogs—and take
the next bus back. I didn't know, though, if there'd *be* another bus that night.
And so when the non-Anglophone driver of some non-American car now pull-
ing up to us seemed to recognize Razi—"he cousin," Razi explained, "from
town"—I reminded myself that neither Dean nor Fatso, back in old Virginia,
had turned out to be maniacs.

The trip, to me, seemed endless. Endless prattle, by both these guys, in what
I assumed—correctly—was Arabic. (Wikipedia: "They use the Arabic language
and follow a social pattern very similar to the other East Mediterraneans of the
region.") No English translation, for me, by Razi. Where'd they live, I won-
dered—Beirut? The so-called cousin, at last, did drop us off—somewhere. It
being so dark, though, I couldn't see a thing—anywhere. No stars or even moon
out. No lights on, either. Razi now took my hand—his, I noticed, was clammy—
and led me on. (Or had I first led him—somehow? Desire is imitative.) Minutes
later—with lights suddenly on—we were home. Standing in front of the house,
by a very large table in a courtyard, were the parents—in I'd guess their sixties
or seventies—along with about twenty siblings, siblings-in-law, nieces, and also
nephews of Razi's. Those parents, I noticed, were in some native garb. The
others were not.

"Hello, everyone," said Razi in Arabic. "This new friend Kevin." (He would
now translate—sometimes.) Everyone, except the father, then said something to
me. Dad—also blue-eyed—just glared at me. That table, I noticed, was *covered*
with food—everything from some lentil dish to some other lentil dish. I knew
instinctively, soon, to sample it all—lest Razi, along with this whole *mishpukha*,
be both insulted and hurt. And then, of course, came coffee.

Dad *kept* glaring at me. He seemed, I thought, to have my number. He must
have known instinctively—like Dr. Svetlov at IDANT—both my true sexuality
and that I hadn't really come here to eat. No one else knew, though. Or, being
both altruistic and ethical, they pretended not to—for both Razi's sake and
mine. Conversation, then, remained impersonal. I was grilled, in Arabic, on—
like some "native informant"—almost anything American: from our non-porn
film industry to various pop stars (Madonna, Michael Jackson) to of course
food. ("'Twinkies'? *Really?*") And they all—apart from both Mom and Dad—
went on and on and on like this for hours. At about midnight, though, the table
was cleared. Siblings, siblings-in-law, nieces, and nephews took off for their own
homes—on foot. Razi and I were taken inside, by the mother, and then to a tiny

bedroom—a closet, really, if not cubicle, next to both parents' own bedroom. In it, there was just one maybe fifty-thousand-watt bulb hanging from the ceiling. And there was just one bed—one mattress, rather, laid right on the floor. Queen-size.

Razi, still, seemed excited. Happy, even. I, though, was not. It was both very bright and very, very hot in that room—with just one tiny window. As that window had no screen, mosquitoes came in. We said goodnight to the mother. We then closed the door. No lock, I noticed. Razi then got undressed—but for his underwear. That's what I then did, too. (Fashion is imitative.) And so now we were *both* nearly naked—not nude. I then touched that hair. It *was* greasy. We then kissed. That was *horrible*. Even worse than with Dean. And so—because of how *repulsive* it would be, for me—the very *last* thing I now wanted, meaningless or not, was *sex*. Plus I was also, by this point, *very* wired. Plus I was also—somehow—very, very *tired*. Plus I was *stuffed*—with all those lentils. Plus some septuagenarian with an axe to grind—some *maniac*, maybe—could hear everything we were doing. And so I said to Razi, "Let's just sleep." He said, in effect, "fine." For some reason, though, we'd have to keep that light bulb on. He then smoked a cigarette—another smell I disliked. (My own dad—as you know from "G712"—smoked, too.) He then just shut his eyes and snored—and never ever stopped. (My dad snored, too.)

Could this, I wondered, get any *worse*? I am *burning* up. I'm being *bitten* by mosquitoes. I am *blinded* by that goddamned light. I'm too *caffeinated*, anyway, to sleep. This room *stinks*. This guy's a *buzz saw*. I have *no* idea—European or not—where I am, no one to come *get* me—no Bill, that is, nor even Woody—no other way *out*, and no way to ward off that *axe*. Just then, though, some cock—some *avian* cock—started crowing and, to quote Svetlov, "never ever *ever*" stopped.

At about six o'clock, the door burst open. It was the father, who, after seeing that the two of us—one of us, brown-eyed, still awake, the other just now opening those blue eyes—were lying here about a foot apart, barked something at Razi. "Time for breakfast," the guy more or less *sang* in translation. A *very* girlish sound, I thought—like some combination of Michael Jackson and Madonna. And then, said Razi, he'd show me the town—something "very special" there in particular. After that, if I liked, he'd walk me back to the bus.

The breakfast, now served inside by the mother, was mostly cake. (Plus some *good* coffee, Dean.) The father, throughout this, stayed outside—in that courtyard, pruning some kind of tree. Razi alone prattled to me in English. I couldn't listen to the guy anymore. I ate, just to be polite, and ate, and ate, and drank some more coffee, and wondered when that bus would get here. And why hadn't it come to town last night?

Razi, on this guided tour, seemed pretty popular. Everyone we met, while walking around, stopped what he was doing to hug and then catch up with him. Almost all, though, seemed confused by my presence. "Is he married?" they'd ask Razi. "Are there children?" The only one not confused, some very ugly date merchant, gave Razi a look, and then a smile, and then gave *me* a hug—which, to be honest, was grope-like—and then just laughed. So did Razi.

He and I came to a small, as yet roofless house. After indicating—and I swear this is true—a *pomegranate* tree by the entrance, he explained that old Blue-Eyes was having this built for him. Taking my hand, once again, he led me inside. "This here," said Razi, "is the bedroom. And this here, kitchen."

"And Kevin," he said, "Kevin no go home to America. Every day, you here, you go to market. 'One kilo of lentils,' you say. 'No, *two* kilos.' Ha, ha, ha."

But his own blue eyes weren't laughing. And it was all too clear, now, what would happen—to me—if I once again said "fine," in effect, to this plan. If, that is, I allowed myself—even after such a night—to imitate Razi's desire. I'd be boiling lentils for the next twenty years—I already imagined myself telling though not writing this story, much as when I'd proposed the perfume name *Emmeline* to Grangerford—never teaching another class on homosexual activity, or its equivalents, nor even writing another book on anything else. Finally, the International Society for the Study of European Ideas would return to Haifa: a conference at which, in *female* native garb, I'd offer a "site-specific" seminar, called "Pomegranates in the Garden," on my life, as a wife, among Druze. It's something I'd connect there, ironically, to my mere bridal *registry* back in New York, with Warren as groom, at Bloomingdale's.

"You have *no* idea who I am," I wanted to say. Or, meaner yet: "We're done now."

But instead, to be nice, I lied.

"I should have said this before, Razi, and I'm sorry, but I already *have* a lover—named 'Mike'—back home."

Razi burst into tears. And so I finally began to see what had happened to *him*. I wasn't just some hook-up with whom he'd something in common—in this case Caballé, just as it had been "Aspercel" for Dean and me or Proust for my "Gide" and "Barthes." (*Yo caballé*, in Spanish, means "I rode a horse.") Nor was I—as in that encounter—playing "Gide" to Razi's "Barthes" or rather "Barthes" to his "Gide" by our *not* having gotten it on. I was one of those soldiers at the beach—even with no Hebrew, plus relatively little muscle-tone, and even at my age—for whom he had only ever fallen, as of yet, from afar. I was one of those *opposites*, for him—who of course would always break his heart, and from whom, for that reason, he may have gone to Berlin to flee. I also began to suspect that if he didn't find some woman to marry, and soon, people here—apart from that date merchant—will stop liking him so much. Maybe they'd even kill him. Or at least that father would.

At the bus stop, Razi—still crying—gave me a wallet-sized photograph of himself. This had his name and telephone number already on the back. As a gentleman, I gave him my own such number—the real one, despite both my experience with Dean and the fact that many men and maybe even women in these situations—ones, that is, like "Dorian" or "Paris"—will give a fake. And when I finally got off the bus, back in Haifa, not so far from my *Gasthoff*, whom should I run into but Woody. "You'll never believe what happened," I told him. But he did believe. In fact—something else I must confess—he found it just as funny as I'd hoped he would.

| | |

On sabbatical, one year later, in Los Angeles, I'd spend mornings at home reading a Liszt biography and then reviewing it (along with *The Romantic Generation*, by Charles Rosen) for the *London Review of Books*. I'd have called that book review: "Warts and All." The LRB, though, called it: "Adipose Tumerous Growths"—meaning warts—"and All." Afternoons, there, I'd be at a gym—called Bally Total Fitness, on North El Centro Avenue—getting soldierly. Every couple of days—depending, once again, on both horniness and happiness—I'd then be at some bathhouse nearby. I'd like to call it the Sphinx. But it's really "Hollywood Spa," on Ivar Avenue. That's where I met both Actor Type and Gym Coach. It's also where that second three-way of mine happened. Evenings, there, I'd hang around at home, sometimes with friends like Jesse Matz, read both J.D. Salinger and David Sedaris, plus biographies of both Lytton Strachey and Dorothy Parker, re-read more Proust, practice Schumann, think about what book to write next, maybe something *conventional*, or at least once again nonfictional, imagine spending the rest of life alone, and then of course masturbate.

Upon return to Iowa City, I taught both the graduate course "Confessional Narrative in Poststructural Perspective" and our undergraduate one on "Reading Criticism." Afterward, I'd read more Sedaris, re-read even more Proust, practice more Schumann, and think about, or dream of, moving with tenure from Iowa City to—oh, what the hell—Paris. But then one morning, as I gardened—or rather, cleaned the outdoors—a neighbor lady came by. Candida, a massage therapist, had had dinner last night, in the town of Grinnell, with her painter friend Bobbi. (This "Candida," by the way, is named after the play *Candida* by Shaw—and not after the yeast.) Bobbi, there, knew some man my age, only recently out, who might like meeting me. "So, I hope this doesn't sound presumptuous," said Candida, "but could he have your telephone number?"

"What does he look like?" I asked.

"Like the pop star Sting, according to Bobbi, or the actor Ed Harris."

"What does he do?" I asked.

"He's a doctor."

David called that night—a sexier voice, even, than Matt's. And so for me, once again, it was love at first audition. As for David: "You sound nice," he said. "Well," I joked, "I *am* nice."

We'd rendezvous, we agreed, the next Saturday at my place. I opened the door—straight blond hair, cornflower blue eyes, very long eyelashes, tight black jeans, powder blue tee shirt. And so for me, once again, it was also love at first sight. The guy looked, in fact—in fantasy, rather, "primal fantasy"—like that handsome, possibly shirtless man from my dream. As for David—what with my curly brown hair and dark brown eyes, but almost no eyelashes, blue jeans and flannel shirt—it was not. (He'd later say—in fact, still says—that my hair and eyes are black.) His own heartbreaker, he said, had just dumped him—a couple of months ago. (Mark, too, like Candida, does massage. Badly, though, I'd imagine.) And so his own—no longer morbid—inclination to romance, or to "use Love's Litany," or to be sentimental, wasn't yet as strong as mine. "Irregardless," though, I pounced. (The word is "regardless," kids.) And he was a *great* kisser. And then . . . down I floated. Down and down and down and down into these big beefy arms. This, I knew, is whom I'd wake up beside for the rest of my life. I also knew, once again—against what Lacan claimed—that there *can* be such a thing as a sexual relation. Between men, at any rate, and maybe even women.

I suppose, though, that you'd like to know David's porn name. It's "Jupiter Kent." And that pet, too—"Jupiter" to my "Oedipus," "Immortal Beloved," to quote Beethoven, to my mortal, Roman to my Greek—was a parakeet. Also blue. And so, for that matter, was Burkhard's "Peter."

Bright One

Even today, in my seventh decade, I meet people forty years younger who are patently more sensible than I was when I set off on my great adventure. I was their age then, but they are my age now: old heads on young shoulders.

—CLIVE JAMES, *Cultural Amnesia*

A recent graduate seminar of mine—on what I called "neo-humanism"—would meet every Friday morning throughout spring semester. My description of this course was:

> The main story we'll consider includes: Roland Barthes' *A Lover's Discourse*; Martha Nussbaum's *Love's Knowledge*; Judith Butler's *The Psychic Life of Power*; Paul Smith's *Discerning the Subject*; Lawrence Kramer's *After the Lovedeath*, which is on sexual violence; and Terry Eagleton's *After Theory*. Students will find, among these poststructural critics, a taking up of the conscience and an abandonment of the "death of the subject." Another story, among non- but also post-poststructuralists, includes: Alan Sokal and Jean Bricmont's *Fashionable Nonsense*, which is really on ignorance; Daphne Patai and Will Corral's *Theory's Empire*, which is what these co-editors call an "anthology of dissent;" and—my own personal favorite, to be read bit by bit over the semester—Clive James' *Cultural Amnesia: Necessary Memories from History and the Arts*.

My requirements were:

> Students will *converse* with one another both thoughtfully and respectfully, using the word "like" and the expression "you know" correctly, and not, you know,

as what linguists call, like, "discourse markers" or "pragmatic particles." Students will *write*—following the model provided by Clive James—four ten-page essays in response to individual critics read for class.

They would also write a thirty-page "final synthesis" of—if possible—every such critic.

One first-year and twenty-something-year-old graduate student, though, soon expressed concern—in class—about how old most of those male critics are. (Having now transferred elsewhere, this student is no longer in our graduate program.) Barthes, for instance, was sixty-two when *A Lover's Discourse* first came out. James was sixty-eight when *Cultural Amnesia* did. (Nussbaum, though, was just forty-three when *Love's Knowledge* came out; Butler was forty-one when *The Psychic Life of Power* did.) "And so what on earth," asked red-haired, maroon-eyed "Arabella Mansfield," "is a *young* critic to do with such examples?" She expressed concern, too, about that requirement of mine to "converse." She preferred, instead, to "learn via polemics." But what this really meant, I suspected, was Arabella wanted to *trash* stuff.

"Why not address this first concern," I proposed to her, "in essays you'll write?" I myself, I promised, would—if appropriate—bring it up for class discussion. As for this second concern: one second-year and thirty-something-year-old student soon complained to me, in a private discussion right after class, that these so-called polemics by Arabella were "wrecking everything."

A few weeks later, in class, Arabella mocked some written comments I'd made on her first—and Martha Nussbaum related—essay. I—stupidly—said nothing in response to this shenanigan. I simply asked the girl—via e-mail after class—to come talk to me. She did so the next Monday, during office hours, saying she had meant "nothing at all *personal*"—which of course meant insulting—by the mockery. It too, she explained, had been "polemical." I myself explained, in response to this nonsense, or perhaps ignorance, that I could *relate* to such discourse. Back at Brown University, as a young yet newly retired litigator, I treated not only texts assigned by my own graduate school professors but even other first-year students there with what I still considered "lawyerly"—which of course also meant insulting—contempt. We scholars, though, as a young yet newly tenured or "associate" professor soon explained to me, should act the way *judges* do—not litigators. "There may not *be* some adversary now," this woman—and also feminist—had said, "to either defend a position you're attacking or attack what you're defending. Plus, Kevin, there's *never* anyone now—other than you—to settle a dispute."

Arabella said nothing in response. And so I simply confessed to her that it had been *years* before I ever applied this probably feminist lesson to writing not so much mean-spirited or "masculinist" hatchet jobs as fair-minded book reviews. I also—not so simply—read something to Arabella. But I'll get to that—by quoting it all—later.

Arabella missed class that Friday—some "scheduling conflict," she had told me via e-mail in advance, with some "faculty colloquium." And yet a third-year and forty-something-year-old student explained to me, in a private discussion right after class, that Arabella had told her—just the day before—that my "stupid little story" about how I acted at Brown must have meant not so much that I "relate" to the girl as that I consider the two of us "exactly alike." It's a thought, Arabella added, that she finds "just horrifying." She added, too, that my unconscious seems "rather violent."

Arabella did come to class the next Friday. In it, though—to my own horror—she was still trashing stuff. And when class discussion moved from Paul Smith's *Discerning the Subject*—which the girl had called "pseudo-intellectual tripe"—to a bit more of Clive James' *Cultural Amnesia*, I noticed her ignoring the rest of us to stare intently, almost theatrically, out the window. I myself—stupidly—also ignored this shenanigan. And then, since next week we'd be discussing—in addition to more of *Cultural Amnesia*—the anthology *Theory's Empire*, I ended the session by asking everyone—including Arabella—to both think and be prepared to talk about how criticism they themselves had written in the past—for other professors—might have contained errors such as "presentism" discerned therein. "Presentism" is the all too anachronistic use of modern-day notions to interpret the past. Some of my own such criticism, I planned to say next week, was in fact all too presentist. I once used, for instance, the modern-day or twentieth-century—plus poststructuralist—notion of the *non*-sense of sodomy to interpret, as you yourselves know from "Kiss and Tell," the eighteenth-century novel *Fanny Hill*.

Arabella, once again, missed class that Friday. Now, though, she hadn't bothered lying to me in advance—via e-mail—about some "scheduling conflict." Nor had she offered any such excuse. I myself, via e-mail after class, wished her well—"if, in fact, you are unwell"—and asked that she still be prepared, next week, to talk about those errors of hers—"assuming, of course, you have ever made any." She responded, via e-mail: "I shall do no such thing."

I began class that Friday by reading or—to invoke Plato—"rhapsodizing" something to everyone. This was an elegy—called "Sentimental Journey"—that I had just written—for the journal *n+1*—on the death of Eve Kosofsky Sedgwick. Sedgwick, you see, had—at age fifty-eight—died of cancer the Sunday before. It's an elegy, rather, that I had just *re*-written. Most of it derived, one must confess, from a section—called "Eve"—in my already published book *Sedaris*. As you can see, though—because I'll quote it all now—I also discuss a critic, named Lee Siegel, who in *Theory's Empire* had trashed the woman:

SENTIMENTAL JOURNEY

Having demonized Lytton Strachey in *The Voyage Out* by making the purportedly straight character based on Strachey misogynist, Virginia Woolf treats him rather well in *Jacob's Room*. Not only is Richard Bonamy, the decidedly gay character based on Strachey, not misogynist, he's the hero Jacob's fondest friend, just as Strachey himself had been to Virginia's brother Thoby. He's also someone with whom Woolf seems to identify: it is Bonamy, after all, who is left alone with Jacob's mother in that suddenly empty room and to whom, holding out a pair of shoes, she poses that suddenly sentimental—unanswerable—question: "What am I to do with these?" Or at least I find the question sentimental, almost unbearably so—which for me happens to be a good thing, and which is why I cherish it more than any other finale in prose fiction.

Yet for Woolf, Bonamy himself is almost unbearably sentimental—a *bad* thing to be. Sentimentality, according to the momentarily ironic narrator, may be one of the things that make "every woman nicer than any man," but it's also something of which gay—or stereotypically effeminate—men like Bonamy can be accused. For instance, when Bonamy, idealizing Jacob, thinks him "more sublime, devastating, terrific than ever," Woolf, despite her own such idealization, throughout the novel, of Thoby as Jacob, remarks: "What superlatives! What adjectives! How acquit Bonamy of sentimentality of the grossest sort; of being tossed like a cork on the waves; of having no steady insight into character; of being unsupported by reason?" One boring word for this maneuver might be projection, and one description of that finale might be the return of the repressed. Woolf tries to dissociate herself from both Victorian femininity and Victorian fiction by attributing the debased sentimentality she finds they share to an effeminate associate, but can't help being sentimental herself when touching upon—and hence touched by—the hero's death. (Jacob—surname Flanders—got killed in World War I; Thoby, though, died of typhus.)

Fortunately, there are—there have been—other, more interesting words, and other descriptions.

What else, for someone like Woolf, is wrong with sentimentality? Apart from being feminine, old-fashioned, and irrational, it's excessive and insincere. Too much emotion: loving something more than God does, to cite J.D. Salinger. Inauthentic emotion: as if one could turn such feelings off and on, like charm. Sentimentality is also, nowadays, and for presumably homophobic people opposed to Woolf and Strachey, excessively—almost exclusively—homoerotic. "Whereas in the nineteenth century," wrote the late Eve Kosofsky Sedgwick in *Epistemology of the Closet*, "it was images of women in relation to domestic suffering and death that occupied the most potent, symptomatic, and, perhaps, friable or volatile place in the sentimental *imaginaire* of middle-class culture, for the succeeding century—the century inaugurated by Oscar Wilde among others—it has been images of agonistic male self-constitution." Images, that is—sexy, *moving* ones—like that of a dying Dorian Gray in the Wilde novel and also, perhaps, in the Woolf, that of dead Jacob.

I first read Sedgwick—it was an article on Henry James—when I was a graduate student at Brown University. I first saw the woman—fell in love with her, really, among other things—when she came to speak there on both Wilde and Nietzsche: material, along with that article, to soon appear in *Epistemology of the Closet*. I first *met* her at a conference on, as we used to say, "lesbian and gay studies." It was later called "queer theory," thanks in large part—of course—to Sedgwick herself. *Rolling Stone*, though, called it "gay studies," with Sedgwick, said the magazine, as our "queen."

At any rate: Woolf's characterization of Strachey, through Bonamy, as sentimental wasn't exactly inaccurate, but it wasn't very accurate either. Strachey's biographical writing now strikes us, as does most Modernist literature, as radically antisentimental. He favors innuendo and irony, caricature and pastiche. He has a "virtuoso" style, according to his own biographer, Michael Holroyd, "with its ornate overstatements, its laconic recording of incongruities, its unpredictable transpositions, its ironic crescendoes and plummetings into bathos"—much like Sedgwick, perhaps. Some contemporaries did see sentimentality there. Bertrand Russell, reading *Eminent Victorians* in jail, found "it caused me to laugh so loud that the officer came to my cell, saying I must remember that prison is a place for punishment." But Russell detected "girls' school sentimentality" as well. Ivor Brown, reading *Queen Victoria*, discovered that the "cool and unsparing portrayer of the Victorian notables" was, at least when it came to *their* queen, "no longer the aloof scrutineer." Following that woman, Victoria, down the decades, Strachey, he said, was "at last engaged in a sentimental journey"—which for Brown happens to have been a good thing. Woolf was not another such contemporary. She saw no over-sentimentality in Strachey's published work. But she did see it in Strachey himself—or in, to cite *Epistemology of the Closet*, the man's very "being." He was too sentimental, thought Woolf, about crusty old men like Edmund Gosse, and far too sentimental about callow young men like Roger Senhouse—views, as it happens, shared by numerous friends of theirs as well as by Strachey himself.

Like Woolf, Strachey was quick to disparage other men's sentimentality, if not to "project" his own onto them. But his reasons differed. Early in life, he'd been impatient with a college friend who used sentimentality to conceal homosexuality. Strachey had been relatively "out." He later complained, to the painter Dora Carrington, that the wonderfully named, or *nick*-named, "Sebastian" Sprott, some "charming" young man with whom he'd been traveling, is "inclined to be sentimental, though too clever to be so in a sickly style"—a complaint presumably generated by the fact that such "sentimentality is not directed towards me."

Strachey also disparaged—yet unlike Woolf clearly identified with—women's sentimentality. His Florence Nightingale, in *Eminent Victorians*, ends her days "indulging in sentimental friendships with young girls" and weeping—in print—over old probationers, which may explain Russell's negative reaction. His Victoria ends the "sentimental journey" Brown relished in similar ways. All of which may explain Strachey's explicit identification with Bonamy. "I am such a Bonamy," he remarked upon reading *Jacob's Room* for the first time. The novel may not involve the character's, *his* character's feelings for suicidal young women, like Carrington, or even for crusty old men like Gosse, but it does involve emotions far more central to his, to *our* sentimental *imaginaire*: Bonamy's barely sublimated sexual feelings for a young male friend and would-be lover, now—like Sedgwick, of late—dying, now—finally—dead. And whereas Strachey may not have been so naive—so bold, rather—as to have said, or written, that Thoby was "more sublime, devastating, terrific than ever," he didn't have to be. Bonamy—that is, Woolf—said it for him.

Apart from *Jacob's Room*, with its surprising finale, and apart from *The Waves*, with its fleeting indication of yet another lovelorn homosexual, I don't see Woolf as a sentimental novelist. I do, however, find Woolf sentimental in her very "being"—to the extent I can know it at all. I also find her closet sentimentality feminocentric, and hence passé by modern standards. Notwithstanding the slighting

of forsaken Fanny Elmer, Jacob's sweetheart, it was suicidal young women—
Carrington in particular—and not doomed young men who really tugged at
Woolf's heart-strings, perhaps because they shared both a gender and a death
wish—as opposed to, say, a terminal illness. As one male friend—straight—re-
marked upon seeing the careful attention she paid Dora after Lytton's death,
"I've been mistaken about Virginia; somewhere she keeps a warm heart."

Could it be, then, that one definition of literary Modernism should under-
score the momentary, deliberate, and often ultimate eruption of an overtly ho-
moerotic—yet covertly feminocentric—sentimentality all the more powerful for
its unexpected inclusion in an otherwise ironic text like *Jacob's Room*? And that,
not so contrary to popular belief, modern irony should be read as inauthen-
tic, modern sentimentality as real? Certainly, the case can be made. One need
only consider such sentimental moments as Frédéric Moreau telling his friend
Deslauriers in *Sentimental Education* that the time they *didn't* make it to some
brothel "was the happiest time we ever had" (distressed young men in the fore-
ground, young women—prostitutes—in the background), or Stephen Dedalus
in *Ulysses* finding his little sister Dilly with a French primer and realizing he
can't save her (distressed young man in the foreground, young woman in the
background).

But it's more complicated than that. Consider, for instance, the sentimental
moment in Salinger's *Franny and Zooey* when the latter does save the former, his
own kid sister, by explaining just who older brother Seymour's "Fat Lady" was.
She was the one idealized if make-believe radio listener for whom Zooey, on air,
would shine his unseen shoes—unseen, that is, by her—and Franny, imagining
the lady with cancer, would try to be funny: distressed young woman in the *fore-
ground* (Franny), *dead* young man in the background (Seymour the suicide), dis-
tressed *older* woman behind him (that Fat Lady), and even older dead young man
behind her. "There isn't anyone anywhere that isn't Seymour's Fat Lady," says
Zooey on the telephone. "Don't you know that?" And doesn't she know—"*listen*
to me now"—who that Fat Lady really is? "Ah, buddy. Ah, buddy. It's Christ Him-
self. Christ Himself, buddy." Fortunately, another such Fat Lady (for she'd come
out that way, as overweight), another *cancer-ridden* Fat Lady (she'd come out that
way as well) can help us understand such a moment, in part by having acted for
so long, yet not long enough, as an aloof scrutineer of her own public, overtly
homoerotic, yet—truth be told—covertly feminocentric sentimentality.

I'm talking, of course, about Sedgwick—who in public (as well as in pub-
lished work) could be funny as well. When, for instance, I last saw the woman,

at a conference on "lesbian, gay, and *bisexual* studies," her talk, which I intro-
duced, was to be a comical deconstruction of Marcel Proust's deconstruction of
what she called, rather perversely, "peri-performativity"—or the seeming capac-
ity of some speech act to *nearly* do something. My introduction, I confess, now
consisted in large part of a limerick—written by me: "A spankable critic named
Eve / Wrote books that made homophobes heave. / She'd give them depictions
/ Of anal addictions / That showed them how *not* to conceive." That "spank-
able," as nearly everyone knew, referred to Sedgwick's own confession, in the
essay "A Poem is being Written," about her having actually—or rather, laugh-
ingly—enjoyed such treatment. She now laughed, too, at my own poem. So too,
then, did the crowd. And then we all laughed at Sedgwick's talk. Of course, not
everyone elsewhere enjoyed such shenanigans. Donald Morton, a gay Marxist,
called such comedy—derisively—"ludic postmodernism." Lee Siegel, a non-
gay near-Marxist, called such confessional work "a reveal-all-hurts-and-wounds
style of writing." I myself, though, quoting the play *Plenty* by David Hare, have
called—in fact still call—both modes combined: "psychiatric cabaret."

What was it about Sedgwick, maybe in her very "being," that made so many
such theorists, younger men in particular, want to please her—and even, with
all due aggression, to emulate her? Or even, as some readers here will know,
to steal from her. She seemed to think, in relation to most gay men, ones with
AIDS in particular, of herself as a mother figure. For those of us who write,
if only criticism, she also seemed to think of herself as *Proust's* mother. Then
again, she could also see herself as—ah, buddy—Proust Himself. She was, there-
fore, well, a kind of fag hag. Or if not fag hag, I'd say *diva*. But I also think, at
bottom, that she became our own Fat Lady, someone we were supposed to do
all sorts of things for—shine those shoes, try to be funny, be *sentimental*—and
that she became her for reasons which reflect Sedgwick's own feminocentric
sentimentality. After all, the woman, we knew, was dying—as perhaps am I. Yet
unlike Salinger's basically pathetic figure, Sedgwick seemed ideal as well. She
was, to invoke both Bonamy's and Woolf's sentimentality, sublime, devastating,
terrific—and never at all crusty.

But what if our sentimentality *is*, if not excessive, inauthentic? To pose a
series of naive and somewhat disingenuous questions, what if some of us *do* turn
it off and on like charm? What if, for some of us, sentimentality *is* our particu-
lar charm? Do we turn it on simply because, as writers who have inadvertently
confused the emotion with pity, we need readers—readers like Sedgwick, that
is—to *love* us? Or maybe to love us *back*. And, to re-pose the final question of

Wilde's *An Ideal Husband*, the oddest—most potent, symptomatic, friable, and volatile—of the plays: "Is it love you feel for me, or is it pity merely?"

The students, one could see, had paid pretty close attention to this "rhapsody" of mine. (Not to brag, but I *do* do such recitation pretty well—as did Ion, writes Plato.) Or rather, all but one of them had. Arabella, one could also see, had both theatrically and—in a literal sense—studiously ignored the thing by, no, not staring out the window again. She had ignored it by both reading and taking notes on some book. Other students, too, had seen Arabella do this—much to, one sensed, their either incredulity or even disgust. (Mr. She's-Wrecking-Every-thing would tell me—in a private discussion right after class—that he'd been "just *furious*.") I myself—stupidly—also ignored *this* shenanigan. And then I began discussion on a bit more of *Cultural Amnesia*. Arabella, though, contin-ued that reading and note taking. And so I asked the girl some question about *Cultural Amnesia*. She confessed—boldly—that she couldn't possibly answer this question. And so I asked—coldly—to know the name of that book she's got. "It's *The Body in Pain*," she said. "By Scarry."

Elaine Scarry, I should explain, is a "full" professor—of English—at Harvard University. Plus the woman was thirty-nine when this book first came out. She has also been—thanks to "Emmeline Grangerford"—a Warbucks Award winner.

"Are you even *here*, Arabella?" I asked rhetorically.

"Well, *Kevin*," she herself asked, "why on earth would I discuss Clive James? I'm not reading the guy anymore."

I then—as Henry James would put it—hung fire. "What to say to the girl?" I wondered. "What to say to her?" "Nice," is all I did say—sarcastically. This meant, of course: "We're done now." And then—stupidly—I just resumed dis-cussion. Arabella resumed reading and note taking. She stopped it only when the rest of us—both thoughtfully and respectfully—began talking about *After Theory* by—and the man was sixty when this book first came out—Terry Eagle-ton. Arabella, though, trashed both *After Theory* and—"that senile old *post*-Marxist"—Eagleton himself.

Picking up on discussion we'd had a few weeks earlier in class of—as prom-ised—age vs. youth, knowledge vs. ignorance, experience vs. innocence, so-phistication vs. naivety, and even wisdom vs. senility, I then sent Arabella—via e-mail after talking to Mr. She's-Wrecking-Everything—the message:

> I imagine you felt quite pleased—at the time—by that little performance of yours. You should, though, now be ashamed of it. And you probably will be one

day. But you'll certainly be ashamed of it if and when some student of yours does something similar. Not wise, Arabella. Not wise at all. In fact, all you really were—at the time—was mean.

For I myself felt I should if not say then at least write something non-sarcastic— by which I mean sincere—hence constructive and even, in a somewhat parental way, *nurturing* to Arabella, so as to if not undo then at least override that de-structive and even abusive "nice" of mine. And yet there was no response from her to this message.

I then—the next Monday—met with "Vera Charles." She is the second femi-nist in this chapter—or the third one after Sedgwick. She is also, like me, a full professor of English at the University of Iowa. At sixty-something, though, she's rather older than I am—by about fifteen years. Vera told me, after having heard this story thus far, that—at the end of my "rhapsody"—I probably should have made Arabella leave the classroom. And so I now sent the girl—via e-mail—the message:

> I have just conferred with a senior colleague to whom I described your disrespect-ful and disruptive behavior on Friday. The colleague, as it happens, is female—a point of no great significance to me, in this case, although perhaps it is to you. She told me, to my surprise, that what I should have done was have you leave the classroom and not come back. I say "to my surprise" because I'd never imagined directing a *graduate* student to do any such thing. Upon reflection, though, I see she's right. You should know, then, that if you display any such behavior again I will in fact eject you. It's something I owe to both myself and, more importantly, other students. You should know, too, that I'm sending this message to them as well, via e-mail, because they've got a right to know now what to expect from me. Finally, as hard as it is for me to not take your behavior personally, I want you to know I'm still at least trying not to. And so please understand: I do want you to continue coming to class, but only if you participate there with all due respect to everyone—myself included. Clive James, for that matter, included.

And yet once again there was no response from her. Nor were there any—to me—from other students.

I then—that Wednesday—met with "Wendy Darling." She is the third femi-nist in this chapter—or maybe, assuming Arabella herself is a feminist, the fourth one. She is also, like both Vera and me, a full professor of English at the University of Iowa. She's also, at fifty-something, only somewhat older than I am.

She's also, more to the point, our Director of Graduate Studies. Wendy told me, after having heard this story thus far, that she herself would meet with Arabella.

Wendy did so later that day. Arabella "acknowledged" in this meeting, Wendy then told me via e-mail, that she had behaved in an "inappropriate manner" in class. The girl "felt," though, that she "cannot return to it." And so I myself e-mailed Arabella: "It is acceptable to me that you not attend our last few sessions. You may also, if you wish, use—instead of the Clive James book—*The Body in Pain* for your final synthesis."

I then, that Thursday, perused Arabella's third—and Lawrence Kramer re-lated—essay. It concerned, too, some man named "Dominic Dromgoole" hav-ing—at age forty-one—both recently and rather "stupidly" trashed both a young Alfred Jarry and an even younger John Lydon. This thing of hers also, to my surprise, concerned Clive James having trashed Lydon. (He recalls, in *Cultural Amnesia*, having found just one look at Lydon's performance of "Johnny Rot-ten" enough to show "why even the SS occasionally court-martialed a few of its personnel for nihilistic behavior beyond the call of duty.") And so, I thought, Arabella *was* still reading the guy.

The essay ended, sincerely:

> Perhaps the biggest problem facing critical work in the humanities is not theory or humanism but rather the indefeasibility of knowledge and stupidity. For any Jacques Derrida or Allan Bloom, there will also be a plentiful stock of mindless emulators hungry for a way out of actual thought, out of the terror of an actual confrontation with the surprising otherness of literature. Indeed, this willing herd is happy to find it in any likely formula, be it feminist, deconstructionist, or "neo-humanist." Stupidity is, if nothing else, resilient. Perhaps the sin, if one really wishes to deploy such a metaphysical metaphorics, of theory was that it's [sic] particular investments in exposing the willful blindnesses of its forebears lent it to more and more open and voracious exploitation. And perhaps this blatant and excessive indulgence in stupidity was a blessing, for it forced the academy to deal headlong with the problem of stupidity in its hallways and not safely outside as it had once assumed.

"But then," Arabella added sarcastically, "this is all, no doubt, merely a fit of youthful nihilism, a simple brushfire useful for clearing the ground, pretty va-cant and out to lunch. Grow up. Choose life. Fitter, happier, more productive."

"What to write to the girl?" I wondered. "What to write to her?" What I did write—both sincerely and sarcastically, as well as ironically—was:

This essay is—as Cicero would have it—both instructive and funny. It is also—
for me—rather moving. Until, of course, you seem to suggest—to me—that *I'm*
"mindless." Being mindless, though, or stupid, how would I ever know it for
sure? Or maybe I'm *not* that daft. Maybe it's just you being *deft* here. Such
insults, or if not insults then implications, are, to quote Sedgwick, "rhetorically
efficacious." They've got a deniable deniability—much like flirtation. Of course
it *is* true what you say, in general, about the "indefeasibility" within the academy
of both knowledge and stupidity. And so if you'd like to pursue such inquiry
further, you should probably read—assuming you haven't already done so—the
book *Stupidity* (2002), by Avital Ronnell [sic]. [The woman's surname is *Ronell*.
And she was fifty when this book came out.] It's one I don't really understand,
I'm afraid, but have at least gotten the gist of.

The wonderfully named Dromgoole does, indeed, sound like a piece of
work. Having just done some rooting around on the Internet, I'm sure what
you say of him is true. That's what comes, I guess, from the guy's having such
theatrical parents. [Dromgoole's father, according to Wikipedia, is a theater di-
rector turned television executive; his mother, an actress turned schoolmarm.
Dromgoole himself—in London—has directed Shakespeare's Globe.] But if you
can stand hearing any more—from me—about Clive James: I wonder why the
man, in *Cultural Amnesia*, seems to be at least a *bit* fond of Barry Humphries
as "Dame Edna Everage," when Humphries' own *non*-parental theater back-
ground is, ironically enough, not very different from that of either Alfred Jarry
or John Lydon. See, on that score, John Lahr's book *Dame Edna Everage and
the Rise of Western Civilization* (1991). [He, too, was fifty when this book came
out.] John, as you may know, is the son of Bert Lahr—the Cowardly Lion in *The
Wizard of Oz*.

Also, Arabella, the critical reception of if not Lydon then Jarry reminds me of
that of Vaslav Nijinsky, whose both precocious—this dancer was born in 1890—
and iconoclastic brilliance as a *choreographer*—in *Afternoon of a Faun* (1912),
Jeux (1913), and *The Rite of Spring* (1913)—also "opened the door," as you say in
relation to the playwright, for other such *modern* dance to come. At the time,
though, these three not so easy pieces were written off by many reviewers, all too
devoted to *classical* ballet, as the immature work of a kind of, as you put it with re-
spect to reviews of both Jarry and Lydon, "idiot"—although I don't know that any-
one charged the poor kid, as you also put it with respect to reviews of these two, of
"fraud." And so if you'd like to pursue *that*, you should probably read *Nijinsky: Sa
vie, son geste, sa pensée* (2006) by Guillaume de Sardes. It's the best book, to date,

on the subject—even including my own. It's also in French, of course, which language maybe you know—or, like me, can at least more or less read.

Guillaume de Sardes, by the way, was just thirty when that book came out. I was already thirty-seven when mine—called *The Queer Afterlife of Vaslav Nijinsky*—did.

I then—before class that Friday—heard from Wendy again. Arabella, the woman had written via e-mail, has agreed to that proposal of mine. ("It is acceptable to me that you not attend our last few sessions," and so on.) There were, though, some additional concerns—"and so I've asked Arabella for a formal statement to which, I'm afraid, you will have to respond." "What on earth," I wondered, "is she worried about now?" And yet after class—sans Ms. Learn-Via-Polemics—came this e-mail from Wendy:

> I've just gotten a message from Arabella. She has decided to consider the dispute settled and so will not, after all, be submitting any formal statement.

"What *dispute?*" I wondered. One new concern, though, had to do with my "evaluating" the girl. "She requests, in short," wrote Wendy, "some 'concurrent review' of the process. But to contest any grade she gets from you, I told her, she can just file a grievance."

I could, I supposed, take this to be one last insult. I could, in other words, take it to mean that since I'm not only too stupid but also too mean to judge Arabella in an—to quote Clive James in my epigraph to this chapter—either "sensible" or fair-minded way, I should be monitored pretty closely. "How, though?" I wondered. "And by whom?" Instead, I took it to be ridiculous. I took it, too, to show that something about one of us, or about the two of us together, had prevented Arabella, unlike—it seemed—everyone else in this seminar, from sensing who I really am: just an—to quote Nietzsche—"all too human" guy doing his—as Epictetus would have it—very, very best to give all of these kids what he sensed they need, much as I'm now doing here with you readers. Much as, for that matter, I've done in all my written work—apart from *Finishing Proust*. Or rather, a guy doing his best to if not *save* these kids—as Zooey Glass does manage to save his little sister Franny but Stephen Dedalus can not save little Dilly—then at least *help* them when possible, or allowed to by them, while imagining that, like him, they're also probably, if at times sadly, doing their own very best.

And what might that "something about the two of us" be? Here was my not so stupid theory: the girl has a problem with father figures. Arabella did once complain, in class, that the reason she "loathes" Clive James—in *Cultural Amnesia*—is that "the guy positions himself there" as a father figure. I, though—upon due consideration—could not see how this is true. Nor could I then credit Arabella's attempted "proof"—to me—of such a positioning. Nor could she appreciate my joke, in response to the proof, that "maybe the guy's being avuncular." Plus I was sure that the girl knew that sometimes—as a teacher—I can't help acting somewhat parental. As I'm male, though—which is also something I can't help—this must have been taken by Arabella, I thought, as acting—despite any effeminacy involved—somewhat paternal. Two only somewhat younger male colleagues, though—one of them newly tenured and the other not yet tenured but both of them, in real life, biological fathers—soon told me, in person, that they had never found Arabella—as a student—at all disruptive or disrespectful. Well, I thought, maybe these guys are still young enough, or are unparental enough in class, to not yet come across—at least to graduate students—as at all paternal.

Of course, I couldn't prove—not even to myself—this not so stupid theory. Unlike when I told her that "stupid little story" about how I acted at Brown, Arabella never deliberately revealed very much of any significance to me about her own background. Nor did she inadvertently reveal very much to me about her psyche. Except, of course, by both trashing stuff and acting out. Acting childish, rather. (You readers, of course, can't possibly have revealed *anything* to me about yourselves. Things such as: Where did *you* go to school? What happened to *you* there? How old are *you*?) I do not know, for instance, what the girl's dealings—if any—were with her biological father. Did the man—in any way—ever abuse her? Did he mock her—superior—intelligence? Did he resent it? Or was *he* the original "idiot"?

How do I know Arabella herself knew that I sometimes—as a teacher—act somewhat parental? Because after telling her, during office hours, that story about how I acted at Brown, I now rhapsodized—to Arabella alone here, sitting just across the desk from me—an essay I'd just written. It, too—like this chapter—is called "Bright One." Plus like "Sentimental Journey," it derives from my book *Sedaris*:

BRIGHT ONE

When asked last week, by the co-editor [Ralph Savarese] most aware of my autobiographical work hence also aware that, in real life over the past ten years, I have helped raise three bright, beautiful, now twenty-something-year-old "boys" named Adam, Seth, and Sam, to write, for some possible post-feminist anthology, a personal essay "on academic *father*hood," I told him, as usual, that I'd sleep on it. The unconscious, at such times, is smarter than you. It'll show, in dreams, what to write or maybe not write. This time, it showed: I'm the perfect fifties house-wife, devoted to my not three but two kids: teenage son, teenage daughter. Unlike Adam, Seth, and Sam, though, they're brats. They don't appreciate anything I do for them, nor do they feel at all sorry for me. Think: Donna Reed on *The Donna Reed Show* plus Divine, in *Polyester* [1981], as "Francine Fishpaw." Today, for example, when I try without success to make a rather difficult cake, the two just *mock* me. Losing it, I punch no, not the boy. I punch the *girl*—punch her hard, in fact, and right in the face: *bam bam bam.* I also, as it happens, punch our mattress— *bam bam bam*—waking both David and me. He's the biological and therefore— to them—completely masculine father of Adam, Seth, and Sam. This—David's existence as such in their lives—has made me a mere father *figure* to them. Plus a somewhat effeminate one at that. It has made me, I've joked, a combination of "Uncle Charley," on the sitcom *My Three Sons*, and Auntie Mame.

This, I mused, can't bode well. I can't write on abuse, by me, or on beat-ing students, especially female ones in relation to whom, on some level and as one or more genders—masculine and or feminine—I may feel somewhat pa-rental. For of course I don't beat them. Nor am I aware—not that I would be aware were the level unconscious—of having ever wanted to beat them. I love most students, especially the girls. My own parents, moreover, never abused me, whether physically or even just—even worse—verbally. Nor did my two oldest, somewhat parental siblings—sixteen years older than I—twins Eric and Mau-reen. Teachers, though, were another story. One, in elementary school, said, or at least implied, that I'll never measure up to brother Bob, a concert pianist who, while thirteen years older, had also had her. Another said so as to brother Steve, just two years older. Nor, needless to say, did I ever abuse Adam, Seth, and Sam—not as their Uncle Charley / Auntie Mame, not even, sometimes, as—as I've also joked—their Peter Pan / Mary Poppins, and not even, more frequently, as myself alone. Instead, I'd teach them to cook, to clean, to read, to write—to read literature, that is, and write essays. I'd also knit sweaters—rather difficult ones, in cable stitch. And nor would David abuse them. And nor would their mother Julie, which is why, for the most part, they *are* so bright and beautiful.

I say *by me*, though—"I can't write on abuse, by me"—because I have, in fact, as some readers here will know, so discussed those schoolmarms (our first piano teacher Mrs. Graa, our fourth-grade teacher Mrs. Keaton). I've also discussed—in print—ones that another David had. David Sedaris, I've written in *Sedaris*, had just *awful* teachers in both elementary and middle school. Marcel Proust, I've written there, did not. Sedaris' third-grade teacher, a Miss Chestnut, tried to shame him—abusively and in public—out of obsessive-compulsive behavior like licking "her" light switch. The attempt, of course, was unsuccessful. His fifth-grade speech therapist, Miss Samson, tried—in private—to shame him out of a lisp. (I too lisped.) The attempt, once again, was unsuccessful. (I, thanks to a good such therapist, no longer lisp.) I've also, more to the point, discussed the man's father—Lou Sedaris—a horrible role model who'd use shame abusively: a weapon to wound, punish, maybe even destroy. These deployments, too, were public, plus sarcastic, aggressive, sometimes hateful. They might, for example, target some semi-competent but totally innocent waitress. Worse yet, they might target daughters Lisa, Gretchen, Amy, and Tiffany. Even more to the point, they'd target David—although not Lou's younger by eleven years and yet non-gay son Paul.

A fairly benign such instance occurred whenever this David—Sedaris—did something stupid. "As a child," he writes, "I'd always harbored a sneaking suspicion that I might be a genius. The theory was completely my own, corroborated by no one, but so what? Being misunderstood was all part of the package. My father occasionally referred to me as 'Smart Guy,' but eventually I realized that when saying it, he usually meant the opposite."

"Hey, Smart Guy—coating your face with mayonnaise because you can't find the insect repellent."

"Hey, Smart Guy, thinking you can toast marshmallows in your bedroom."

That kind of thing. A mainly malign instance occurred when, after dropping out of college for the second time and then traveling across the country, he found himself back home, in North Carolina, and also living at home. Loafing, really. After six months spent waking at noon, getting high, and listening to the same Joni Mitchell record (*Hejira* [1976]) over and over again, he was called into Lou's den and, not surprisingly, told to get out. "I felt," writes Sedaris, "as though he were firing me from the job of being his son." Surprisingly, this eviction—this termination, in effect—had nothing to do with laziness. "I wouldn't know it until months later, but my father had kicked me out of the house not because I was a bum but because I was gay."

Our little talk was supposed to be one of those defining moments that shape a person's adult life, but he'd been so uncomfortable with the most important word that he'd left it out completely, saying only, "I think we both know why I'm doing this." I guess I could have pinned him down, I just hadn't seen the point. "Is it because I'm a failure? A drug addict? A sponge? Come on, Dad, just give me one good reason."

Who'd say that?

As far as we readers know, Lou never apologized. (I, as a bit more than just a reader, suspect he'd also *beat* David—and publicly.) But Sharon Sedaris, their now dead mother, did apologize, at the time, and more or less *for* Lou. "'I'm sorry,' she said. 'I'm sorry, I'm sorry, I'm sorry.'" Sharon, of course, was the boozy, chain-smoking champion of neither abusive nor sarcastic but ironic, nurturing, constructive shame. She'd use words not to wound, punish, or destroy, but to cure. Unlike Lou, that is, she'd make kids realize both how foolish or vicious they were being *and* that they could do something about it. In particular, she'd make them realize how selfish or snobbish they were—how non-benevolent, non-egalitarian. (Sharon, unlike Lou, was a terrific role model, with benevolence and egalitarianism—if not the drinking and smoking—her two best virtues.) Such fostering of self-consciousness, though, required the suspension— for just the right amount of time—of what Sedaris, meaning some kind of love, calls "attention." The kind of love, that is, that Sharon just couldn't—or wouldn't—verbalize:

> "Of course you love Ya Ya," [Lou] would say. "She's your grandmother." He stated it as a natural consequence, when to our mind, that was hardly the case. Someone might be your blood relative, but it didn't mean you had to love her. Our magazine articles and afternoon talk shows were teaching us that people had to earn their love from one day to the next. My father's family relied on a set of rules that no longer applied. It wasn't enough to provide your children with a home and hand over all your loose change, a person had to be *fun* while doing it. For Ya Ya it was too late, but there was still time for my father, who over the next few years grew increasingly nervous. He observed my mother holding court in the bedroom and wondered how she did it. She might occasionally snap, but once the smoke cleared we were back at her feet, fighting for her attention.

Such fostering of self-consciousness, that is, required the suspension of—biologically—*maternal* love. Other kinds, Sharon *would*—if drunk—verbalize. *"Love?"* she'd ask in such condition. "'I love a good steak cooked rare. I love my cat, and

I love . . . ' My sisters and I leaned forward, waiting to hear our names. 'Tums,' our mother said. 'I love Tums.'"

I, however, was both physically and verbally abused—up until when he hanged himself—by brother Steve. He'd bash me against walls, stab me with pens, mock my—inferior—intelligence. "Hey, Bright One," he'd say, "thinking Wittgenstein played *piano*." (Ludwig, of course, did not. Older brother Paul did, with just the one arm.) Or again: "Hey, Bright One, thinking Julia Child is *French*." He'd also, all the while, mock our own mother, Ida, as, I'm afraid, would Dad. "Hey, Bright One," they'd both say to her, "thinking toast should *burn*." Or again: "Hey, Bright One, using ketchup as *soup*." I, though, would not. I'd just watch Child, as *The French Chef*, and then read a few cookbooks, and then at age thirteen, to Mom's relief, take over the kitchen.

After Steve's death, plus fourteen years later that of Dad, Bob took over, verbally, from both of them. Mom, he'd call a "freak." Me, he'd call a "pseudo-intellectual narcissist," which, in truth, to my own at least somewhat black kettle, was really rather pot-like of him. Losing it, I then told or rather wrote the man off—a letter never answered. Shame on him. *Nurturing* shame.

One's older siblings, then—either male or female, good or bad, di- or I suppose monozygote—can have acted somewhat like parents. One's teachers, then—either male or female, good or bad—can have acted somewhat like either parents or somewhat parent-like siblings. As such, they can have also identified with students—and, if such teachers are either biological women or somewhat effeminate men, with female students perhaps especially. And so if we, as teachers now, have learned—if only consciously—to not channel in the classroom any abusive parents (like Lou Sedaris), somewhat parental siblings (like my brother Bob), or somewhat parental teachers we have had (like Miss Chestnut or Mrs. Keaton) and to channel there, instead, any nurturing ones (like Sharon Sedaris, or my brother Eric, or my sister Maureen, or my mentor Robert Scholes), then students of our own—whether or not we identify with them—should both survive and thrive. (In my dream, then, I'm not just Donna-Francine but that abused daughter of hers as well. That son, I suspect, is both brothers Steve and Bob—as, again, is the daughter. The cake, there, represents not my own cooking, of course, but Mom's.) Better yet, we should channel David Sedaris there. (He himself—in print—channels Sharon.)

Even better, channel yourself in the classroom. Pretend there that you're still at home with—as is my case—some boys or—as is not my case—girls in relation to whom you can not so much—sincerely—*be* either paternal or maternal but

rather in relation to whom, when their biological parents happen to be off some-
where playing hooky, you can—ironically—*do* both paternity and maternity or,
more frequently, both avuncularity and, well, English has no feminine version
of this word to describe not so much what Uncle Charley does, with his nephews
Mike, Robbie, and Chip but what ("Life's a banquet!") Auntie Mame does with
her nephew Patrick. You can also, ironically, do a kind of magic—for students—
the way Mary Poppins does with Jane and Michael Banks or the way Peter Pan
does for Wendy, John, and Michael Darling.

Proust, though, when just as young as—at some point—all of my own Da-
vid's kids have been for me, reminds us that it may be even better yet for any
of us—anywhere—to not "channel" or role-play anyone else—whether real or
imaginary—at all. In answer, at age fifteen, to the question "If not yourself, who
would you be?" on the now famous, if mislabeled, "Proust Questionnaire,"
young Marcel wrote: "Since the question does not arise, I prefer not to answer
it. All the same, I should very much have liked to be Pliny the Younger." Just
five years later, though, at twenty (or almost Steve's age when he died), he wrote:
"Myself—as those whom I admire would like me to be." First Dad, for me, then
Steve: so bright, they were; so beautiful, in fact; so admirable.

Why on earth, though—or in heaven's name—would I rhapsodize this to Ara-
bella? Because I thought it would, as I've said before, help the girl. Help her
sense, that is, who I really am and so what I'm, like, at least trying to do for her.
Maybe, though, given who, you know, *she* really is, or was, or who she at least,
like, *might*, in the girl's or even woman's very "being," really have been, this
wasn't, like, the very best, you know, *idea* I've ever had.

Arabella's final synthesis, by the way, concerned both *The Body in Pain* by
Elaine Scarry and Avital Ronell's book *Stupidity*. The grade that I gave her on
the thing, as well as—being a coward—for the course, was an "A."

Salome

Volodya is to enter the University in a few days. Tutors come to study with him separately and I listen with envy and involuntary respect as he, tapping the blackboard briskly with the chalk, speaks of functions, sines, coordinates, and so on, which seem to me to be the expressions of an inaccessible wisdom. And then one Sunday after dinner all the tutors and two professors assemble in Grandmother's sitting room and in the presence of Papa and several guests stage a rehearsal of the University examinations in which Volodya, to Grandmother's delight, reveals extraordinary knowledge. I am also asked some questions in several subjects but I cut a very poor figure and the professors make an obvious effort to conceal my ignorance from Grandmother, which fact embarrasses me still more. However, little attention is actually paid to me: I am only fifteen years old; therefore, I still have a year until my examinations. Volodya only comes down to dinner and spends all his days and even his evenings upstairs at his studies, not because he is compelled to, but of his own free will. He is extremely ambitious and wants to pass the examinations with honors, not merely satisfactorily.

—LEO TOLSTOY, *Childhood Adolescence Youth*

All four of my grandparents, as any biological children of mine reading this might wish to learn, came from Russia. They all, moreover, came from villages there—or *shtetls*—that were kind of like "Razi's." My father's father—a waiter who, like both Robert Schumann and Oscar Wilde, would die at about age forty-six of syphilis—came from one somewhere in "White Russia." His name was Isidore Kopelson. My father's mother, named Sally Goldfarb, came from one somewhere in the Ukraine near the city of Kiev. So, too, had Vladimir Horowitz come from near there. This concert pianist, though, claimed to have been both born and raised in Kiev itself. My mother's mother, Esther Lieber, came from one somewhere in Lithuania. My mother's father had also come—in the year 1913—from near Kiev. He was a tailor. And his name—here in America—was Harry Goldstein.

Who knows, though, what it had been in Russia. This grandfather used to tell us grandchildren—repeatedly—a story about how some man just ahead of him on line at Ellis Island, after having told immigration officers there that his name is "Harry Goldstein," was let into this country. And so he himself said the same thing.

Harry, at the time, was about age fifteen—like Leo Tolstoy (as fictionalized) in the epigraph to this chapter. His own father, a few years earlier, had already left that *shtetl* of theirs—sans wife—for New York City. He then somehow earned enough money to send for both Harry and a younger son named Boris. Boris, though—en route—went missing. And so shortly after Harry himself—sans Boris—arrived in New York City, the father went back to Russia to find the boy. After searching there without success, he consulted, according to my mother, some "gypsy fortune-teller." (I only ever heard this story from Mom—once. Plus I heard it from her a few years after Grandpa Harry died—at about age seventy-eight—of heart disease. And so I couldn't say for sure what, if anything, he still—so many decades after this younger brother's disappearance—felt about it. I can only say—or if not quite say then simply suggest here—what I myself would have. Mom, these days, has Alzheimer's disease. She therefore cannot recall her own father's original name. If fact, she no longer recalls it as "Harry." And nor does she even recognize me.) That fortune-teller then told this unfortunate man where he could find Boris: up in them thar hills—or Carpathian Mountains—and near some "river" she described. (It was a stream, probably.) But instead of finding Boris—alive—he then found only a dead body here. Harry's brother, it seemed, had been kidnapped, and then robbed, and then stabbed to death by Cossacks. It is Czar Nicholas II, also known as "Nicholas the Bloody," who I now know was ultimately responsible for such a thing.

Other relatives who like Boris never got to leave Russia—many of them, and on both sides of our family—would also get killed there. Some were killed— thanks, again, to Nicholas—in various pogroms over the years. Others, though, were shot to death at Babi Yar—it's a ravine near Kiev—in the year 1941. The marksmen there, as you may know, included SS—or *Schutzstaffel*—officers. But it's Hitler who—as *der Führer*—was ultimately responsible for this.

We grandchildren, at any rate, included my brother Bob, a not quite concert pianist, my brother Steve, and me—a would-be pianist. Steve, as you might recall, was two years older than I am; Bob is thirteen years older. We included, too, our two oldest and therefore somewhat parental siblings: the twins Eric and Maureen—or "Ricky" and "Micky"—who are three years older than Bob. Micky, as it happens, was a Russian major in college, Brandeis University, and then rather surprisingly became a spy. Well, that's, no, not a lie exactly. It's an exaggeration. She really went to Brown University, for a master's degree in literature. (Her thesis compared the novel *The Idiot*, by Dostoevsky, to Herman Melville's *Billy Budd*.) She then worked—broadcasting pro-capitalist propaganda over to the Soviet Union—at Radio Liberty. This radio station, as she must have known, was not so secretly run by the CIA. She got engaged to a research chemist named Arthur, got married to him, got pregnant by him, and quit. She would later, after a few years, change careers to become—perhaps motivated by that old lisp of mine—a speech therapist. (Their son Stephan also lisped.) Ricky, as far as I know, has never been a spy. He's an architect—now retired—just as Steve would have been. For where Ricky had majored in architecture at Columbia University, Steve, as I've said before, double-majored—at MIT—in both architecture and urban planning. And so there were, as it were, twin identifications: Steve emulated Ricky, and I—while subject to all the usual vicissitudes of adulation, aggression, and ambivalence or, to quote Tolstoy in that epigraph, "envy and involuntary respect"—emulated Bob. I have therefore always thought of us five siblings as a lot like those seven in stories by J.D. Salinger—with me as "Franny" Glass, but now many years later as her oldest living brother "Buddy" as well. I thought so especially during the first five years after Steve's death, when, like Seymour Glass, he still seemed to us, as I've also said before, to have killed himself on purpose. And yet I've also considered us four brothers—minus Micky—to be a lot like those "Brothers Karamazov" in that other novel by Dostoevsky, with Ricky as Dmitri, Steve as Ivan, and me as Alyosha Karamazov. This, as you may know, would make Bob the brother or rather *half*-brother in it called, rather nastily, "Smerdyakov"—even though of all of them it's Smerdyakov who, by hanging himself, will die the way Steve did. (The name "Smerdyakov" means: "son of the stinky one.") Seymour, in the story "A Perfect Day for Bananafish," shoots himself—at age thirty-one. Steve, as you do know, was only twenty-one when he died. (Note that Smerdyakov, not unlike Lauren Slater in her memoir *Lying*, is a possibly fake epileptic—whereas Dostoevsky himself had been an actual one. David Foster Wallace—a very successful writer and yet actual suicide—once described Smerdyakov, moreover, as "un-believably repellant." He is, wrote Wallace, a "living engine of shining resent-ment in whom I personally see parts of myself I can barely stand to look at." Note, too—as the critic Peter Brooks has—that those "Brothers Karamazov" are all, minus Alyosha, rather *troubling* confessors. So, too—perhaps—am I.) Ricky, at any rate, would sometimes tease me about such thinking. He'd say that, unlike those Salinger kids—Seymour, the suicide, "Buddy," a not very successful writer and yet narrator of those stories about the kids, "Boo Boo," a housewife, the twins "Walt" and Waker, "Zooey," a rather handsome and yet elfin actor, and the rather beautiful actress "Franny"—we ourselves had never had "old heads on young shoulders." ("Volodya's" math, for his younger brother, had seemed—to quote that epigraph again—"the expressions of an inaccessible wisdom." "Not wise, Arabella," I told that graduate student of mine. "Not wise at all.") He would say, too, that—unlike any Karamazov and also Tolstoy himself—nor had we been aristocrats. Plus if either the Kopelsons, and or "Goldsteins," and or Goldfarbs, and or Liebers could ever—as Jews—have had a coat of arms, its shield, joked this oldest living brother of mine, would show borscht.

Of course, I'm not the only "New York Jew" to have—using Dostoevsky—ever thought such a thing. Michael Greenberg, the author of the memoir *Hurry Down Sunshine*, writes in a recent *Times Literary Supplement*:

> I first read *The Brothers Karamazov* at the age of sixteen, absorbing it with greater intensity than any novel I have read since. I had just moved away from home, setting myself up in a tiny studio above a shoe shop on Eighth Street, with a night job at a bookstore on the Upper East Side. The copy I read was a used hardback, translated by Constance Garnett, that I found for ten cents in one of the sidewalk bins that lined Fourth Avenue at the time. It was water-stained and had an acrid, smoky odor, as if it had been carried out of a fire. Sometimes the pages tore away as I turned them.
>
> I had little idea of who Dostoevsky was, and was unprepared for what seemed to me a feverish dramatization of the aggression my four brothers and I felt towards each other, and towards our father. There appeared to be great similarities between the Karamazov and Greenberg brothers. We were equally magnetized by our father's moods, seeing our most troubling traits in him, lingering in his orbit, perhaps, to get a glimpse of our future selves. I made no secret of the fact that I didn't like what I saw, ridiculing my father's outbursts that frightened my brothers but made him seem weak to me and out of control.

We were quick to forgive each other, and quick to go at it again. My mother used to say that I was the son most like him. In *The Brothers Karamazov*, Dmitri, the eldest brother, rails against his father's depravity because it is just like his own. He compares his carnal hungers to that of an insect driven to feed. "In short—a Karamazov!"

While reading the novel, it became clear to me that I had left home to let my brothers and father battle it out among themselves. The murder of old man Karamazov made me feel that the unraveling of my family was inevitable, that we had no chance of surviving our animosities—though of course we did survive them. I could easily imagine the brother most outwardly devoted to my father committing the crime, like Smerdyakov in the novel, Karamazov's bastard son and servant. My eldest brother was like Dmitri, I thought, loudly contending for our father's business, and ending up taking the rap due to an accretion of cleverly planted evidence that he is unable convincingly to explain. My younger brother, too young to be corrupt, was the saintly Alyosha.

"And I," Greenberg concludes, "fancied myself like Ivan, the intellectual atheist who lays out the cynicism of the Grand Inquisitor, then coolly leaves town with the idea of making a name for himself in more exalted circles."

My own father, though, had no such moody "outbursts." Nor was he "weak." And then Dad, too—like Grandpa Harry—died of heart disease. Plus he did so, as you might recall from "Hatchet Job," at the age of seventy.

| | |

I, as you know, majored—at Yale University—in neither Russian nor French nor even English but music. I did, though—as you'll have inferred from the chapter "Veritas"—join a group there called the Yale Russian Chorus. To quote its current website:

> The Yale Russian Chorus is a tenor-bass a cappella choral ensemble specializing in both sacred and secular Slavic music. Chorus members are Yale University students from a variety of academic disciplines. Founded in 1953 by Denis Mickiewicz, a Yale student at the time, the Yale Russian Chorus is recognized as one of the world's premier ensembles. The repertoire spans the twelfth century to the twenty-first, and stretches across Eastern Europe from Slovakia to Georgia. This includes ancient chant, folk songs, and works by Tchaikovsky, Bortnyansky, Kedrov, and Chesnokov.

That's true, mostly. Yet what this doesn't quite say is that up until recently—
long after the school itself let women in—only men could join the group,
making it more of a fraternity, really, or, this being Yale, "secret society" than
some "ensemble." (Like both Harvard University and Princeton University,
Yale doesn't have fraternities. Harvard, instead, has all-male hence fraternity-
like "final clubs;" Princeton has—recently co-ed—"eating clubs.") And so the
group has never been recognized as a "premier" anything by anyone whose
opinion mattered. Nor does this say that most of those men—at least during my
years in the Yale Russian Chorus, from 1977 to 1979, by which time the school
itself no longer had such a quota—were Jewish. (Yale still, though, had—and
probably still *has*—one on students from my high school.) This, for audience
members in the know, gave an interesting twist if not shall we say *spice* to our
singing of "sacred"—or church—music. Nor does it say that many of us, in a
rather better kept secret, were gay—even if also, as in my case, still virgins.
Nor that the chorus, too—like Radio Liberty—had at one time been run or
at least financed by the CIA. This Agency, during the very hottest part of the
Cold War, would pay us—at that point still predominantly Protestant—chorus
members to both learn Russian at Yale, under spies, presumably, and then
go visit either Moscow or Leningrad. (Had it, though, paid Micky that way
at—mainly Jewish—Brandeis? She says no.) While there, they would huddle
together in some square . . . and then suddenly burst into some folk song, like
Kalinka, which means "bush," and then, switching back to English, into some
"negro" or even, like "Old Man River," pseudo-negro spiritual. (See "Khoris-
toria," on YouTube.) A crowd, by now, would have gathered to enjoy or maybe
even ridicule this shenanigan but then, when the singing or rather *scream-
ing* stopped, be subjected—back again in its native tongue, more or less—to
anti-communist propaganda. (Just *listen* to "Khoristoria," for such screaming.)
Russian, says Micky, is a very hard language to learn—or at least harder than
French. (It's just as hard, though, for people to learn English.) I now presume
that at least a few of these screamers, like those Russian teachers they had at
Yale, would then, unlike this only sister of mine, become actual spies upon
graduation. Even two of my own cohort—both kids, like Micky, were Russian
majors—seem to have done so: the bass Danny Grossman and the baritone
Mark Vecchio. Danny was Jewish; Mark, Catholic. Mark was also, though, a
nephew of the then soon to be Governor of New York State: Mario Cuomo.
And Cuomo, at the time—in case anyone reading this is interested—still lived
just down the block from my parents in Queens, New York.

My friend Jesse Green, though—who double-majored in both Theater Stud-
ies and English—was not so secretly gay. (He sang tenor in the Yale Russian
Chorus—as did I. Plus he, too, was Jewish.) Jesse, in fact, was quite openly gay.
Plus he was independently wealthy, which no doubt facilitated—I thought—
such boldness. It also, doubtless, facilitated Jesse's own less dangerous career—
upon graduation—than espionage. For he now became, as you might recall, a
somewhat successful writer: the novel O Beautiful, the memoir The Velveteen
Father, the memoir My Bar Mitzvah Year, plus lots of stuff in the New York
Times. Jesse's own paternal grandfather, you see, had—like some Rothschild—
created this country's first savings and loan association and then—many years
later—trust funds for both Jesse and a brother of his, older than Jesse by two
years, named Tony.

And yet nor, despite having never been rich, was my friend Bill Watson se-
cretly gay. Bill, too—like Danny—sang bass with the group. Bill, too—like both
Danny and Mark—was a Russian major. Unlike them, though, he could never
have become a spy. Security clearance, for non-closeted homosexuals, was
then—as even now, perhaps—simply out of the question. (Danny was straight,
while Mark at least seemed so. Bill, incidentally, was Protestant.) In fact, whereas
Jesse spent hour after hour up in his de facto dormitory room—idling, I sensed,
with other Theater Studies majors like David Hyde Pierce and Bronson Pinchot
(later Serge in the film Beverly Hills Cop [1984] and Balki on the sitcom Perfect
Strangers [1986–1993])—Bill, I knew, had almost no free time. When not in
class, or in the library studying, or either rehearsing or performing with the
Yale Russian Chorus, he was in some dining hall or other washing dishes. Or at
least he did those dishes when not dancing somewhere—which you may have
inferred from "Kiss and Tell." ("Was I hoping, that night," I asked there, "for
some as we now say 'hook-up'? I'm not sure, anymore. It is true, though, that—
unlike Bill—I wasn't much of a dancer.") And to quote my book on Nijinsky,
where—like my friend Wayne Koestenbaum—Bill makes a cameo appearance:

> Of course, not everyone, not even every gay man, not even every nostalgic gay
> man, would describe unmarked female impersonation as sexually titillating.
> Many gay men turn off the camp, or wish their partners would, when trying to be
> either seductive or seduced. Leo Bersani, for example, complains if "the butch
> number swaggering into a bar in a leather get-up opens his mouth and sounds
> like a pansy, takes you home, where the first thing you notice is the complete
> works of Jane Austen, gets you into bed, and—well, you know the rest." [Lincoln]

Kirstein associated the sensuality of the *lezginka* with Nijinsky's provocative "fe-rocity" but ignored the most famous feature of the dance—famous because jump-ing on toes sheathed in soft boots looks painful if not impossible and transgres-sive if not transgendered. He even denied that the *lezginka* involves any type of impersonation. The Captain [in *Danse caucasienne*], Kirstein asserted, is "not the imitation of a particular personage but the embodiment of a regional vitality."

As if regional vitality were ever gender-trouble free. Russians found Moscow masculine but St. Petersburg, their capital, feminine. The French found Russia the way Russians found Persia—feminine—but Paris, their capital, feminine as well. Americans, especially ones who've lived through the Cold War, find Russia both masculine and feminine, militaristic yet artsy, which problematizes Kir-stein's complacent suggestion that the Captain is merely as wild as the moun-tains he's supposed to inhabit [the Caucasus Mountains]. Yet for every Kirstein or Bersani there's at least one gay man who needn't ignore the unmarked female impersonation in the *lezginka*. Take Bill Watson, fellow Slavophile, Yale Russian Chorus cohort, and traveling companion on the choir's 1979 tour of the Soviet Union. Bill, having been given *lezginka* boots by a dancer we met in Moscow, ran to our hotel to try them on, claimed they fit perfectly, and, imitating a par-ticular personage (Nijinsky), jumped on his toes—a pose he too chose not to hold. Bill knew ballet and could match *pointe* for *pointe* with any Trockadero transvestite but preferred to approximate Nijinsky's unmarked female imperson-ation, just as he preferred unmarked female impersonation when seductive. So if Kirstein wasn't haunted by the faux pas in the *lezginka*, Bill was.

Not that Bill ever seduced me, nor I him. And not that Bill, like Nijinsky, ever danced professionally—or even wanted to. What he wanted, like Jesse, was to be a writer. He'd wanted, in particular, to translate poetry by Osip Mandelstam and Yevgeny Yevtushenko—whom we had also met in Moscow. We'd met Yev-tushenko, that is, whose most famous poem, from the year 1961, is called "Babi Yar." (Mandelstam, being Jewish, was of course dead by 1979. He'd been killed, somehow—by some of Stalin's henchmen—over forty years earlier. But it's Sta-lin who was ultimately responsible for that.) "Over Babi Yar," the thing begins, "there is no monument."

Just a cliff, like some headstone.
I am afraid.
I'm as old, today,
As all of Jewry.

The translation, here, is by my sister. Bill, from what I could tell, or now recall, did such work even more beautifully—much like either poetry or translations by Richard Howard and either poetry and or fiction and or creative nonfiction and or journalism by Jesse—and yet he ended up, upon graduation, as a mere secretary.

The Yale Russian Chorus, at night, would rehearse up in a tower: the gothic-style Hall of Graduate Studies. Some chorus member, most often a graduate student, would have brought a liquor bottle. If a graduate student, he would also—apart from chorus life—have been trying to write a doctoral thesis for the last ten years. The liquor would of course be vodka. The vodka would be used for an opening toast. The toast, most often, involved some story about some chorus alumnus that most of the rest of us neither knew in person nor, to judge from what we were hearing about him, even cared to know. The bottle would be passed around. Actual singing—such as it was—would begin only after all the contents thereof had been guzzled. This done, our (Jewish) conductor Steve Lipsitt—on whom, one must confess, I had a pretty serious crush—would have us, in fact, scream our way through some repertoire. (Steve's own brother Eric, also older than he by two years, was in the chorus too. Both of them were straight. Both were tenors as well, although Eric—much as my brother Bob is a better pianist than I—had the better or rather *even* better and hence more operatic voice. Eric, in solos, did particularly good work with both *Kalinka* and our own *Lezginka*. The irony of these two having the same names as my own brothers, minus Bob, had upon my joining the group—at the beginning of sophomore year—struck me right away. You, it'll strike later.) That done, we would take a break during which even more vodka appeared. Those of us, though, who would not now drink—including Jesse, Bill, and me—would huddle together and gossip, quietly, about those who still would. And then—all together—we'd scream a bit more, ending rehearsal most often, arms draped drunkenly across shoulders, with the sacred song by Bortnyansky—Dmitri Bortnyansky—called "Mnogaya Leta." "Oh, Lord," it means, "grant us many years."

This Steve and I, despite my crush, were also friends. For a time, as you'll soon see, we were the only two music majors in the group. Plus we both lived in the same de facto dormitory—or, this being Yale, "residential college." Plus we both sang in the Yale Concert Choir: a truly premier not to mention both booze-free and co-ed ensemble. Here, though, I sang bass—as my vocal range back then was not unlike that of Barbra Streisand. Now, it's more like Cher's. Here, moreover, was where I met Bob's old graduate school friend Jon Bailey—as this group's conductor. (Bailey, at the time, at least seemed straight—a

married man with a couple of adopted children. He would later, like Bob, be
denied tenure—at Yale—and then unlike him leave the wife and kids, move
to Los Angeles, and—finally "out," out there—conduct that city's Gay Men's
Chorus.) Steve Lipsitt, at the time—unlike me—took singing very seriously. He
planned, in fact, to soon—upon graduation—do it professionally. (Eric Lipsitt, I
thought, could have done such a thing quite easily, but chose to become a doc-
tor instead. An *actual* one, that is, unlike "Svetlov" at IDANT. Steve, now—in
Boston—does not sing professionally. He conducts orchestral music.) And so—
apart from chorus life—he was studying voice under the soprano and also Yale
School of Music faculty member Phyllis Curtin. He did so, in fact, for course
credit—just as, as you'll soon see, I was studying piano for it. (My own voice
teacher at Juilliard, or the Pre-College Division thereof, had been—although
probably no relation to the poet by this name—the soprano Elizabeth Bishop.
There is now, apparently, a young mezzo-soprano also by this name.) And so
when Steve, as a favor, asked me to accompany his so-called lessons for credit
with Curtin, I of course said yes. Plus that would be my own form of dining
hall work. The pay was lower—or even lower—than Bill's there, but of course
the work itself was nice. (I have no idea, though, what Bill would soon earn as a
secretary, but it must have been a lot lower than what I would as a lawyer.) It was
here, for instance, that—as I recall—I first both heard and played *Dichterliebe*.

Phyllis Curtin, incidentally, had many years earlier, at both New York City
Opera and then later the Metropolitan Opera, been a very light-voiced rival
of the somewhat heavier-voiced but also simply heavier—plus Jewish—soprano
Beverly Sills. ("Sills' trills thrill," I recall, was an answer in some *New York
Times* crossword puzzle from about 1968.) Her signature or at least favorite role,
I sensed, was Salome—in the opera *Salome*, based on Wilde's play, by Rich-
ard Strauss. For hung beside the piano in this studio was a gilt-framed photo-
graph—in black-and-white—of the woman herself impersonating that girl: a
nearly nude and yet, I thought, gorgeous woman and so by now, I also thought,
a perhaps self-regarding if not just narcissistic one who could not only really
sing back then, when this picture was taken, but also it seemed really dance.
(Montserrat Caballé, being not just heavy, like Sills, but rather obese, I'm told
could merely record—and never actually perform—*Salome*. Curtin, too, re-
corded it.) Or to quote the woman herself, in a recent interview:

> The first person who asked me to sing Salome was [the conductor] Joseph
> Rosenstock at New York City Opera. He was a very difficult, irascible man, but

he was crazy about the opera. Before I ever looked at the opera I had read the Oscar Wilde play and had always adored it. After doing it at City Opera, I did some productions with Dino Yannopoulos and his concept was to play her as young and willful. After all, Salome is a young woman—she's in her teens and a virgin. She shouldn't sound like [her mother] Herodias. My teacher was horrified, of course. He had me learn it all vocalizing on my finest *ah*. He wanted all the technical problems to be solved so that I would be on secure footing with all the emotional and dramatic stress. It got to the point with that piece where I could sing it as easily as anything I did.

The last name "Rosenstock," by the way, was also that of Grandma Sally's second husband—probably no relation to the conductor. No, wait: *third* husband—the only one of hers I ever met. And John the Baptist, being proto-Christian, was of course killed—decapitated—by one of Herod's henchmen. But it's Herod who was ultimately responsible for that. Or rather, it's Salome who was. At any rate, when at the beginning of our last year together at Yale—senior year—Steve asked me to also accompany Yale Russian Chorus auditions—plus help judge them—I again said yes. These, though—with three exceptions I'll get to—I cannot recall.

| | |

After college graduation and then shortly after—in early November—my brother Steve's death, I did see Bill Watson pretty often—maybe four or five times a year. I would go, sometimes, to Washington, D.C., where as you know from "Kiss and Tell" he lived over by Dupont Circle—also called the "Fruit Loop"—and as you now know he worked as a secretary. Or, visiting both Jesse Green and me, Bill would sometimes come up to New York City. Jesse and I—as just roommates, not lovers—lived together in Greenwich Village while I was studying law at Columbia University but not eating very much and Jesse, therefore, kept trying to feed me. (I was also, as you also know from "Kiss and Tell," studying some porn Jesse had.) Bill, though, would always come up—in late June—for Gay Pride: the parade down Fifth Avenue and then festivities over by the Hudson River. (It's an actual river. The so-called East River, on the other side of Manhattan, is a tidal strait.) Bill, you see, was in a rather campy marching band called "Different Drummers." But he didn't play an instrument. He led this group's flag corps, called "flagettes," making good use, from what I could see en parade route, of all those many years he'd spent learning ballet at the *barre*.

Well, you already know that Bill and I—after that oral argument before the United States Supreme Court, in *The Board of Education of Oklahoma City vs. The National Gay Task Force*—once went to a different kind of bar called the Phoenix. You also know what then happened to me with both horse-trainer "Dean" and choirboy-like "Warren": unsafe sex—as a bottom—with the one, pseudo-marriage to the other. You do not know, though, from "Kiss and Tell," and nor could anyone really tell this from my Nijinsky book, what then happened to Bill. It was this, sadly. I was dancing, badly, with Dean while Bill was with some black guy I'd never seen before. And nor, I later learned, had Bill ever seen him before. And nor would I, after meeting him here briefly, ever see the guy again. For despite the fact that those two soon became non-roommate lovers, "Smerdyakov," as I'll rather nastily call him too, was much too closeted to want to get to know some—by that point—openly gay guy like me. Or at least to want to know one, said Bill, other than Bill himself. And the only other things I ever heard, also from Bill, about this Smerdyakov were that he had some "Himalayan" cats named Mumbo and Jumbo and that the man himself—as he'd told Bill—had "a type of cancer." (I therefore do not know what his job was. Such cats, as you may not know, are a cross between "Persian" and "Siamese.") What the man really had, though, was of course AIDS.

This soon, unfortunately, did him in. And that left Bill with both Mumbo and Jumbo . . . and AIDS. Because for some stupid reason he had believed that line of Smerdyakov's about "cancer" and for another stupid one he too—as a bottom—must have been having unsafe sex with the guy. This, eventually, did Bill in. I confess, then, that whereas I may not have killed either Warren or myself by accident by being sodomized by Dean and then later doing so myself to this soon-to-be pseudo-husband of mine, I did—to invoke that awful two-part film, from the years 2003 and 2004—kill Bill. (Compare, if you like, this "speech act" of mine to the memoir *The Future Lasts Forever*. Louis Althusser, in it, will never confess or rather take any responsibility for having strangled his wife—Hélène Rytman, a Lithuanian Jew—to death.) Or at least I *think* I killed him, because—in legal parlance—although I may not have been the "proximate cause" of this death, as Bill's Smerdyakov was, I am, in fact, its "cause-in-fact"—much as, if he *has* been killed for being gay by that awful father of his, I'd be the "cause-in-fact" of Razi's. (I no longer seem to have that photograph of Razi, with both his name—including last name—and telephone number on the back. And so how could I now ever know for sure?) Not, of course, that I should have stayed with Razi—in that village of theirs—as a kind of wife. ("'Kevin no go home to America. Every day, you here, you go to market. "One kilo of lentils," you say. "No, *two* kilos." Ha, ha, ha.") I should, though, if not have invited Razi to come live with *me*—in Iowa City, Iowa—and be my love then at least have suggested that he move once more, only this time for good, to Germany. Maybe to Berlin, again.

Have I, though, ever—in print—confessed such guilt before? Not exactly. For all I said in concluding that cameo—from *The Queer Afterlife of Vaslav Nijinsky*—was:

> Bill knew ballet and could match *pointe* for *pointe* with any Trockadero transvestite but preferred to approximate Nijinsky's unmarked female impersonation, just as he preferred unmarked female impersonation when seductive. So if Kirstein wasn't haunted by the faux pas in the *lezginka*, Bill was. As am I, who at this point am more haunted by the friend, now dead, who was haunted by Nijinsky than I am by Nijinsky himself.

Call the omission, as I'm told Eve Kosofsky Sedgwick would, a "blockage involved in mourning." Or call it, perhaps—like that Egyptian river—denial.

| | |

The only musicology I've cared for nearly as much as either *The Classical Style* or *The Romantic Generation*, by Charles Rosen, is by someone I'll call—rather nastily—"Stalin." (Others in the field, as it happens, also call the guy this. I bring Stalin up now because, as you'll see soon enough, he played an awful role in the life—and death—of one of the three would-be choristers whom I can recall having auditioned.) He too, like Rosen, is Jewish. He, too, is older than I am—but by just fifteen years. (Older than Bob, then, but younger than either Ricky or Micky.) Unlike with Rosen we two have never even met. And so when the *London Review of Books*, about ten years ago, asked me review Stalin's latest book, on "discerning" Russia musically, I said yes, read the thing once—only once, I'm afraid, because it's about a thousand pages long—and then churned out something I considered clever. "Get Real," the thing is called—and with by now signature self-regard or just narcissism it begins:

> I'm the kind of critic who reads epigraphs symptomatically. I also write them symptomatically. For example, by opening *Beethoven's Kiss* with Proust ("The rapid, nervous, charming style with which the Baron played the piano had its

equivalent in the man's nervous weaknesses"), I meant to imply that my writing style is rapid, nervous, and charming—and also that it expresses my sexuality. So when [Stalin] opens this book with Salman Rushdie ("I feel that everything I say or do is treated as an allegory of my situation. But I'm trying to not be defined by this situation."), I find I must consider his own situation, treat the book as an allegory of that situation, and wonder why he would resist such treatment.

[Stalin] is the preeminent authority, in the United States, on Russian music—which is quite a situation. But it's not that situation by which he's trying to not be defined. His other, equally long books include treatments of both Stravinsky and, as he spells it, "Musorgsky." This one, a collection of essays on Mussorgsky and others, can be paraphrased as follows. The European tendency to orientalize Russian culture, including Russian art music, is countered by a Russian tendency to occidentalize European culture—and by a Russian tendency to emulate European culture. The tendencies are ideological, but quite real. Russian composers use European means to convey non-European meaning, including the meaning of Russian nationality. Western audiences both fathom and feel these meanings. Yet Western musicologists denigrate the otherwise meaningful music "itself." As do ex-Russian composers, for political reasons. "The Cold-War Stravinsky," [Stalin] writes, "insisted not on music as metaphor but on 'music itself'—a very strange notion indeed." Its history has yet to be written, but it does not seem to be a very long one. In fact, "the term has nothing to do with the nineteenth century's 'absolute music,' with which it is now often mistakenly interchanged; for the absoluteness of absolute music, as Wagner (yes, Wagner) first envisioned it, was an absolute expressivity, not an absolute freedom from expression." I would not call this writing style rapid, nervous, and charming. I'd call it commanding, erudite, and sly. And I'd suggest it enables that preeminence here of his.

I continue in a similar, "symptomatic" vein. But this, apparently, wasn't what the journal wanted in some review by me. The thing, they said, was "too academic"—much as, perhaps, this here book by me is. And so they paid what I believe is called a "kill fee." Nevertheless, I soon published "Get Real"—somewhat revised—in some scholarly journal that I'll call, well, *Kill Fee*.

When this came out, Thomas Christensen—the friend and music theorist who would also explain fugues or rather quadruple fugues to me—warned me to expect a postcard. This Stalin, apparently, is notorious for not taking critique well. Hence, in part, that alias. Anyone, therefore, who says anything at all negative, in print, about the man's work, even or perhaps especially something "symptomatic," is told by him on such a card—if, that is, such critique gets Stalin's attention—to, in effect, go fuck yourself. (In Russian, says Micky, this would be *poshol ty na khuy*—literally, "go sit on a prick." Some other prick, that is, than your own.) Sometimes, as I'd later learn from three consecutive issues of the *Times Literary Supplement*, he is also told so—by Stalin—in print. In the first issue, the musicologist Hugh Wood reviewed some books on the English composer Edward Elgar. Stalin then accused Wood, in the next issue, of "insularity, anti-intellectualism, know-it-all-complacency, proud ignorance, [and] blimpish spite." Wood responded, in the one after that:

> I greatly admired and have favorably reviewed elsewhere [Stalin's] achievement in [a book he wrote on supposedly all of Western music.]. The often remarked-on omission of Elgar's name from it surely puts him in a rather invidious position now. What is really bugging him? Why does he resort once again to the sort of random, indiscriminate abuse with which colleagues who have displeased him in some way are only too familiar?
>
> I suspect that behind the chuckles and the *fausse bonhomie* lurks the fury of one who hears unwillingly a voice other than his own. Honestly, I never knew it was quite so easy to draw blood. I guess I'm kind of honored to be his target this time, but wish I could rate the tirade as the measured judgment of a distinguished scholar rather than the self-indulgent reaction of someone suffering from an ill-digested lunch.
>
> A few questions remain. Just what type of second-rateness in these books [on Elgar] is he intent on promoting? Has he any interesting thoughts about Elgar? What did he have for lunch?

I, though, was not told—in print—to in effect go fuck myself. Not by Stalin, at any rate. And nor did I even get that postcard from him.

|||

This, then, is what I recall about three of the auditions that—at the beginning of our senior year—both Steve Lipsitt and I conducted. Some "Jim Van de Velde," a rather handsome freshman with short blond hair and small blue eyes, sang "Old Man River" for us—yes, "Old Man River"—and then said that although he was also "rushing" a couple of other "singing groups" he'd really like to join ours. We, to Jim, seemed to be the "coolest one." This kid, Steve and

I decided, should be let in—by us—to sing baritone. He then did join our group, did sing baritone with it, and even helped organize its tour the next summer of the at that point—1979—not yet former Soviet Union. Many years later, Jim would return to Yale as both an Instructor in the Political Science Department and the dean of some residential college other than Steve's and mine. He would also, though, in the winter of 1998, be falsely accused by both administrative officers at the school and New Haven, Connecticut, police officers of having stabbed some "Suzanne Jovin"—a student and also mentee of Jim's who had been double-majoring in both Political Science and International Studies and who also, under him, had been writing a senior thesis on "Osama bin Laden and the Terrorist Threat to U.S. Security"—to death. The school then fired Jim. No criminal charges, though, were brought against him—nor anyone else. And so the girl's actual murderer is still unknown—except maybe to gypsies.

Guy Brewer, another freshman, had been a Juilliard Pre-College friend of mine. Plus he too—like both Steve and me—was a music major. Therefore he, too—after singing some sacred song by Bach—was let in to the Yale Russian Chorus by us. In Guy's case, though—unlike that of Jim—this was for him to sing bass. In fact, he would soon—the next year—take over from Steve and start conducting.

Like "Charles," my best friend from elementary school, Guy—as it happens—had been just about the only black kid at Juilliard. And this was, unfortunately, also true for him at Yale. Like me, Guy had studied piano at Juilliard: I under Kathrine Parker; he with Edgar Roberts. (My voice teacher, once again, was Elizabeth Bishop. Guy, there, had none.) He, though, and even more so than my brother Bob, was a brilliant pianist—brilliant, that is, in terms of both physical dexterity and musical intelligence. This first struck me in the fall of 1974, in a piano class about which I have already written in both a letter to Wayne Koestenbaum and then, by simply quoting this letter there, my book *Beethoven's Kiss*:

> I studied improvisation at Juilliard with Sylvia Rabinof, a friend of Mrs. Graa [my first piano teacher]. Mrs. Rabinof taught us harmonic progressions over which we could make up various dances—mazurkas, polonaises, what have you. I was never very good at this (I could only recreate the progressions in either C major or A minor) and so was relieved when Mrs. Rabinof, whose husband [Benno] had just died, was replaced by Miss Rosette. Miss Rosette couldn't have cared less about tonal harmony and encouraged cacophonic abandon. I remember with particular fondness my *Playground Suite*, with its zany "Slide-Upon" movement.

You might recall from "Kiss and Tell," though, that this apparently solo suite was really a duet—played by me with my friend Beth Sussman. And so I should have said as much before, or not have made *this* omission in *that* book. Nor even have first made it in that letter to Wayne. Guy, at any rate—like Beth—had unlike me truly learned stuff from Sylvia Rabinof. They both, that is, could improvise any dance in any key—major or minor. Plus they could sight-read either piano or even orchestral scores at the keyboard. Plus they could transpose—and to remote keys—such scores there.

Guy, moreover—again like Beth—had studied composition at Juilliard. In fact, writing music—not just playing it—was his main interest. Main passion, perhaps. This struck me that next spring, at a recital featuring what I believe Guy called his "Sunrise" String Quartet. Or maybe it was—with no reference here to the show *Fiddler on the Roof* intended by me—the "Sunset" Quartet. ("Sunrise, sunset. Sunrise, sunset. Swiftly fly the years. One season following another, laden with happiness and tears.") This thing, I thought, sounds like something that when at Guy's age—which was about fourteen years old back then—Mozart might have written. Or, I now think, it was like something that at this age either Schubert and or Saint-Saëns and or Reynaldo Hahn might have. And nor, I later learned, was I alone in such thinking. The composer Vincent Persichetti, who taught in the college division of Juilliard, had been at this same recital and invited Guy—upon the kid's pre-college graduation in three years— to study with him. Other such Persichetti students have included the composers Philip Glass and Peter Schickele—better known as "P.D.Q." Bach. (The latter, by the way, came—to New York City—from Ames, Iowa.) Guy, though, chose— for college—Yale over Juilliard. This may or may not have been a mistake for him in the long run but was definitely a problem—at least for me—at the time.

What happened was this. Guy, too—as a music major—wanted piano lessons for credit. Such instruction, supposedly, meant that you already either sang or played some instrument at the graduate level and so could be taken on as a student by some Yale School of Music faculty member—like Phyllis Curtin—both "for free," meaning one's undergraduate tuition covered it, and in order to help meet this major's course requirements. I, as a freshman, had auditioned—successfully—for such lessons by playing a rather easy concert etude by Liszt. It's called *Un Sospiro*. (That means: "a sigh.") Guy now played a very hard one by Liszt—called *Forest Murmurs*—and yet failed the audition. This, I thought, was outrageous. He'd *had* to have done a better job than I did—plus probably better than any other freshmen pianists now trying out. Were those professors—the pianists Ward Davenny and Donald Currier—who judged Guy's audition *deaf*? Were they *racist*? (Or, I now think, does Guy's alleged failure there suggest, to quote Hugh Wood, the "fury" of not one but two men who hear unwillingly some voice other than their own? Does it also suggest, to misquote Tolstoy in the epigraph to this chapter, their "envy and involuntary *dis*respect"?) Guy, though, wasn't outraged. He didn't even seem surprised to me. And at least Music Department faculty—including the composer Martin Bresnick, that old high school friend of Bob's, who'd soon start giving Guy composition lessons for credit—turned out to be if not deaf, of course, then color-blind. As would the Yale Russian Chorus.

It was Ward Davenny, by the way—not Donald Currier—who in the fall of 1976 had taken me on as a student. (Davenny was straight, while Currier at least seemed gay. All of the latter's male students, both graduate and undergraduate, had—against all odds—rather beautiful green eyes. Emerald eyes, in fact—or fantasy, rather. Mine, of course, are brown.) Davenny, at that freshman-year audition of mine, had—he himself later confessed to me—remembered a "*Robert Kopelson*" from an equally successful but much more impressive one that the kid, while still a senior at Harvard, had done about ten years earlier. (Bob, as you know, chose—for graduate school—U.C., Berkeley, over Yale. Which probably *was* a mistake for him in the long run.) Davenny had also then—he added—assumed that we two are related. And this, of course, was true. But he had also therefore assumed, as was not true, that we're equally good pianists. Or so I myself—after such, to again quote Hugh Wood, not so "random, indiscriminate abuse"—now assumed Davenny had assumed. Which may be why, apart from the fact that he's not female and also from his having been otherwise abusive to me as well, I'd be omitting him—twenty years later—in *Beethoven's Kiss*. Take, for instance, this passage in that book—one also at first written to Wayne:

> Diana Graa, the teacher Dr. Train demonized, is a widow. Kathrine Parker, the teacher I shared with David Nish, is a spinster. Arlene Portney, the teacher—and friend—through whom I trace my Lisztean lineage (Portney studied with Sascha Gorodnitski, who studied with Alexander Siloti, who studied with Liszt), is a wife and mother, but was a "maiden" when I studied with her. I hate these mind-warping and male-oriented stereotypes. They misconstrue women, and make women misconstrue themselves. Why, then, do I use them?

Nish, too, incidentally, is both Jewish and gay—neither of which I knew at the time. Guy, I believe, is not gay. But nor have I known him—unlike my friend

"Charles" at Harvard—to ever have a girlfriend. And not that it mattered, most likely, but Guy—unlike me—hasn't got an older brother, impressive or not, whom either Davenny or Currier could have remembered at that otherwise unsuccessful audition Guy had with them. He's got a younger one whose name really was Charles, whose nickname was "Chuck," whom Guy—unlike my brother Steve in relation to me—had always actually liked, and whom, there-fore, I myself can recall Guy having described, one time back at Juilliard, as a "rather handsome devil."

"Gregor Samsa," as I'll call him, now auditioned for the chorus. This kid, too—like both Jim and Guy—was a freshman. Like Jim, he was a blond. The hair was longer than his, though. Plus unlike Jim he had glasses—wire-framed ones. Like Guy—as well as both Steve Lipsitt and me—he was a music major. He sang "Aura Lee" for us. This is an American Civil War song the tune of which Elvis Presley had later used, ignobly, in the hit song "Love Me Tender." We let Gregor in—as a tenor. Although I don't recall anything he then said to us, I do know that both Steve and I found the kid rather charming—smart, funny, very enthusiastic, but also kind of goofy. And this, by the way, would also describe—in part—the "Pushkin" whom both "Emmeline Grangerford" and I would later teach.

Neither Steve nor I, as seniors, would get to know Gregor—or for that matter Jim—very well. Guy I already knew. We two did, though—when billeted there during spring tour—spend a night with Gregor at his parents' house. This was a middle-class but also kind of gloomy place in New Jersey. Gregor's mother, I thought, seemed rather nervous; the father, I thought, seemed both nervous and depressed. Gregor, though, still seemed goofy to me. Has Dad, I wondered, just been *fired*? Have the two of them—both Mom and Dad—been *drinking*?

Gregor—along with both Jim and Guy—went on tour with the chorus that summer: from Leningrad, or the former St. Petersburg, to Novgorod, or Ve-liky Novgorod, to Moscow—where Bill got those boots and also where, with both Bill Watson and Danny Grossman translating for us, I met my deceased Grandpa Harry's two living siblings, his only sister Nina and his youngest brother David—to Yerevan in the Armenian Soviet Socialist Republic, and then to Tbilisi in Soviet Georgia. (I can't say why I didn't then ask either Nina or David what Harry's name had been in Russia. My husband David's son Sam, by the way, spent the summer after his own freshman year in college in Tblisi. That city is in the so-called Democratic Republic of Georgia.) But the next and also last time I saw Gregor was in Carnegie Hall, two years later, when and where the Yale Russian Chorus, along with alumni including me, helped the conductor Eve Queler's New York Opera Orchestra do a concert version of Mussorgsky's opera *Khovanshchina*. The chorus impersonated, although not at the same time, both drunken musketeers and some so-called Old Believers, who at the end of this thing burn themselves to death. An all-female chorus—from that Juilliard School rival the Manhattan School of Music—impersonated both Old Believers and musketeer wives.

Mussorgsky, who died at age forty-two from alcoholism, had left *Khovan-shchina* both unfinished and, except for two fragments, unorchestrated. The first performing edition was done by the composer Rimsky-Korsakov. This was the version used at the opera's world premiere in St. Petersburg—in the year 1886—under some conductor named Eduard Goldstein. It was also the one used in that same city at the "Maryinsky" but later "Kirov" and now once again Maryinsky Theater—in the year 1911—with the bass Feodor Chaliapin as "Dosifey." He is the leader of those Old Believers. A variant of this version, by both the composers Stravinsky and Ravel, was used two years later for the French premiere of *Khovanshchina*—staged, in Paris, by the impresario Serge Diaghilev—with Chaliapin once again as Dosifey and some contralto named Elizaveta Petrenko as "Marfa." She is a gypsy fortune-teller. The composer Dmitri Shostakovich—having been denounced, through henchmen, by the real-world Stalin in 1936 and then again by him twelve years later—scored, for a Kirov Theater production in 1952, some scenes from the opera that had for some reason been omitted by Rimsky-Korsakov. Shostakovich—in the year 1958—later re-scored the whole thing for some film of the thing. And it was this last version that—for the first time on at least any American stage—Eve Queler used.

Like *Boris Godunov*, which is also by Mussorgsky, *Khovanshchina* is a meditation on history. (So too, are *War and Peace* by Tolstoy and then—as an operatic version of this novel—the composer Prokofiev. So too, for that matter, are *Eugene Onegin* by the real-world Pushkin and then—as an operatic version of this novel in verse—the composer Tchaikovsky.) Conceived in the bicentenary of Czar Peter I also known as "Peter the Great"—or the year 1872—it reflects a moral controversy that has always surrounded him. (Peter used Western models to create, in effect, a suddenly Western country. And so he has always been seen—by Russians—as either the best or the very worst thing that ever happened to them.) To quote Mussorgsky himself, in a rather cryptic letter to the critic Vladimir Stasov: the work concerns "the power of the black earth" and its

resistance to ploughing "with tools wrought of alien materials"—"dark rumina-
tions," writes the musicologist Richard Taruskin in *The New Grove Dictionary
of Opera*, that are really all we have to go on "if we want to understand, as a work
of history, the sprawling, unprecedented opera-chronicle that gestated over the
nine years that remained to the composer, since his early death left crucial
holes in the scenario," and yet which nonetheless suggest, to Taruskin, how
spurious may be any progress narrative revisers later made for it.

Unlike *Boris Godunov*, though, *Khovanshchina* is tuneful—making it, once
again for Taruskin, "aristocratic." Except for scenes involving some lowborn
scrivener, he writes, "it is full of 'noble' melody in place of the radically realistic
speech-song" that one finds in at least the first—or 1869—version of this earlier
work.

> In part this is a continuation of a tendency, already noticeable in the revised
> *Boris* [1872], toward a more heroic scale and a more authentically tragic tone—in
> short, toward a more traditionally operatic style. But Mussorgsky refused to call
> it a retrenchment; on the contrary, in one of his late letters to Stasov he pointed
> with pride to his *advancement* toward what he called "thought-through and jus-
> tified melody," meaning a kind of melody that would embody all the expressive
> potential of speech. Yet these sinuous melodies, unlike the idiosyncratic recita-
> tives of his earlier manner, are curiously impersonal. The characters who sing
> them (Marfa throughout, Shaklovity in Scene iii, Dosifey in Scenes iii and vi)
> do not speak, it seems; rather, something akin to a Tolstoyan notion of impassive
> historical forces (what Mussorgsky, in his sphinx-like way, had called "the power
> of the black earth") speaks through them.

And this is perhaps the main message of a work "in which personal volition
is everywhere set at nought; in which everyone plots and strives and everyone
loses; in which the final stage picture shows the last survivors of the old order,
the opera's only morally undefiled characters, resolutely stepping out of history
and into eternity, where Peter cannot touch them."

Gregor, ten years later, died at age thirty. I learned this, though, only ten
years after that—when I myself, finally, was at Harvard as a "Bunting Fellow." I
happened to mention, here, to a female composer—let's call her "Marfa"—that
I used to be in the Yale Russian Chorus. She teared up and asked if I'd known
her good friend Gregor. He, as a "musicological genius" focused on both eigh-
teenth- and nineteenth-century Russian music, had been to graduate school
with the woman. And as far as such music went, said Marfa, he had much

preferred "that genius Tchaikovsky to, say, Mussorgsky"—whereas she herself, as far as such *twentieth*-century music goes, preferred Prokofiev to Shostakovich.

Gregor's genius, at any rate, had been recognized—at I'll say U.C., Berkeley—not just by other graduate students there but also by faculty members. "Including by [Stalin]," who—said Marfa—would have been his dissertation director. And yet, seeing Gregor "as a type of rival," Stalin also felt threatened by him. (The man was furious, perhaps, at—to misquote Hugh Wood—having *willingly* heard a voice other than his own.) Rather meanly, he posed—at Gregor's pre-dissertation oral comprehensive examination—some very hard question about some very obscure composer. (My own such director, Robert Scholes, did no such thing to me—nor to anyone else I know.) Gregor failed, claimed Stalin, to answer this question correctly. And so he directed or rather— I'd say—*exiled* Gregor to spend the next year in, as it was still called, though not for many years longer, Leningrad. He was, she said, to do general research on the so-called Mighty Handful or *Moguchaya kuchka* of composers—Mily Balakirev, Alexander Borodin, César Cui, Mussorgsky, and Rimsky-Korsakov—who used to work there together. (Stalin, as you'll soon see, has a different story.) Shortly after arrival, though—in Leningrad—Gregor died in a car crash.

Marfa was crying by now. I therefore expressed condolences and asked if Gregor had had any siblings. She didn't know if he had. I changed the subject, but even having changed it, I told myself: "So, Kevin, you're the cause-in-fact of yet another death—although the proximate cause, in sending Gregor on that stupid trip, was Stalin. For had you, or had both Steve Lipsitt and you, not admitted Gregor to that stupid chorus, he may never have come to both know and love such music—Russian music—so well. Or to love it so tenderly. Or at least the melodic forms of it." I also, for some reason, told myself that Gregor himself hadn't caused this accident. I imagined, that is, that he couldn't possibly have been at the wheel. And although I could, I suppose, ask Marfa—via e-mail—if this is in fact the case, I never got to know her very well either. Or at least not well enough to ever pose such a question.

I have, though, just asked Guy Brewer this. He's not sure. (He is, though, sure that Gregor had a younger brother.) And nor can he think who might know. I then looked—via the Internet—into Gregor's involuntarily aborted and hence only apparently less dangerous career—in academia—than espionage. While at Berkeley, I learned, he had co-founded a scholarly journal that I'll call *Echoes*. The first issue—opening with an article by Lawrence Kramer on "absolute musicology" and ending with one by Gregor himself on "idiocy" in

Mozart—came out shortly after the car crash. This "idiocy" piece seems to have been the poor kid's only such publication. As for subsequent work, in print, by Stalin—subsequent, that is, to this *Echoes* issue—there's only one reference therein to this graduate student of his. It's in that book about "Musorgsky," which, one must confess, I had not read any of before writing—for the LRB and then *Kill Fee*—that review called "Get Real." Chapter Seven thereof—called "The Power of the Black Earth"—is, Stalin claims: "dedicated to the memory of [Gregor Samsa], a graduate student at [the University of California, Berkeley], who died on October 29, 1991 in an automobile accident in St. Petersburg, Russia, where he was conducting research for a dissertation on *Khovanshchina* and Musorgsky's idea of history."

| | |

What's this all about, really? What's with all the—*ah*—"emotional and dramatic stress" here? Having read—symptomatically—this book thus far, you've probably "discerned" something I myself have known for about thirty years: that I used to see myself as the cause-in-fact of my brother Steve's apparent suicide and also to see Steve himself, like some Old Believer, plus like Seymour Glass, as our family's "only morally undefiled character, resolutely stepping out of history." For whereas I did both truly and tenderly, with all the usual vicissitudes of adulation, aggression, and ambivalence, not just like but actually *love* my brother, he—unlike Eric in relation to Steve Lipsitt, or Guy in relation to "Chuck" Brewer, or Seymour in relation to "Buddy" Glass, or "Buddy" in relation to "Zooey" Glass, or "Zooey" in relation to "Franny" Glass, or both Dmitri and Ivan in relation to Alyosha Karamazov, but rather like, I'm afraid, their "repellant" half-brother Smerdyakov in relation to those three and also like, I believe, Tony in relation to Jesse Green—did not love me. Nor, I thought, did he even like me at all. In fact—again like that Smerdyakov—he just *hated* me, going so far, from time to time, as to say, or scream, that I and I alone, somehow, made his life on earth "miserable." And yet, I now think, I'm no "Stalin." Steve, unlike Gregor, would be exiling *himself* to Israel. He would also go so far, or further, as to often, and into our own teenage years, rather immorally beat the shit out of me. Well, that too is an exaggeration—like saying Micky spied. He did, however, often *try* to do this. And so I often thought, or felt, that figuratively speaking he *had* done so. (Consider this, then, my own Wilde moment—or one of a few such in this book. The Oscar Wilde, that is, of the letter *De Pro-*

fundis—and not the play *Salome*—who would confess, for him, all the awful things that Lord Alfred Douglas had done. Wilde, by the way, was sixteen years older than that guy.) You may not, though, have also discerned that I probably still see us this way—despite my having also known, for about twenty-five years, as you yourselves know from "Veritas," that Steve's death, or rather autoerotic asphyxiation, was like Gregor's really just an accident. Nor may you have discerned—to invoke both what happened to Grandpa Harry's brother Boris when killed at just—said Mom—age twelve and what Harry himself all those decades later may have felt about it—that I still see myself as a murderer. The accusation or rather self-accusation is of course false, as was that one of Jim by both administrators and policemen. And yet dreams, recurrent dreams, keep making it: punitive or rather self-punitive nightmares in which Steve doesn't just beat the shit out of me but literally kills me—and always, like Seymour or rather like Hitler's marksmen at Babi Yar, with a gun. My awakening from these has been, as you might imagine, like—. It has been like—.

There's that "blockage" again, Eve. Eve Sedgwick, that is, not Eve Queler. And so to quote the journalist—and Austrian Jew—named Alfred Polgar:

> Abel, if he had fled from the murderous attentions of his brother Cain, would as an emigrant have had to put up with an even more bitter inconvenience. He would have had to wander for the rest of his life with the brand of Abel on his forehead.

Polgar, by the way, is someone you can learn about from the Clive James book *Cultural Amnesia*—the one that my student "Arabella" said she just "loathed." You'll learn there, for instance, that all of the man's writing—especially in its original German—is just as beautiful as this quote in translation. You'll learn, too, that Marlene Dietrich—a first cousin, as it happens, of my husband David's mother—once asked the man to write her biography. That book, though, was not to be—much as buildings or even entire cities by Steve were not, and nor other poetry translations by Bill, and nor Gregor's dissertation on *Khovanshchina*, and nor whatever Suzanne—Suzanne Jovin—would have accomplished in life. Polgar, you see, having just escaped the Nazis . . . died at age eighty-one—in the year 1955—and hence, unlike those four, of some so-called natural cause. Perhaps it, too—as with both Grandpa Harry and Dad—was heart disease.

Death to Gumby

If not yourself, who would you be?
Since the question does not arise, I prefer not to answer it. All the same, I should very much have liked to be Pliny the Younger.

—MARCEL PROUST, 1886

If not yourself, who would you be?
Myself—as those whom I admire would like me to be.

—MARCEL PROUST, 1891

"I am, at heart," said Marlene Dietrich, "a gentleman." (The woman, of course, was German. At age thirty-eight, though—thanks to Hitler—she chose American citizenship.) And yet the so-called French Feminist Luce Irigaray—a student of those *anatomical* gentlemen Jacques Lacan and Jacques Derrida—wrote that there is just one "initial path" for anatomical *ladies*. (Irigaray is Belgian. Julia Kristeva, another "French Feminist," is Bulgarian.) It's the path, she explained, that is "historically assigned to the feminine." It's the path, in other words, "of *mimicry*." And so one must "assume the feminine role deliberately"—which means "to convert a form of subordination into an affirmation, and then to begin to thwart it."

True enough, I suppose. It's true, that is, for lots of women—whether or not they also happen to be heterosexual, as is Dietrich on film, or to be homosexual, as Irigaray is in real life, or to be bisexual, as Dietrich was in life. And yet it's also true for some men. Or for some gay men. In my own case, for instance, I first imagined myself to be—well, to quote *Beethoven's Kiss*:

> Up until a year ago, when I discovered it was also [Muzio] Clementi's birthday, I'd always thought of January twenty-third as the day [that] Anna Pavlova died. Why recall this coincidence (my birthday, her death day)? Because I dreamt of being a ballerina long before I ever dreamt of being a [piano] virtuoso. One of my earliest impressions is of Pavlova, on film, dancing *The Dying Swan*. The suture involved—not to mention the terpsichorean necrophilia—was, of course, fundamentally queer. I was a four-year-old boy who saw himself as a forty-year-old woman. It was seamless as well. All of a sudden, I *was* Pavlova, and so had my brother [Bob] play Saint-Saëns' *The Swan* over and over again, perfecting my own dying swan as he did so. Bob, to his credit, never ridiculed the routine. My parents, however, having had us perform for them, did. Unaware of my incompetence (I didn't know I needed [ballet] lessons) as well as of my abnormality (I didn't know I was too young, and too male, for the part), I was stunned by their laughter, but pretended I'd been in on the joke all along. Needless to say, I retired from that particular stage and began to worry about other ways my body would betray me.

This began, for me, disembodied such identifications, which for many years were no longer with dancers of either gender—until at nearly thirty-eight I imagined myself to be the Russian Vaslav Nijinsky (born in Kiev, Ukraine)—nor even with female pianists—such as very sexy Martha Argerich, an Argentinian, or somewhat comical "Hildegarde" (*née* Hildegarde Loretta Sell in Adell, Wisconsin)—but rather—and also rather exclusively—with women in opera. While listening—and yet not singing along—to full-length opera recordings, I would imagine myself to be, say: Gilda, from Verdi's *Rigoletto*, dying at last of stab wounds that had really been meant for her ex-lover "Gualtier Maldé," a man better known—to everyone there except the poor girl—as the Duke of Mantua; or to be Mimi, from Puccini's *La Bohème*, dying—of "consumption"—while in Paris with her ex-lover Rodolfo; or to be Lucia, from *Lucia di Lammermoor* by Donizetti, dying offstage—somewhere in Scotland—after having first completely lost her mind and then stabbed her new husband Arturo to death; or— and here recall from both "Kiss and Tell" and "Salome," the sopranos Montserrat Caballé and Phyllis Curtin—to be the Richard Strauss heroine Salome as she's crushed to death—in Tiberias, Galilee—by some of Herod's henchmen after having first danced all too seductively for the poor man and then forced him to have John the Baptist killed. (That last bit, by the way—the killing of Salome—isn't in the Bible. It's something that Oscar Wilde—in the play this opera is based on—had devised.) But after—at the age of eighteen—coming out as gay to my parents, I left both opera and such death-driven sentimentality behind. I left them, in fact, for out and out *camp*. I would now, for instance, imagine myself, as you might recall from "My Cortez," to be Marie-Hélène de Rothschild—plus I'd imagine my law-firm friend "Albertine" to be Guy de Rothschild. I would imagine myself, as well, to be "Esperanza Jujube," a Charo-like and hence Spanish version, devised by me, of a then well-known American "Trend Spotter" named—both allegedly and rather funnily—Faith Popcorn. (Charo's real name is: María Rosario Pilar Martínez Molina Moquiere de les Esperades Santa Ana Romanguera y de la Najosa Rasten. She's a both very sexy and somewhat comical *guitar* virtuoso—who studied with Andrés Sego-via.) "Popcorn," though, turns out to be the woman's own version of the Jewish or rather—I suppose—for her *too* Jewish last name Plotkin. Faith, though, is her real first name.

What Irigaray, at any rate, did not then write—quite truthfully—is that for many gay men, as for women of whatever sexuality, there can be a second, historically *masculine* path. And nor did she write that these two seemingly opposite paths—either masculine or feminine—can in some ways be the same path. And nor that where there is such "mimicry," or *mimétisme* in the original French—which means both impersonation and what Irigaray along with other feminists, such as Gayatri Spivak (*née* Gayatri Chakravorty in Calcutta, India), have called "strategic essentialism"—there might be *mockery* as well.

Take *Remembrance of Things Past*, from which Irigaray probably derived that "path." (She wrote, in French: *un seul chemin*.) Proust's narrator—who is an alter ego of that author and so who's also, possibly, named Marcel—notes that the little town of "Combray"—based on an actual town that used to be named Illiers—featured two seemingly opposite walks or *deux "côtés" pour les promenades*: the first—called "Swann's Way"—took him, in childhood, to the upper middle-class estate of Proust's other main alter ego in the novel, the character named Charles Swann; the second, called "The Guermantes Way," took him to that of aristocrats with whom—unbeknownst to Marcel the nar-rator—this Swann, in Paris, used to hobnob. (I am not concerned here, very much, with alter egos—even female ones—of whom, as such, Proust may have been unaware: with the original Albertine, for instance.) Also unbeknownst to narrator Marcel, for a time, these two walks meet up somewhere past those two estates—much as Gilberte, Swann's daughter by his erstwhile mistress and now wife, Odette, will one day marry Robert de Saint-Loup, a Guermantes who also happens to have been a friend—maybe the only friend—of Marcel, and then with him have a daughter of her own. As for imitative mockery or *pastiche* in Proust, here for instance is Marcel—rather meanly and also many years after his victim's younger brother as well as erstwhile collaborator Jules had died—playing the critic Edmond de Goncourt:

> The day before yesterday [Gustave] Verdurin drops in here to carry me off to dine with him—Verdurin, former critic of the *Revue*, author of that book on Whistler in which the workmanship, the painterly coloration, of the American eccentric is interpreted sometimes with great delicacy by the lover of all the refinements, all the *prettinesses* of the painted canvas, that Verdurin is. And while I am getting dressed to accompany him, he treats me to a long narrative, almost at moments a timidly stammered confession, about his renunciation of writing immediately after his marriage to Fromentin's "Madeleine," a renunciation brought about, he says, by his addiction to morphine and which had the result, according to Verdurin, that most of the frequenters of his wife's drawing-room did not even know that her husband had ever been a writer and spoke to him of Charles Blanc, of Saint-Victor, of Sainte-Beuve, of Burty, as individuals to whom they considered him, Verdurin, altogether inferior.

I, in childhood, had no such "Combray"—nor even an Illiers. (Illiers, by the way, is now named—thanks to Proust—Illiers-Combray.) All I had back then was Hurleyville. It's a town, in the Catskill Mountains of New York State, where Grandma Sally Rosenstock *née* Goldfarb used to live but—believe me—no one like Swann let alone any Guermantes ever did. (Three women at some Catskills resort—maybe Grossinger's—sit in rocking chairs on its veranda. The first of them sighs, "Oy!" The others nod in agreement. Then the second sighs, "Oy vey!" The others nod. Then the third sighs, "Oy gottenyu!" The others nod. And then, finally, a fourth woman here—exasperated—says, "*Enough* about the children!") Nor did I have Marcel's tea-soaked madeleine—it's a shell-shaped cookie—the taste of which, of course, when coupled with other such physical sensations, will later—via "involuntary memory" or *souvenir involontaire*—help him recall all of Combray. (For Proust, in reality, that cookie was toast.) All I had back then were untoasted bagels dipped—by Grandma Esther "Goldstein" *née* Lieber—in what used to be called "regular coffee." That's black coffee with cream and sugar. Plus *she* lived—with Grandpa Harry—in the Bronx.

As a student at "Bronx Science," though, I did as you might recall from "My Cortez" have—for English—both very sexy Florence Dragnet and as her own seeming opposite very comical Joseph Scavone. I myself would—deliberately— mimic these two. But this was sans mockery—and therefore not at all mean. Plus it was only when I too—many years later—first became a teacher. Where Dragnet, for instance, had once spent an entire week explaining to us—all too seductively—the scene from Edith Wharton's novel *Ethan Frome* in which Ethan and his wife's cousin Mattie eat pickles and donuts together, I myself, as you might recall from "Kiss and Tell," spent entire semesters explaining—some-what seductively—at least *sublimations* of "homosexual activity." And where Scavone had explained to us at least certain funny insults in literature that we'd read—such as "purple-hued maltworm," which means drunkard, from Shake-speare's *Henry IV, Part One*—I myself at least tried explaining camp. I tried, for instance, explaining scenes such as the one from Ronald Firbank's novel *The Flower beneath the Foot* in which the Countess of Tolga gives the Queen of Pisuerga "a glance that was known in Court circles as her *tortured-animal* look." These days, though, when lecturing or even just "rhapsodizing" to college kids, I no longer play—either sexily or comically—these two high school teachers of mine. And I certainly don't play them those ways when conversing—in class— with graduate students. I now play, so to speak, myself alone. Or rather, I play myself conversing—at home—with my husband David's sons: Adam, Seth, and Sam. Plus with Seth's best friend, Keaton—to whom both David and I are father figures. And so—I'd imagine—I do not now, in class, play myself as the either Auntie Mame and or Uncle Charley and or Mary Poppins and or Peter Pan of these four "boys" of ours. (David's mother, as you might recall from the chapter "Salome," is a cousin of Marlene Dietrich.) And yet when—both non-sexily and non-comically—either lecturing to undergraduate students or conversing with graduate ones, I still, as you might have just inferred, do something that both Dragnet and Scavone used to. I still, that is, *explain* plenty of stuff. Firbank, for instance—as I've said before in class as well as written in that review, titled "Tawdrily, I Adore Him," of my friend Wayne Koestenbaum's book on opera— deploys such italics as "her *tortured-animal* look" both to be suggestive and to indicate citation . . . but of no source in particular. And so what you might call Dragnet's Way and Scavone's Way were really—if only in *this* way—the same Way. They were both, as I've just implied: Ways of Explanation.

When I too—like either Jules or Edmond de Goncourt, or like Charles-Au-gustin Sainte-Beuve, with his so-called *causeries* or "conversations" on writers, but also like Proust's Verdurin—became a *critic*, now that's of course a related but much more complicated story. Here, again, I have moved from playing other men as well as women—like both Roland Barthes and Eve Kosofsky Sedgwick in my first book, *Love's Litany*—to playing myself alone. In the next book, *Beethoven's Kiss*, I myself "speak"—so to speak—with Wayne, primarily. In the next one, *The Queer Afterlife of Vaslav Nijinsky*, I speak mainly to my at that point soon to be ex-lover "Matt." (I am using, by the way, these *to's* and *with's* on purpose.) In the next one, *Neatness Counts*, I speak mainly—despite that book's dedication to my at that point not yet husband David—with my by then long dead brother Steve. It's a nickname for "Stephen." In *Sedaris*, as you know, I speak mainly to Sam—the last named because youngest of four dedicatees there: Adam, Keaton, Seth, and then Sam—and yet through the poor boy to myself as well. In this book—despite the dedication to, as you must have figured out, by now recently dead Eve Kosofsky Sedgwick—I speak mainly to David, plus of course to any *biological* kids of mine: both boys and girls. This should, well, explain—finally—the first of those three subsequent epigraphs here. It's an otherwise private "thank you" to the poor man for his having recently suggested that I now try not just to "speak" in writing but to—so to speak—*converse* in it. Much as Sainte-Beuve did. And so for both "Swann" and "Odette" in this passage, all you readers other than David can now put our own two first names:

> The bonds that unite us to another human being are sanctified when he adopts the same point of view as ourselves in judging one of our imperfections. And among those special traits there were others, besides, which belonged as much to [Kevin's] intellect as to his character, but which nevertheless, because they had their roots in the latter, [David] had been able more easily to discern. [He] complained that when [Kevin] turned author, when he published his essays, these characteristics were not to be found in them to the same extent as in his letters or in his conversation, where they abounded. [He] urged him to give them a more prominent place. [He] wanted this because it was these things that [he himself] most liked in him, but since [he] liked them because they were the things most typical of him, [he] was perhaps not wrong in wishing that they might be found in his writings.

I have also moved, in writing, from assuming the role—or persona—of if not total "ignoramus" then the role of "know-it-all" to the Socratic role of these two types combined and then to one that's much less dishonest, for me, than any of those three: the role of "know-a-thing-or-two." I have therefore also moved from what the British philosopher J.L. Austin called "constative"—which means merely descriptive—to "performative" writing, and then from performative writing *tout court* to the type of it called *confessional*, and then—even or especially "as we speak"—from confessional writing *tout court*—"stammered," perhaps, like that "long [oral] narrative" of Verdurin's, although not, one must hope, quite as "timid" as it—to confessional *satire*.

All I have ever written, though—including this long narrative *book* of mine—are essays. Plus, as you can see, I keep on quoting a lot—just as when "rhapsodizing" to students. Make that: either "to" or "with" them, because where I both lecture and rhapsodize *to*—to me—child-like undergraduates, I not only converse but also, one must confess, both lecture and rhapsodize *with* the relatively mature—and yet still, to me, child-like—graduate ones. But then so, too, did Michel de Montaigne quote a lot. (My own Albertine, when in graduate school, had as you might recall from "My Cortez" plagiarized an article on him.) He is the world's first essayist. (He was also, of course—unlike either Irigaray or Kristeva—French.) He's even, perhaps, the greatest such writer. Take that famous thing he wrote on a terrific example, taken from his own life, of what we would now—citing Sedgwick—call not homosexuality but "male homosociality":

> *Si on me presse de dire pourquoi je l'aimais, je sens que cela ne se peut exprimer qu'en répondant: "Parce que c'était lui; parce que c'était moi."*

In English, it's: "If you press me to say why I loved him"—by whom Montaigne means his by then long dead and also best friend, Étienne de La Boétie—"I can say no more than it was because he was he, and I was I." The name *Étienne*—in English—is "Stephen."

|||

Of course, no one—including unconventional critics like either D.A. Miller or his own role model Roland Barthes and even conventional ones like either Charles Rosen or the musicologist I've called "Stalin"—seems to "know it all" more than lawyers do. Some lawyers—like my friend Evan Wolfson and his role model, Laurence Tribe—even, I believe, really do know everything. And so it was more from men like them than one like Rosen that, as a lawyer myself, I first learned—sans mockery—to at least mimic omniscience:

> Clearly, speech about homosexuality does not necessarily, or indeed ordinarily, fall within any category of speech held by this Court to be excluded from the protection

of the First Amendment. When speech about homosexuality constitutes defama-
tion, obscenity, or "fighting words," such expression may be prohibited because
these categories of speech fall outside the protection of the First Amendment. Any
fortuitous content involving homosexuality, however, is irrelevant.

And then after I left law behind, it was *still* more from such men—and not one
like Roland Barthes or even a woman like Eve Kosofsky Sedgwick—that, as a
graduate student, I continued learning to do it:

> Could it be that the "it" to which this perspicuous lyric refers—"What's love got
> to do with it?"—is sexuality? Followers of Michel Foucault consider sexuality to
> be a vexed and vexing cultural construction formed by, at the very least, three
> powerful discourses: theology, medicine, and law. The male homosexual, for
> example, is at once a sinner, an invert, and a sodomite. Unfortunately, most Fou-
> cauldians fail to suspect, even though common sense should tell them it must,
> that another powerful (if nowadays undervalued) discourse inflects sexuality as
> well: love, or more specifically, erotic philosophy. What does love have to do
> with sexuality? Leave it to poststructuralists, Tina Turner might snicker, to fail
> to ask this question—or to suggest "nothing" as its answer.
>
> Whence that failure and that answer? Why is "love" less fashionable than
> "sex" or "desire"? Critical theorists tend to see love as an outmoded and incoher-
> ent epistemological anomaly that has no place among the discourses that con-
> struct sexuality as an epistemological field. According to Roland Barthes, the life
> of the lover is one of "'philosophical' solitude, love-as-passion being accounted
> for today by no major system of thought (of discourse)." Even though popular
> culture is obsessed with love, love—according to Stephen Heath—is "not con-
> temporary," it is "left aside or disparaged by the actuality of theoretical systems."
> According to Julia Kristeva, "today we have no love discourse" and "lack a code
> of love" because "social consensus gives *little* or *no* support to . . . amatory ideal-
> ism." But even if conceptions of love are now passé and fragmentary, they are not
> necessarily inconsequential. They are active, if residual, cultural elements that
> have played and continue to play a crucial and under-examined role in the con-
> struction of sexuality. As Oscar Wilde, who had more to say about sexuality than
> he himself realized, once put it: "Do you wish to love? Use Love's Litany, and the
> words will create the yearning from which the world fancies that they spring."

This, no doubt, explains why my friend Wayne Koestenbaum, in his blurb for
the book—*Love's Litany*—that opens with those two paragraphs just quoted,

associated its "voice"—by which he means my persona there—with "a litiga-
tor's clean panoptic brio." (Recall, though, my female teacher's advice—not
yet heeded by me, at Brown University, but recently repeated by me, at the
University of Iowa, to the female student I've called "Arabella." Scholars, this
non-French feminist told me back then, should at least try to be judicial. "There
may not *be* some adversary now," she also explained, "to either defend a posi-
tion you're attacking or attack what you're defending. Plus, Kevin, there's *never*
anyone now—other than you—to settle a dispute.") Because Wayne, you see,
has always known better than anyone else I know—including my best friend,
Doug Trevor—how to read me "symptomatically." Then again, he also knew—
back then—that I myself, as a litigator, had actually practiced law.

Wayne could, though, have written: "a *pianist's* brio." (He knew too, based
on my letters to him later in *Beethoven's Kiss*, that I actually played the in-
strument. Plus he did not yet know, based on hearing me play it, that I *lack*
such brio.) Because long before I ever mimicked—or feigned—omniscience
in court papers, I had already done so—non-linguistically—at the keyboard.
"I'm creative, or rather re-creative," I confessed—non-timidly—in "My Cortez":
"not Chopin, but someone who *plays* Chopin—and in both senses of the verb:
to perform, to impersonate." And what this means is that as someone—unlike
either brother Bob and or Guy Brewer and or Beth Sussman and or especially
Charles Rosen—with not just pretty poor physical dexterity but also pretty dim
musical intelligence, I've only ever been someone who impersonates other peo-
ple—including women like Martha Argerich—who themselves seemed to me
to impersonate Chopin. (As bright or even brilliant musicians, as well as skilled
technicians, such people are of course not—in reality—mere mimics.) Or who
seemed to impersonate Schumann. *My* Schumann Fantasy, for instance, is—in
reality but also fantasy—a reproduction of *Bob's* Fantasy, primarily. But it is
also a reproduction of the one by Martha Argerich, on the Russian—or Soviet,
rather—label *Melodiya*; and of the one by Maurizio Pollini on *Deutsche Gram-
mophon*; and so on.

Of course, feigning omniscience wasn't the only thing I did as a lawyer.
I also, as you know, claimed—at my first law firm, and not on paper—to be
black. Nor was it the only thing I did back then to have later shaped my criti-
cism. Both Albertine and I, as I've said, imagined her to be Guy de Rothschild
and me to be Guy's wife—and also cousin—Marie-Hélène: fantasy escape from
reality at that firm. But other aspects of this persona—of this *role*, rather, or
rather of *both* roles—need further, well, explanation here. First of all, unlike

that of "panoptic litigator," they are decidedly gendered. As such, they are by no means independent of one another; for just as there is no such thing as "masculinity" without "femininity" or as "femininity" without "masculinity," to both name and deconstruct the basic opposition at work or rather at play here, there is no Guy without his Marie-Hélène nor Marie-Hélène without her Guy. Second of all, these gender roles got inverted: with a man playing a woman, a woman playing a man. Third of all, in an "affirmation" that if not Luce Irigaray then at least Marlene Dietrich might have appreciated, this inversion itself got flipped: with Albertine playing Guy as rather feminine and me playing Marie-Hélène—campily—as rather masculine. (Of course, most such drag involves phallic women or "viragos." They are your broad-shouldered, deep-voiced Joan Crawford types, and not, say, your Deanna Durbins. Charo-like Esperanza Jujube, though, is feminine. Or rather, she *was* feminine. I no longer play her—as at least this woman of mine had always been a solo act. No friend of mine, that is, ever played some *Señor* Jujube. Nor did one also play the woman herself.) We would pretend, for instance, that although the two are now divorced—in reality they were not—it's Marie-Hélène who had always had all the money. In reality, of course, Guy had it. Albertine's Guy, therefore, would now have to beg me for alimony. We would pretend, too, that—to Guy's not quite understandable chagrin—Marie-Hélène had been unfaithful during the marriage. (Hence their divorce.) In reality—to my pseudo-husband "Warren's" chagrin—so too had I been. We would pretend, as well, that Guy was gay—"fag-haggery," on Marie-Hélène's part, that of course explained this infidelity and also that in a just a couple of years Eve Kosofsky Sedgwick would explain. ("An excessively refluent and dangerous maelstrom of eroticism," she writes in the article and then book chapter "The Beast in the Closet," "somehow attends men in general at such moments, even otherwise boring men.") And this was all—for me—to feel a lot more powerful than I really was at work. It was also, for me, to feel both wealthier and classier than I was in life. (For Albertine, I'd imagine, it was to feel masculine. It is true, for instance, that she was the only female associate at the firm—back then—to ever wear pants there. Or to have very short hair. She's straight, by the way—as are most "fag hags." She's thin, as well.) It was also— even with that obviously Warren- and later also Matt-inspired "divorce" of ours, as well as with the deaths of the actual Marie-Hélène in 1996 and then that of her Guy in 2007—for me to feel closer, in fantasy, to some woman in general and in particular to this woman, Albertine, than as a gay man I felt I had been, in reality, to my erstwhile girlfriend "Naomi" and so for many years afterward thought I could ever really be. Both my own Marie-Hélène and Albertine's Guy still live on—non-sentimentally—for the two of us. Or rather they do, as a big part of our history together, whenever—and however—we now communicate long-distance: in phone calls, via e-mail, via regular mail.

I moved from feigned omniscience—in writing—to feigned ignorance plus omniscience—in writing—for a couple of reasons. It struck me that lines like—in my book *Love's Litany*, with reference to Roland Barthes—"Every back room habitué can get what he wants" or—in my letter to the *London Review of Books*, with reference to Edward Said—"If this literary critic knew as much about music as he pretends to, he'd know that you can't compose a quadruple fugue without writing the ending first" are not that different from ones I had found—as quoted in "My Cortez"—in college-level work. ("Every mother wants what's best for his or her son," wrote a male student of mine. "Feminists believe that women should reap what they sew" [sic], wrote a female student.) It struck me, too—when now reading such lines of mine "symptomatically," not to mention entire essays or even books of mine this way—that they're oblivious. Not every such "habitué," for instance, can get what he—or she—wants. Plus unbeknownst to itself—or rather, unbeknownst to *me* throughout the thing's composition—*Beethoven's Kiss* is really a self-help book: not so much *I'm OK - You're OK* as *I Can Play - You Can Play*. (So, too—among other things—is *this* book such a book: "Stop feeling like a *fraud*, Kevin," it says. "Or like a *failure*. Stop feeling like a *thief*, as well. Stop thinking, too, that you've *killed* other people. And don't pretend, anymore, to *be* other people." Or to quote—not sarcastically—my student Arabella on the singer "Johnny Rotten": "Grow up. Choose life. Fitter, happier, more productive.") Plus despite what I imagined throughout its composition, *The Queer Afterlife of Vaslav Nijinsky* represents not so much an identification on my part with this male dancer—with Nijinsky, that is, as opposed to Pavlova—as, because of Matt, an identification I had with the dancer's own soon-to-be not just ex- but in effect brutally dumped lover. And so I was now concerned, when reading myself or rather my old work "symptomatically," with an alter ego—with Serge Diaghilev, that is—of whom, as such—like with Proust and his Albertine—I really should have been aware when writing this thing but, being stupid or maybe just in denial at the time, was not. *I, Serge*, therefore, might have been a better title. My inspiration: *I, Tina*—by Tina Turner.

And so—in both self-mockery and self-defense—I now came to use Socratic irony. I would, that is, address readers smart enough to get that—like the character "Socrates" in Plato's *Ion* but also like many law professors of mine back at Columbia University—I myself, in print, am smarter than I'm pretending to be there. (It's called, in fact, the "Socratic Method" by such teachers. See *The Paper Chase* [1973], with John Houseman as the—fictional—Harvard Law School professor "Charles W. Kingsfield, Jr.") This is why, for instance, the "Kevin Kopelson" who narrates *Neatness Counts* takes so long to figure out— much as I myself figured it out only when finishing that thing up at Harvard— that the book is an elegy. (See "G712," on Paula Marantz Cohen—in her review for the *Times Literary Supplement*—who never ever figured it out. Perhaps she hadn't finished *reading* the book.) This is also why the narrator of my book *Sedaris* never figures out—whereas I myself knew it even when beginning to write it—that the work is also, by which I mean *primarily*, about Proust.

I was, of course, already familiar with fictional incarnations—or if not full-blooded incarnations then at least somewhat alter-ego-like approximations—of such a maneuver. All of these, in fact, are either writers or would-be writers. There is, in the novel *Middlemarch*, the character "Casaubon." "For my part," narrates the gender-flipped author "George Eliot" (*née* Mary Ann Evans) about him there, "I am very sorry for him."

> It is an uneasy lot at best, to be what we call highly taught and yet not to enjoy: to be present at this great spectacle of life and never to be liberated from a small hungry shivering self—never to be fully possessed by the glory we behold, never to have our consciousness rapturously transformed into the vividness of a thought, the ardor of a passion, the energy of an action, but always to be scholarly and uninspired, ambitious and timid, scrupulous and dim-sighted.

There is "Charles Swann," as I've mentioned, who—like Proust, more or less— can never ever finish his own life's work. It's an essay on Vermeer. There is "'Buddy' Glass," who as a narrator is more of a comedian than the author J.D. Salinger—throughout their I suppose joint composition of stuff like *Franny* and *Zooey*—knew he himself had to be, plus who as an author himself is less successful—by which I mean both rich and famous—than Salinger already was.

I was familiar, as well, with at least one *theatrical* approximation of such a maneuver: the character "Louis Ironson" in the play *Angels in America*. This guy talks even more than the playwright Tony Kushner—I'd imagine—does. But as a mere word processor, at some federal courthouse, he never really— unlike Kushner—writes anything. All he does, there, is (if not quite plagiarize judges who—truth be told—just plagiarize their law clerks) the kind of transcription that my now dead friend Bill Watson—a would-be translator—had done as a secretary.

I was also familiar—more to the point—with "autofictional," no, not just approximations of such a maneuver. (Wikipedia: "*Autofiction* is a term used in literary criticism. [It] refers to a form of fictionalized autobiography.") I was also familiar with autofictional and hence full-blooded incarnations thereof. There is, of course, the narrator possibly named Marcel who, until those other physical sensations happen to him, can't quite figure out—whereas the author Marcel Proust could—what the taste of that soggy cookie had meant. Plus—unlike Proust, unlike Swann for that matter—he might never ever even begin, as far as we know, his own life's work. It's a novel to be something like *Remembrance of Things Past*. There is also the narrator actually named "Roland Barthes" whom the author Roland Barthes tells us, in an epigraph to *Roland Barthes by Roland Barthes*, to consider "a character in a novel." (*Tout ceci doit être considéré comme dit par un personnage de roman.*) "Roland Barthes," moreover, never seems to realize just how depressed or at least pessimistic the two of them— both Barthes and "Barthes"—are. There is also the narrator named "David Leavitt." But since the author David Leavitt, as you know from "G712," thought or at least acted like the "commitment ceremony" that Warren and I had was about Leavitt himself, primarily, I'd say the two of them—both Leavitt and "Leavitt"—deserve nearly an entire paragraph to themselves. Or rather, a *satirical* paragraph. As satire, though, it'll be if not quite mean then at least far more pessimistic—or maybe cynical—than what my most recent role model, David Sedaris, does—in his confessional satire—with characters other than himself. Or at least with most such characters. His father Lou, for instance, is an exception to this rule. And so let me just add, at the end of this paragraph, that there is also the narrator—of what other critics call "creative nonfiction" more so than "autofiction" or even just "confessional satire"—named "David Sedaris." But I have already—in my book *Sedaris*—said everything I have to say about the two of them: both Sedaris and "Sedaris." Unless, of course—as promised or perhaps threatened by him—the first of these will now write *only* fables.

Plagiarism, it seems, can run in couples. Not, of course, that I'm accusing anyone connected to *me* of this. I'm accusing, first of all, David Leavitt's necking partner at that commitment ceremony, a man who—to a mutual friend's chagrin—transcribed much of his first and only novel, called let's say *Years Ago*, from ostensibly private conversations that he had had with her. (The novel, thus plagiarized from those conversations, was published in the year 1987—or the same one during which both the autobiography *I, Tina* by Tina Turner and the essay "Is the Rectum a Grave?" by Leo Bersani first came out.) I know this, as you might have guessed, from my own such conversations with the woman. Leavitt then—"allegedly," to quote the comedian Kathy Griffin—took much of one of his own novels, called *While England Sleeps* (1993), from the auto-biography *World within World* (1951) by Stephen Spender. This both "outed" and irritated Spender. ("I don't see why [Leavitt] should unload all his sexual fantasies onto me in my youth," the by then quite elderly man complained. "If he wanted to write about his sexual fantasies, he should write about them as being his, not mine.") Spender now sued, with the matter quickly settled out of court. Leavitt then wrote a novella, called *The Term Paper Artist* (1997). It's about and yet also narrated by a writer—named "David Leavitt"—who has just done something not quite identical to this. Like "Buddy" Glass in relation to J.D. Salinger, though, "Leavitt" is less successful—as an author—than the author by that name. Unlike both "Sedaris" and Sedaris, though, he's no less scru-pulous than Leavitt. Or rather, he's no more *un*scrupulous. "I was in trouble," the man begins by admitting and yet minimizing the theft of Spender's work. "An English poet (now dead) had sued me over a novel I had written because it was based in part on an episode from his life." To nonetheless atone for that transgression, "Leavitt" must now write or rather *ghost*write papers for—and in exchange for sex with—his own students. (Ghostwriting, like forgery, is the flipside of plagiarism: instead of wrongly claiming, "I did this," it wrongly claims that someone else did.) They are at UCLA. And yet what neither "David Leavitt" here nor the author David Leavitt anywhere admits is that the idea for such an exchange—plus a lot of the work's dialogue—was taken by them from a gay porn video, and later DVD, that first came out in the year 1991: Falcon Stu-dios' *Score 10*. (It "stars," among others, both "Ryan Idol" and "Dcota." "Idol's" real name is: Marc Anthony Donais. But if your name is *Donais*, shouldn't your porn name—anagrammatically—be *Adonis*?) I know this, as you might have guessed, from having once watched the thing. Or twice. Or—well, you get the picture. "Not that there's anything wrong with that," to quote the sitcom *Sein-feld*'s "Jerry Seinfeld" on anyone—or rather, on anyone else—being gay. I know it, too, from having read "The 'Imitation David': Plagiarism, Collaboration, and the Making of a Gay Literary Tradition in David Leavitt's 'The Term Paper Artist.'" It's an article that I just happened to review—in manuscript—for the scholarly journal called *PMLA*. I then, one must confess, told the editors there to publish the thing. And they did.

David Leavitt, the author, is no longer with the plagiarist of *Years Ago*. And
yet his current partner, a would-be pianist and also writer named Mark Mitch-
ell, isn't—either personally or professionally—much of an improvement. Not
that I ever met the guy. Nor could I ever finish reading his book called *Virtuosi:
A Defense and (Sometimes Erotic) Celebration of Great Pianists* and published
in the year 2000 by Indiana University Press. ("Wayne Koestenbaum's *The
Queen's Throat* and Kevin Kopelson's *Beethoven's Kiss*," sneers Mitchell there
early on, "are not so much about music as about their author's obsessions: in
the first case with divas, in the second with Wayne Koestenbaum.") For not
only was Mitchell quite mean to the brother, whom he'd just brutally dumped,
of another friend of mine—I know this, as you might have guessed, from con-
versations with that friend—he also later claimed to have both researched and
written his next book—called *Vladimir de Pachmann: A Piano Virtuoso's Life
and Art* and published in 2002 by Indiana—in just under six months. This,
turns out, was—allegedly—a lie. But it's one not because Mitchell—naturally
enough—took a bit longer to do such work. It was a lie because, to "write" the
book, he took—or rather, stole—work-in-progress done over a period of fifty
years by some by then quite elderly—and also reclusive—biographer named
Kuznetsov and then without the poor man's permission merely redacted it. (To
compare this redaction with that work-in-progress, see the website of the Inter-
national Piano Archives.) Oops. Not "Kuznetsov." I meant to say, Edward Blick-
stein. (It was Anatoly Kuznetsov—and not that plagiarist D.M. Thomas—who
wrote the "documentary novel"—first published in 1966—called *Babi Yar*. The
life—if not the art—of Vladimir Pachmann had previously inspired a fictional
story—called "Bachmann"—by Vladimir Nabokov. This story, like the novel
Babi Yar, was originally in Russian. And it was first published by Nabokov—
in 1924, in Berlin, and in a Russian émigré paper called *Rul* that had been
founded by his father—under the *nom-de-plume* "V. Sirin." Both Vladimir and
his son Dmitri later translated the thing into English.) This, of course, irritated
Blickstein, who unlike "Leavitt" had—I'd imagine—no need let alone desire to
ghostwrite anything. Plus—I'd also imagine—who never even got sex out of the
deal. Blickstein now sued both Mitchell and Mitchell's publisher, Indiana Uni-
versity Press, with the latter quickly withdrawing the book from circulation. But
then, in the year 2005, the very same press published—and even I find this hard
to believe—Mitchell's next book. It's called *Moriz Rosenthal in Word and Mu-
sic*. (Like Vladimir Pachmann, Moritz Rosenthal was a piano virtuoso. Plus he
taught the instrument—to among other students Charles Rosen.) And then, the

following year, Mitchell got—something I do not find hard to believe—a Guggenheim Fellowship. It pays, I guess, to sleep with either "Leavitt" or Leavitt: with the one—if you're a college boy—you get term papers; with the other—if you're a plagiarist—you get both book contracts and awards.

I was also familiar with non-autofictional, well, let's just say incarnations of at least one wish fulfillment that David Leavitt's creation of "David Leavitt," in *The Term Paper Artist*, must have—quite fleetingly—achieved for him. The wish itself is erotic—as Leavitt, there, seems to imagine he looks like "Dcota" and so could seduce someone like "Ryan Idol." The incarnations, as with Casaubon, Swann, "Buddy" Glass, and Louis Ironson, are either fictional or theatrical. Like "Leavitt," moreover, but unlike Proust's Albertine, each such incarnation—I thought—involves *conscious*, which is also to say deliberate, identification by the author. Each, that is, involves an alter ego of whom—as such—he must have been aware. Each, in fact, involves a male author's *female* alter ego. For unlike "Leavitt" and even Casaubon—and yet like both my Marie-Hélène de Rothschild and Esperanza Jujube—each also involves male-to-female inversion. As such—unlike "Leavitt" and Casaubon but like Marie-Hélène and Esperanza— each enabled my move from "confessional writing *tout court*" to confessional satire. Sedaris, of course, has done this too—but without any such drag. (Well, that's not true exactly. There is, as you'll soon see, or have already discovered in my book *Sedaris*, at least *some* drag in the man's work. Or rather, some *closeted* drag there.) Plus unlike Sedaris and even Leavitt, each also enabled me to write—finally—about sex. Or rather, about both sexual "fantasy"—to quote Stephen Spender—and sexual conduct. Plus one of them "herself" writes books. Or at least wrote the one book.

The first of these incarnations—also the one "writer" among them—is that mid-eighteenth-century whore "Fanny Hill." "Fanny," as the ostensible author and also "autodiegetic" narrator of *Memoirs of a Woman of Pleasure*, is, as you know from "Kiss and Tell," both mask and mouthpiece for what both gay and later "queer" critics, perhaps unloading our own fantasies onto him as there's no corroborating evidence, infer to have been the actual author John Cleland's otherwise closeted, no, not *homosexuality*. (In "autodiegetic" fiction, the narrator is also not just some relatively minor character but the protagonist. *Remembrance of Things Past*, then, is both autofictional and autodiegetic. So, too—if you believe its epigraph—is *Roland Barthes by Roland Barthes*. So, too, is *The Term Paper Artist*.) She is both mask and mouthpiece for what we infer to have been the man's otherwise closeted *proto*-homosexuality:

Slipping then aside the young lad's shirt, and tucking it up under his clothes be-
hind, he showed to the open air, those globular, fleshy eminences that compose
the mount-pleasants of Rome, and which now, with all the narrow vale that in-
tersects them, stood displayed, and exposed to his attack: nor could I, without a
shudder, behold the dispositions he made for it. First then, moistening well with
spittle his instrument, obviously to render it glib, he pointed, he introduced it, as
I could plainly discern, not only from its direction, and my losing sight of it; but
by the writhing, twisting, and soft murmured complaints of the young sufferer;
but, at length, the first straits of entrance being pretty well got through, every-
thing seemed to move, and go pretty currently on, as in a carpet-road, without
much rub, or resistance: and now passing one hand round his minion's hips, he
got hold of his red-topped ivory toy, that stood perfectly stiff, and showed, that
if he was like his mother behind, he was like his father before; this he diverted
himself with, whilst with the other, he wantoned with his hair, and leaning for-
wards over his back, drew his face, from which the boy shook the loose curls that
fell over it, in the posture he stood him in, and brought him towards his, so as
to receive a long-breathed kiss, after which, renewing his driving, and thus con-
tinuing to harass his rear, the height of the fit came on with its usual symptoms,
and dismissed the action.

"Homosexuality" per se, they say, had not yet been "discursively constructed."

The second of these incarnations is that late-nineteenth-century princess
"Salome." "Salome," as the eponymous heroine of a play written beautifully in
French by Oscar Wilde but then very badly translated into English by his own
soon-to-be ex-lover, Lord Alfred Douglas, or "Bosie," to use the nickname the
man's mother first gave him, is both mask and mouthpiece for what we critics
know, in fact, and from external evidence, to have been both Wilde's and Doug-
las' otherwise closeted "inversion"—as homosexuality back then was for the
most part still called. (Wilde's urge to write actual pornography—and yet while
using no such mask—is corroborated by his at least editorial involvement with
the novel *Teleny*. It was Douglas, of course, who dumped Wilde. And the nick-
name "Bosie," it seems, was short for "Boysie.") She is mask and mouthpiece,
that is, for both Wilde's and Douglas' either self-destructive or self-attractive
desire for men like the play *Salome*'s John the Baptist: with Douglas, given his
narcissistic as well as borderline personality, this desire was *self*-attractive; with
Wilde, it was self-*destructive*. (The play's Herod, after all, has Salome killed—
whereas the Bible's Herod, as I've already said, does not. And so Wilde, more

like me with Diaghilev in the Nijinsky book than like Proust with Albertine, must have had an unconscious identification with the man. Douglas, in turn, might have had one with John the Baptist—or to use the name Wilde had used, "Jokanaan.") To quote a new—and I'd imagine excellent—translation by Richard Howard, who had also done *Roland Barthes by Roland Barthes*:

> SALOME: Ah, John, John, you were the only man I ever loved. All the others disgusted me. But you . . . you were beautiful. Your body was a column of ivory on a silver pedestal. No, it was a garden filled with doves and silver lilies. No, it was a silver tower set with ivory shields. Nothing in the world was so black as your hair. In all the world there was nothing so red as your mouth. Your voice was a censer scattering strange perfumes, and when I looked at you I heard strange music! Ah, why didn't you look at me, John? You hid your face behind your hands and your blasphemies. You covered your eyes with the blinders of a man who wants to see God, John, but me, me . . . you never saw me. If you saw me, you'd have loved me. I saw you, John, and I loved you. Oh, how I loved you. I love you still, John. I love only you . . . I'm thirsty for your beauty. I'm hungry for your body. And no wine, no fruit can satisfy my desire.

The same passage as not just rendered but—I'd imagine—ruined by Douglas had been:

> Ah, Jokanaan, Jokanaan, thou wert the only man that I have loved. All other men are hateful to me. But thou, thou wert beautiful! Thy body was a column of ivory set on a silver socket. It was garden full of doves and of silver lilies. It was a tower of silver decked with shields of ivory. There was nothing in the world so white as thy body. There was nothing in the world so black as thy hair. In the whole world there was nothing so red as thy mouth. Thy voice was a censer that scattered strange perfumes, and when I looked on thee I heard a strange music. Ah! wherefore didst thou not look at me, Jokanaan? Behind thine hands and thy curses thou didst hide thy face. Thou didst put upon thine eyes the covering of him who would see his God. Well, thou hast seen thy God, Jokanaan, but me, me, thou didst never see. If thou hadst seen me thou wouldst have loved me. I, I saw thee, Jokanaan, and I loved thee. Oh, how I loved thee! I loved thee yet, Jokanaan, I love thee only . . . I am athirst for thy beauty; I am hungry for thy body; and neither wine nor fruits can appease my desire.

That's just "a lavender version of the King James Bible," to quote Howard, "an English both elaborate and archaic." Whereas the passage by Wilde—in French—had been:

> Ah! Iokanaan, Iokanaan, tu as été le seul homme que j'aie aimé.
> Tous les autres hommes m'inspirent du dégoût.
>   Mais, toi, tu étais beau.
> Ton corps était une colonne d'ivoire sur un socle d'argent.
>   C'était un jardin plein de colombes et de lis d'argent.
>   C'était une tour d'argent ornée de boucliers d'ivoire.
> Il n'y avait rien au monde d'aussi blanc que ton corps.
> Il n'y avait rien au monde d'aussi noir que tes cheveux.
> Dans le monde tout entier il n'y avait rien d'aussi rouge que ta bouche.
> Ta voix était un encensoir qui répandait d'étranges parfums, et quand je te
>   regardais j'entendais une musique étrange!
> Ah! pourquoi ne m'as-tu pas regardée, Iokanaan?
>   Derrière tes mains et tes blasphèmes tu as caché ton visage.
>   Tu as mis sur tes yeux le bandeau de celui qui veut voir son Dieu.
>   Eh bien, tu l'as vu, ton Dieu, Iokanaan, mais moi, moi . . . tu ne m'as
>   jamais vue.
>
> Si tu m'avais vue, tu m'aurais aimée.
>   Moi, je t'ai vue, Iokanaan, et je t'ai aimé.
>   Oh! comme je t'ai aimé.
>   Je t'aime encore, Iokanaan.
>   Je n'aime que toi . . .
>   J'ai soif de ta beauté.
>   J'ai faim de ton corps.
>   Et ni le vin, ni les fruits ne peuvent apaiser mon désir.

That's "of an almost Beckett-like simplicity," to continue quoting Howard, "its lyricism intense rather than intricate, its perversity authentic rather than archaic."

The other such incarnations are early twentieth-century characters by that would-be Oscar Wilde, Ronald Firbank. And these include not just his "Countess of Tolga"—with "her *tortured-animal* look"—in *The Flower beneath the Foot* but also his "Princess Mary"—whom Firbank himself saw as a would-be "Salome"—in the novel called *The Artificial Princess*.

| | |

So that's what enabled my move to satire—or rather, to *confessional* satire. What inspired it, in general, was my having become more and more—to quote both Oscar Wilde and Richard Howard in *Salome*—"disgusted" by academic culture. I became disgusted by—to invoke Samuel Johnson—either vicious or foolish conduct. I became disgusted by people, such as either Mark Mitchell or—to be honest—myself, stealing other people's work. I became disgusted by people, such as either Paula Marantz Cohen or—to be honest—myself, trashing other people's work. Or rather, I became disgusted by our doing so for—primarily—personal reasons. I became disgusted, as well, by people doing their own work and yet doing it horribly—by which, in at least some cases, I mean just lazily. I became disgusted, too, by such people then getting promoted for mainly political reasons. I became disgusted, too, by people such as either Emmeline Grangerford or Stalin causing pain to either graduate students or mentees. You can only take—or see other people take—just so much of this, well, shit, before you have to stop either saying or writing, in confessional mode, "shame on *me*" and now write "shame on *you*, as well." (Confession's Way and Satire's Way, then, like those of either Swann and the Guermantes or Dragnet and Scavone, are also really—if only in *this* way—the same Way. They are both, as I've just implied: Ways of Shame. Those of Plagiarism and Forgery, once again, are Ways of Fraudulent Attribution.) You have to now write, that is: "Shame on *you*, as well, you so-called scholars. Shame, as well, on you *administrators*. On those administrators here, for instance, at the University of Iowa, who must have said—to one another—about our undergraduate students: "They've got to major in something—and they *speak* English." And who, along with every other tenured member of my department here, agreed to tenure Carol. And yet who, along with that "someone in 'exercise science,'" did not agree—after the first publication of "My Cortez"—to fire me. They all knew, I'm now sure, that—as an erstwhile litigator—I'd sue them if they had. (When just a few months ago as of this writing—on January 22, 2010—the Italian magazine *Internazionale* reprinted the essay of mine that I'd called "My Cortez," they instead used the title "L'uomo che citava troppo." This means: "The Man Who Quotes Too Much." Google, though—via an automatic translator—renders it: "The Man Who Sued, Too.") Or perhaps those administrators were being kind—to me. Or perhaps, unlike that exercise woman, they were wise.

And so that's what I did, but only—initially—in *limerick* form. I would now write, that is, ones like:

A gallic mentality reigns
When gaggles of *soi-disant* "brains"
   Assemble to brood
   On subjects as crude
As: "Haussmann: Lord of the Drains."

And then I'd circulate the things—in private—among friends. Too *mean*, I thought at the time, to publish anywhere. Not to mention too *obscure*. This one, for instance, is on the Nineteenth-Century French Studies Conference—held in the year 2000—at which I first met Elisabeth Ladenson and hit it off with her. It is also on Baron Haussmann, *Préfet de la Seine* during the Second Empire, who initiated and organized the urban redevelopment—including the sewers—of Paris.

| | |

The conference—hosted by Yale University in the year 1989 and so not on queer, yet, but rather on "lesbian and gay" studies—at which I first met and hit it off with Wayne Koestenbaum was also, as you know, where D.A. Miller wouldn't give me the time of day. This, I recently realized, may have had as much to do with Miller's own soon-to-be not just ex- but dumped lover being there too as with my not being the man's—by which I mean Miller's—type. At any rate, we two—that lover and I—now met and hit it off as well. I'd even develop—one must confess—a crush on him. He looked, I only now realize, a lot like my husband David. Plus like David, he was very sexy, very funny, and very bright.

Of course, I loved more about "Michel"—as I'll call him—than just his looks or humor or even intelligence. He was, at that point, still a graduate student in French—although not one at the University of California, Berkeley, where Miller taught. (Miller later went to Harvard. Now, though, he's back at Berkeley.) I myself, as you know, was still a graduate student in English. Michel's French, I'd been told, was "impeccable." (Seductively so, I felt.) So, too—I found—was his sense of camp. And that's why when, not long after this conference, we were both invited to a costume party—hosted by other academics—I devised drag personas for us to "deploy" at it. *Scholarly* such personas. I would now pretend to be, that is, not either Marie-Hélène de Rothschild or

Esperanza Jujube but—anagrammatically—"Aviral Tonell." She, I claimed, is the somewhat crazed, perhaps evil twin of Avital Ronell. Ronell, in reality, had just published an all too theoretical and therefore unreadable tome—called *The Telephone Book: Technology, Schizophrenia, Electric Speech* (1989)—which as far as I could tell was really on Heidegger. (Wayne, though, says he understood that book. And Ronell, too, taught at Berkeley.) My *shtik*, then, as "Tonell," was to complain to anyone at this party who would listen that Ronell, therein, had stolen and then taken credit for something that at first was *my* idea: "the dial tone as *a*tonal." What this idea meant, of course, I couldn't explain. It just sounded to me—in parody form—like the kind of cultural studies then most popular. It sounded silly.

Michel would now pretend to be "Mireille Dujardin." It's a last name I took from the—little known fact—actual creator of "stream-of-consciousness" technique: not the Irish novelist James Joyce, as most people believe, but a French one named Édouard Dujardin. The first name, "Mireille," I took from "French in Action." That's a by now quite famous language-acquisition course that had been devised—for Yale—by a professor there named Pierre Capretz. I, as a student there, took three years of the class—but to pretty much no avail. David Sedaris, elsewhere, took what sounds an awful lot like it:

> Before leaving New York, I enrolled in a month-long French class taught by a beautiful young Parisian woman who had us memorize a series of dialogues from an audiocassette that accompanied our textbook. Because it was a beginning course, the characters on our tape generally steered clear of slang and controversy. Avoiding both the past and the future, they embraced the moment with a stoicism common to Buddhists and recently recovered alcoholics. Fabienne, Carmen, and Eric spent a great deal of time in outdoor restaurants, discussing their love of life and enjoying colas served without ice. Passing acquaintances were introduced at regular intervals, and it was often noted that the sky was blue.

Mireille Dujardin, I explained to Michel, was—not unlike Luce Irigaray—a fully crazed feminist, which apart from the woman actually being French is all I knew about her at the time. This gave Michel the idea—which of course I loved—of wearing nothing but a bath towel to the party, plus another, smaller towel on his head, plus some rhinestone earrings he just happened to have. As Tonell, I wore both a mini-skirt, borrowed from my friend and also fellow party guest Geeta Patel, and sunglasses—while of course holding a telephone book. The towels suggested, to Michel, a *shtik* of his own: he, as Mireille, would say that she has just reclaimed—in writing—"the bathroom as a site of liminal desire." But what that idea meant, of course, he couldn't explain. It just sounded to him—in parody form—like the kind of what is now called *"sexuality* studies" then most popular. It sounded silly. Turns out both Michel and Mireille were ahead of their time. New York University, where Avital Ronell now teaches, now offers its undergraduates a course—taught by a "Harvey Molotch"—on *The Urban Toilet*. Molotch's syllabus, in part, reads:

Week 3: Intimate Pollution (Contemporary)
Jo-Anne Bichard, Julienne Hanson, and Clara Greed. "Please Wash Your Hands." In *The Senses and Society*.

Week 7: Race, Class, and Gender
Barbara Penner. "A World of Unmentionable Suffering: Women's Public Conveniences in Victorian London." In *Journal of Design History*.
Mitchell Duneier. "When You Gotta Go." In *Sidewalk*.

Week 8: Sexual Spaces
Lee Edelman. "Men's Room." In *Stud: Architectures of Masculinity*.

Not long after this party—where at least Geeta says we were "quite the hit"—both Wayne and I went to a performance—at Yale—by a group called "The V-Girls." (Wayne taught there back then. He now teaches—as did Eve Kosofsky Sedgwick up until her death—at City University of New York, Graduate Center.) These were five graduate students—all of them female—who had devised *non*-drag, "autofictional" personas not otherwise unlike my Tonell. (The "V," it seems, was meant to be the roman numeral for five.) For what the "girls" or rather young *women* did—*as* women—was parody a kind of panel discussion that you'll still find at cultural studies conferences as well as parody the kind of discourse that a Ronell or even an Irigaray—in both speech and writing, or by rhapsodizing some "talk" they've already composed—might deploy on it. The script for this performance has never—alas—been published. But a later alleged "conversation" by the "girls"—with the scholarly journal called *October*—gives a good idea of the not just intelligence but brilliance and also humor that it involved:

MARTHA BAER: I'm sorry. Before we begin, if we could just sit . . .

ERIN CRAMER: Oh, yes, like this . . .

BAER: Yes, longways. That's much better. I'm sorry, you see, we
               prefer to sit longways. Over the years, having participated
               in, or shall we say, frankly, simulated, or more frankly re-
               ally, concocted, trumped up, a number of panel discus-
               sions, we've found that the panel format, as you see here,
               as you trace the sweeping, authoritative gesture of my
               hand with your eyes—the panel format is an ideal one for
               our speech as a group.

OCTOBER: As a group you've done considerable research and writing
               about the academic panel discussion.

BAER: Marianne, for one, has written extensively on the history
               and uses of the panel format. I believe it was she who
               wrote—correct me if I'm wrong—that "the term *panel dis-
               cussion* first appeared in 1938, only one year after the de-
               velopment of the panel truck but lagging ten years behind
               the invention of panel heating." Jessica? Andrea? Are you
               comfortable down there?

JESSICA CHALMERS: Yes.

ANDREA FRASER: Lovely.

BAER: I myself, incidentally, have written on the subject of the
               structure and value of the panel. In a paper entitled "Miss-
               ing Floorboards: Surfacing Panels in Nineteenth-Century
               Children's Literature," I called the panel discussion, if I
               remember correctly, "the scene in which dialogue and
               pedagogue are one." I think that's quite apt, don't you?

OCTOBER: That was in your panel on Johanna Spyri's *Heidi*, "Aca-
               demia in the Alps: In Search of the Swiss Mis(s)."

BAER: Right. Later, in our panel "The Question of Manet's
               Olympia: Posed and Skirted," I wrote, "The panel is an
               ideal pedagogical vehicle, which effectively counters the
               usual signifiers of individual expertise and demands a
               long table."

MARIANNE WEEMS: You see, we're most comfortable along this side of the ta-
               ble, comfortable theoretically that is, or comfortable with
               theory, talking about it. Positioned here, we are at once

commissioned to speak, to be heard, we are *specified* as speakers, and yet we are generalized as a group, a group of speakers all with the same status, the same location, the same orientations or frontage, if you will, the same color hair . . .

CHALMERS: Right, Marianne, although I might point out at this point, this juncture, we are not at present sitting on a panel, but rather are being interviewed.

ALL: Ahaaa.

BAER: And why not then consider for a moment, not the panel, which takes place elsewhere, but this interview itself—its precedents, for example, its expectations or requirements, its, can we say, more directly, *desire*, its historicity, and perhaps, to begin with its existence or ontology, or better, its taxonomy, that is to say its positivity, its mutability (?), in short, its legibility or legibilities, that which despite all its invisibility, makes it possible.

ALL: Yes.

OCTOBER: Right.

BAER: Historically, we have been interviewed quite regularly over the years. In the seventies, for example, we were interviewed twice by a remarkable little New York journal, *Too Many Paroles*, which has since folded. That was a biannual, I believe, modeled after the famous German review of the fifties, *Culture, Knowledge, Capitalism, Order, Art, and Spontaneity*. That magazine, if I am not becoming confused, had, instead of page numbers, different words in the upper right-hand corner of each page, yes. A few years back, we were interviewed in a magazine that had a similar format.

FRASER: In fact it was called *Format*. Or was it *Schema*?

CHALMERS: *Topos*?

BAER: In any case, in any case, I think what we've come to here, after rethinking our history as subjects of such a range of

interviews, is that we *like* the format of *October*, the odd
size, the breadth, the clarity. In general, I think I speak for
all of us when I say that we feel, we feel, we feel . . .

WEEMS: . . . pleased . . .

BAER: . . . yes, we feel pleased to be here. Now, as you were
saying.

As you can see, it's hard for me when quoting or rather *transcribing* this to stop.

| | |

While becoming "disgusted"—ethically—by even other scholars within aca-
demia plus administrators here behaving badly, I had also become if not dis-
gusted by then disenchanted—intellectually—with my own specialty. For
where the V-Girls' disenchantment—call it "Tonell Vision"—had seemed to
me to be with *cultural* studies, mine—or "Dujardin Fatigue"—was with, as it
was now called, "queer" studies. And then it was with, as I've said, "sexuality
studies." This began, I think, upon the publication—in the year 1997—of my
book on Nijinsky. I had now pretty much said—or written—everything I ever
thought about *male* queerness. And then other current work, except for that of
Sedgwick, Koestenbaum, Edelman (even including his "Men's Room" article),
Ladenson, and, yes, D.A. Miller, seemed to me to be either beyond silly and just
ridiculous or beyond ridiculous and just—like Carol's *Sassy*—horrible. (The
thesis there, as you might recall, is that Sarah Vaughan's "operatic" voice made
race, gender, sexuality, and above all class indeterminate.) Such work, that is,
either treats trivial subject matter, and or it makes very stupid arguments, and
or—like Ronell's work, or like "Bosie's" for that matter—it is very badly written,
and or—like my own work—it is too close to being either Sedgwick or Barthes,
and or it's too close to being or if not being then impersonating Judith Butler.
Plus political claims made, as in Butler's book *Gender Trouble: Feminism and
the Subversion of Identity*, seem deluded: as if analyzing television shows—even
campy ones like *Batman* or *Pee-wee's Playhouse*, in an article actually called
"Pee-wee Hermeneutics"—could ever disturb, outside of the campus, what we
now, citing Butler, began calling, no, not homophobia. We began calling it
"heteronormativity."

    To express this disenchantment, or rather to *vent*, I now began writing and
also showing friends—but still wouldn't publish—such limericks as:

"Helping her cousin on wheels
Broker a couple of deals
  Made the first lady
  A little tribade-y,"
Eleanor chronicler squeals.

Crippled Franklin and his wife Eleanor Roosevelt were fifth cousins, once re-
moved. The "chronicler" here is Blanche Wiesen Cook, a historian generally
believed to have "outed" the latter in a multi-volume biography. (*Tribade*, a
French term derived from the Greek *tribas* and *tribein* [to rub], is a by-now
quaint word for "lesbian.") In fact, though, Cook doesn't say for sure there that
Eleanor's close friendships with two lesbian couples and also with a mannish,
possibly purple-hued journalist named Lorena Hickok—nicknamed "Hick"—
were sexual. What she says—or writes, rather—is that the these friendships "em-
braced amorosity."

Or I'd write such limericks—which you've already seen in "Kiss and Tell"—as:

A power-crazed prof who knew Greek,
Apparently phallicly weak,
  Told an old Brahman
  With insight uncommon:
"I can't make my subaltern shriek."

This "prof," once again, is Michel Foucault; the "Brahman," Gayatri Spivak—
who actually coined that phrase "strategic essentialism." Plus she's the author of
the article, or maybe it's an essay, called "Can the Subaltern Speak?" Spivak's
answer there, to this question, is "no." And it was the V-Girls—one must con-
fess—from whom I stole that punch line. One of them, at Yale, had asked of the
novel *Heidi*'s protagonist: "Can the subaltern shriek?"

  I also began telling friends—just for fun, plus as an *obvious* joke—that my next
books, after the one on, well, Serge Diaghilev, would be: *Henry James and the
Rectal Sublime, Notes on Siegfried and Roy*, and—my own personal favorite—
Lesbian Lacemakers of the Middle Ages. All of these, to us, sounded—in parody
form—like "queer studies" work then most popular. Ridiculous work. *Horrible*
work. But what I most liked about the last of these in particular was the obvi-
ous *anachronism*. For not only were there no "lesbians" per se—as discursively
constructed—back then, in the Middle Ages, there weren't even any lacemakers.

| | |

I first met Carolyn Fay, a friend who's now an ex-academic, about a decade ago. As yet another graduate student in French, at the University of Virginia—a mentee there, as it happens, of my then soon-to-be friend Elisabeth Ladenson—auburn-haired and emerald-eyed Carolyn was working, for her dissertation, on nineteenth-century representations of sleep. (Elisabeth, now, teaches at Columbia University.) I, supposedly, was working on Proust. And both of us, for that entire fall semester, were doing so—while on sabbatical, for me—at the Camargo Foundation in Cassis, France. ("Camargo," like the sperm bank name "IDANT," is a nonsense word.) Carolyn, after such work, would tell me about her then lover and now husband nicknamed—monogrammatically— "AC" and also about their cat named "Camus." I'd tell Carolyn about Matt, my by then ex-lover, and also about "Razi," my then would-be husband, and also about Carol, my nowadays former colleague, and also about Mireille Dujardin. Carolyn, she said, just *loved* Mireille, or rather the idea of her, and so the two of us—much like Albertine and me back at the law firm—began fleshing out her background. Or rather, fleshing out now auburn-haired and *blue*-eyed Mireille's background. Or rather, fleshing out Mireille's background—like that of Esperanza Jujube—alone. Because Mireille, unlike pre-divorce Marie-Hélène de Rothschild, was single. In fact, we decided, she had never been married. In fact, she had never even dated anyone. And so it began to be very unclear, to me, whether the woman—along with or possibly instead of Aviral Tonell—was now my own alter ego, as well as that of Michel, or whether she was also Carolyn's.

Mireille's father, at any rate, had—we decided—been a butcher in Fontainebleau. (That's the town, near Paris, where the composer Ned Rorem and others had studied with Nadia Boulanger.) As such, he was rather dimwitted—maybe even retarded. Her mother, a very bright woman, worked with the poor man and was quite the cook at home—where needless to say she also, said Carolyn, "ruled the roost." (My own mother's cooking, as you know from "Bright One," was very bad.) And so we had young Mireille surrounded by the—for her—rather disgusting sight of meat, to avoid which she'd often go— said Carolyn—to the local public library. For college and then also graduate school, Mireille went to Paris. Here, I myself said, she studied with Roland Barthes and also fell head over heels in love with another—but male—student of his named, of course, "Guy." (I had that proto-queer theorist named Guy Hocquenghem in mind—and not Guy de Rothschild. I had Matt in mind

too.) She even confessed as much to, no, not Guy. She confessed as much
to Barthes. He, in turn, outed student Guy—who at any rate, said Barthes to
Dujardin, "is involved with someone else." (Barthes did not, though, confess
to her that—as was in fact the case—he too was in love with the boy.) She, in
turn, became very depressed. She may even—like me, after being dumped by
Matt—have sung to herself:

> It's the old story,
> and it's always new;
> and the one who [he] turns aside,
> [he] breaks [her] heart in two.

Or to quote the original German—lines by Heine that were then set by
Schumann in *Dichterliebe*:

> *Es ist eine alte Geschichte,*
> *doch bleibt sie immer neu;*
> *und wem sie just passieret,*
> *dem bricht das Herz entzwei.*

Except that Mireille, I thought, would have sung this in French.

And yet a few months later, said Carolyn—*eureka*! Mireille now fell head
over heals in love with, no, not Luce Irigaray. She now fell for *work* by the
Belgian feminist. For stuff, that is, like this stuff on—supposedly—fluid
mechanics:

> It is already getting around—at what rate? in what contexts? in spite of what
> resistances?—that women diffuse themselves according to modalities scarcely
> compatible with the framework of the ruling symbolics. Which doesn't hap-
> pen without causing some turbulence, we might even say some whirlwinds, that
> ought to be reconfined within solid walls of principle, to keep them from spread-
> ing to infinity. Otherwise, they might even go so far as to disturb that third
> agency designated as the real—a transgression and confusion of boundaries that
> it is important to restore to their proper order.
>
> So we shall have to turn back to "science" in order to ask it some questions.
> Ask, for example, about its *historical lag in elaborating a "theory" of fluids*, and
> about the ensuing aporia even in mathematical formalization. A postponed
> reckoning that was eventually to be imputed to the real.

Now, if we examine the properties of fluids, we note that this "real" may well include, and in large measure, *a physical reality* that continues to resist adequate symbolization and/or that signifies the powerlessness of logic to incorporate in its writing all the characteristic features of nature. And it has often been found necessary to minimize certain of these features of nature, to envisage them, and it, only in light of an ideal status, so as to keep it/them from jamming the works of the theoretical machine.

But what division is being perpetuated here between a language that is always subject to the postulates of ideality and an empirics that has forfeited all symbolization? And how can we fail to recognize that with respect to this caesura, to the schism that underwrites the purity of logic, language remains necessarily meta-"something"? Not simply in its articulation, in its utterance, here and now, by a subject, but because, owing to his own structure and unbeknownst to him, that "subject" is already repeating normative "judgments" on a nature that is resistant to such a transcription.

And how are we to prevent the very unconscious (of the) "subject" from being prorogated as such, indeed diminished in its interpretation, by a systematics that remarks a historical "inattention" to fluids? In other words, what structuration of (the) language does not maintain a *complicity of long standing between rationality and a mechanics of solids alone*? (Emphasis original.)

Such nonsense, for some reason, both enabled and inspired Mireille to—just like that—emerge from her depression. It also, for some reason, caused her to now consider herself—like Irigaray, in real life—a lesbian, or *tribade*, plus to decide to write her own dissertation on—of course—the *bathroom*. That dissertation became—when published—a book, called *Jeux d'eau*, that made her the kind of Koestenbaum-like, Sedgwick-like, and maybe even Sedaris-like celebrity that I myself—if not Carolyn—still wanted to be at the time. *Jeux d'eau*, by the way, is also a piano piece by Ravel. Mireille's *Jeux d'eau*, at any rate, generated an even more successful but also more focused book by her—on the *bidet*. It is called, of course—in English translation—*Irigaration*. But then—my having also told Carolyn about *Henry James and the Rectal Sublime*, *Notes on Siegfried and Roy*, and so on—events conspired to generate a third, ultimately incomplete, and hence Proust-like project.

The events, Carolyn and I decided, were as follows: (1) Mireille, while visiting her parents in Fontainebleau, reads the novel *Dentellière d'Alençon* by Janine Montupet—it's a blockbuster from the year 1984; (2) Mireille, on holiday after that in Venice, has what she calls an "erotic vision" in some of course non-medieval lace museum—it's on the island Burano; (3) Mireille, later on vacation in Boston, comes across an Adrienne Rich interview—in French translation—where the poet with reference to "lesbian historiography" states:

> We need a lot more documentation about what actually happened: I think we can also imagine it, because we know it happened—we know it out of our lives.

The third project, then, is *Lesbian Lacemakers of the Middle Ages* (*Les Dentellières lesbiennes au moyen-âge*)—also known, to us, as *Tit for Tat*. Mireille—we also decided—has come, for work on the thing, to the Camargo Foundation. And so here in Cassis—we imagined—both Carolyn and I now first meet and hit it off with her. (In fantasy, I both read and speak French fluently. Carolyn, of course, does so in reality.) But the work, unfortunately, is driving Mireille nuts—which we imagine we can tell from post-work conversations we're always having with the woman as well as from reading her by now enormous manuscript. The novelist Evelyn Waugh, by the way, had once said pretty much the same thing about reading *Ulysses*.

Upon leaving Cassis, I said, Mireille will become obsessed with death. She will fantasize, in fact, having a rather tragic one—something like the author Camus' car accident—but like Proust will also be terrified that it'll happen before she can finish writing this latest and undoubtedly last book of hers. Hoping then to render such a demise "questionable"—and so cause a stir among both scholar and non-scholar fans of hers alike—she will arrange to have, said Carolyn, a series of—non-Stalin-like—postcards mailed to the two of us afterward. Post*mortem*-cards, if you like. Unfortunately, she will fail to foresee that she'll soon die in an ironic, not to mention shameful, not to mention non-sentimental way: by having a heart attack while straining too hard on some toilet in Bruges, Belgium. There'll be some conference there on "Alternative Textiles." Or so Carolyn also said. I said that Mireille will get killed there—or maybe just seem to get killed—in a bidet explosion. The mechanics of this, though—fluid or otherwise—I have never quite understood. *Can* bidets explode? If so, then *how*?

Needless to say, this was all—for me—in order not just to mock queer studies, and not just to deal with my Matt (as Mireille's "Guy") having dumped me, and not just to feel famous, it was also—and rather, I now realize, like the queer afterlife of Marie-Hélène—to fantasize my brother Steve's death as "questionable." For Carolyn, though, it was . . . Well, to quote the woman herself:

Dear Kevin,

Ah, Mireille Dujardin. Sometimes I miss her.

I did enjoy playing Mireille with you, in France, and in our letters and post-cards over the past ten years. That's the first thing that comes to mind, when you ask me about Mireille: play. Our conversations about her, our imaginings and inventions—it was a form of play. And I've been playing that way for a while. Before I met you, a friend and I had developed an entire imaginary world in which we were famous theorists. We had an imaginary daughter together (it was never clear which one of us was the biological mother) named after Violette Leduc—that literally and perhaps literarily crazy author of a number of autobiographical novels, and a Simone de Beauvoir devotée with stalker-like tendencies. The imaginary Violette was not a stalker, but she was a troublemaker, and we never knew where she was. We played the busy, harried, neglectful mothers, too enveloped in our big theory heads, to pay attention to a little girl who seemed to not need us anyway. Imaginary Violette was part Eloise, part Dennis the Menace.

And in my mind, and in my play world, she was Mireille's forebear, psychologically, if perhaps not chronologically. Mireille may not have been a troublemaker, but she was crazy. That's what I loved about her, and frankly, what I feared. I went from playing absent-minded mother and rebellious daughter (is it a coincidence that during that time I was working on Colette?) to playing the crazy French theorist with you . . . while I was writing my dissertation in France. Where writing also means—agonizing, fretting, searching, groping around in the dark. You remember. Yes, I was writing about sleep in nineteenth-century French literature. And mere months earlier, Elisabeth Ladenson had said to me, after I'd spun some cockamamie literary argument that did contain a kernel of insight, "You know, sometimes you go too far. You grab the bull by the horns and run." She was right. But oh, the shame. Here I wanted to be the dutiful daughter Simone and not the loony Violette. And here you and Mireille came into my life. And Mireille is crazy. Mireille is that which goes too far. Mireille du Jardin, a garden—her own backyard—that she excavates looking for knowledge, knowledge she pulls triumphantly from the dirt, soil clinging to its roots . . . but it turns out to be garbage, or a partially-decomposed gourd, or, knowing her, an irrigation pipe. And *Irigaration* is born. She goes too far.

To stick with the plumbing imagery for a moment, Mireille was my safety valve: a way for me to experiment, to go too far into going too far, all without leaving the safety of our conversations. She was a way for the dutiful daughter to play crazy.

Would that it were that simple . . . as simple as "the madwoman in the attic"—my Jane [Eyre] to Mireille's Bertha [Mason Rochester]. Perhaps I should leave it at that, but no. I'm going to go past [Sandra] Gilbert and [Susan] Gubar. I'm going to go a little farther.

Into the French. That's how I learned it in college: first wave Anglo-American feminism, followed by second wave French feminism. [Hélène] Cixous, [Xavière] Gauthier, Irigaray. Mireille's models. And my own? Here's where the dutiful daughter stumbles onto her ambivalence. And I had been the dutiful daughter: the straight-A student, the good little Catholic girl. The nuns taught me French, and I soaked it up. Suddenly there was this whole other language to play in. And I did. I went to France. I majored in French. I went to grad school. I taught French. I got a Ph.D. I got a tenure-track job [in Lancaster, Pennsylvania]. Then I quit.

I stopped playing. What happened? I'm still figuring it out myself, and while Mireille does not figure heavily into my decision to leave the academic profession, she does read as a symptom of my ambivalence about what I was doing, who I was, and what I wanted to be.

When you and Mireille arrived, I was committed to the path of the French professor. French had always been, at heart, a form of play for me. I was a good little mimic. It was easy to be someone else when I spoke French. It wasn't just a language, but a performance. I donned the mask every time I walked into the classroom. My students ate it up. I was quite good at playing *Madame le professeur*—vibrant, rigorous, know-it-all, with just a soupçon of crazy.

Playing the scholar of French was another matter. One of the problems was language. I had learned French through imitation and study. But how to imitate the language of theory? And if I couldn't reproduce it, could I understand it? Try as I might, I couldn't master it. Of course, that's the point. No one has the Phallus, right? Lacan, Irigaray and their ilk practice a deliberately obscure, sometimes poetic, always *illisible* discourse that defies all of the rules of good writing that the dutiful daughter had learned. Even though I had peeked through the veil, French theory—poststructuralist and particularly feminist theory—continued to frustrate me. And seduce me. And unsettle me. Everyone else in the profession seemed to get "it." I couldn't play along. I couldn't wear that mask. I was settling into the Impostor. The Poseur. I didn't like the personas hanging in my closet anymore. Even my writing felt like a sham—and a bad one at that. When I arrived in France to write ten years ago, these were barely acknowledged feelings, of course. For the dutiful daughter was still on her mission: to be the best academic she could be, or appear to be.

Then you and Mireille came along.

Like me, Mireille doesn't get "it;" unlike me, she thinks that she does. Unhampered by notions of rationality, clarity, organization, and logic, Mireille effortlessly spews her ideas onto the page. She makes connections and associations that only a lunatic, or a dreamer would see. Her writing is *illisible*, in the fullest sense of the word, as neither you nor I ever got around to scripting her nonsensical books. She is the Impostor who fools herself so well that she believes. She believes. And she is passionate about that belief. I loved that about Mireille. Loved it, and mocked it. Mireille was at once what I wanted to be, never wanted to be, and knew that I could never be.

So, in some subterranean way, our musings about Mireille would eventually help me get clear on the kind of writer I wanted to be, and the kind of scholar I didn't want to be. Of course, it would still take years before the dutiful daughter would abandon her mission. That's a *much* more pernicious alter ego. But there again, Mireille helped. Why not step off the tenure track? Why not move across the country? Why not do something crazy? I wasn't desperate. I wasn't depressed. I don't even have the excuse of an erotic vision in a lace museum. But the moment I resigned, I parted company with both the dutiful daughter and the *illisible* French feminist, whose very insanity gave me the guts to quit a tenure-track job in the profession I had pursued all of my adult life. I chose a different path.

And so today I'm the woman who walked away. It's a fun new persona to play with, though less scripted than the French celebrity-theorist. I now find myself interested in people who change their minds, who switch gears, who leave one world for another, as you left the law for literature. Perhaps "Kevin Kopelson" will be my new model. Though I will always play "Mireille Dujardin" with you, just for fun.

Love,
Carolyn

P.S. I met a playwright in San Francisco last month. He is fascinated by Mireille's life story, and thinks it would adapt beautifully to the musical theater. He suggested the title "Out of the (Water) Closet" and plans to have all the actors in drag. What do you think?

As you can see, it was *impossible* for me to stop quoting or rather transcribing here. "What do I think," though? I think I should take Carolyn as my own new role model—after Sedaris—and leave both academia and confessional satire behind for perhaps . . . well, for what now? For *professional* knitting? For *espionage*?

At this point, after leaving Cassis, I began getting postcards—clearly *not* postmortem—from "Mireille" in first Charlottesville, Virginia, and then Lancaster, Pennsylvania, and then San Francisco:

Coucou, mon chéri!

> *J'ai pensé à toi récemment quand j'ai visité le musée moderne. J'ai un nouveau projet! "Lectures à la toilette"—tu sais, l'analyse du bidet n'est pas encore épuisée. De toute façon, tu me manques et j'aimerais savoir de tes nouvelles. Quoi de neuf? Ma nouvelle vie en Californie me convient très bien, mais j'ai hate de retourner en France.*

> *Gros bisous, mon chéri!*
> Mireille

Coucou, chéri!

> *Je t'envoie ce petit mot juste pour te remercier pour ton admirable Sedaris. C'est "brilliant," comme on dit en anglais, et non parce que tu as choisi de l'ouvrir avec quelques mots de mon très humble ouvrage. Non, non, chéri, si j'ose dire, tu es même plus drôle que ce pauvre type David qui a tant de mal à s'exprimer en français (et voilà, donc, pourquoi on l'adore aux Etats-Unis). Quand vas-tu écrire quelque chose sur la soeur, Amy? Celle-là . . . ! disons que je n'aurais jamais pu finir Les Dentellières lesbiennes au moyen-âge si je l'avais rencontrée quand j'étais plus jeune. Elle est délicieuse . . .*

> *Alors, sérieusement, après le succès certain de Sedaris, que vas-tu faire? As-tu envie de collaborer sur mon prochain projet? Il s'agit d'un terrain tout nouveau pour moi—et pour la critique en générale—le sauras-tu? La queue. Oui, la queue des animaux. La queue, que possède presque chaque espèce d'animal, mais qui nous manque. Il me semble que notre cher Freud, en se concentrant sur la biologie actuelle de l'homme, a complètement négligé un manque, ou à vrai dire, une perte évolutionnaire. Où est notre queue? Qu'est-ce qu'elle est devenue? Que signifie cette perte dans l'imaginaire humaine? Voilà, chéri, mon point de départ. Mon*

trajet? Je ne sais, sauf que je commence à fréquenter le zoo, pour chercher de l'inspiration, et peut-être des réponses.

En t'embrassant bien fort, je suis comme toujours, ton amie.

Mireille

Yet by now I'd thought of Mireille—childishly—as mine alone: as *my* alter ego, and *not* as that of either Carolyn or Michel. I also thought of her as real, or at least as more real than either Marie-Hélène or Esperanza ever were. And so I—alone—continued fleshing out her background. There had been, I decided, a maternal grandmother whose own Fontainebleau home, despite the woman's narcissistic and or borderline personality, was another place young Mireille might avoid meat. There had been, too, a ne'er-do-well younger brother—now dead. Plus Mireille herself plagiarized.

Maybe, then—I began thinking—I should now write Mireille's "biography." Or I should actually write—*as* Mireille—the book *Lesbian Lacemakers of the Middle Ages.* Or rather, I should "translate" the thing for her and then, like "Charles Kinbote" in Nabokov's *Pale Fire* (1962), pose as its crazed and also rather obsessive commentator. Carolyn, I figured, could if necessary turn my English back into Mireille's "original" French. Or Michel could. Or my friend "Swisher-Tingley" could. Both texts, of course, would have the same ostensible targets: Mireille Dujardin, as both author and queer-theorist; "Kevin Kopelson," as either her biographer or translator-commentator. But would anyone else—I soon wondered—want to read such a book? Such a *satire*, that is. Or rather, would anyone other than friends of mine want to? And why should they—what with that Nabokov novel still around. Still, though—one must confess—I actually told the English Department and hence our administration here, in an official report on myself that I had to do for the year 2007, that "I am translating the late Mireille Dujardin's as yet unpublished book, *Les Dentellières lesbiennes au moyen-âge.*" Which, you must admit, was not just ironic—as opposed to sarcastic—but also somewhat crazed of me. In fact, it was fully crazed. Then again—one must also confess—I had already done something related to this that was even more so.

Perhaps you recall, from "G712," the *Neatness Counts* passage: "But where are we, really, when we masturbate? And who are we? Who when we write? Who, rather, are we pretending to be?" Well, I had decided—just before publication—to use this as the second of now not just one but two epigraphs to my book *Sedaris*, concerning as the thing does if not masks worn then at least roles played by—or both "autofictional" and "autodiegetic" personas of—the man: the role, in particular, of his somewhat virago-like mother. (There's that "closeted" drag by Sedaris that I mentioned before.) And yes I did soon worry that, after his unfortunate porn-movie theater incident, Paul Reubens—or "Pee-wee Herman"—might take offense. But that man hadn't really read *Sedaris*—with at that point just the one epigraph, taken from Proust—in manuscript. (Reubens' blurb, once again, is: "If I were to read a book on David Sedaris it might be this one.") So I imagined, he'd probably never read the thing in print. And yes I did realize that you shouldn't quote *yourself* as an epigraph to something else you wrote. Who—other than friends of yours, or maybe Mark Mitchell—would ever read the rest of it? Instead, then, I had Swisher-Tingley translate the passage—"back"—into French and pretended Mireille wrote it:

> *Mais où sommes-nous, au juste, quand nous masturbons? Et qui sommes-nous? Qui, en écrivant? Ou plutôt qui faisons-nous semblant d'être?*
>
> —MIREILLE DUJARDIN, *Lesbian Lacemakers of the Middle Ages*

Hence "her" line, in that last postcard I transcribed: "*C'est* 'brilliant,' *comme on dit en anglais, et non parce que tu as choisi de l'ouvrir avec quelques mots de mon très humble ouvrage.*"

I imagined, there would—upon publication of *Sedaris*—be other people—people, that is, who are *strangers* to me or rather who are *readers* of me or rather who are readers of this *work* of mine—to think that Mireille is real. And now that my *own* words—about Roland Barthes—from a previous book had in a new one become this alter-ego-like *woman's* words, I really *was* her . . . if only, no, not for readers. I was really her for *me*—or rather for me alone, in my own little mind—while at least first transcribing those words, in French thanks to Swisher-Tingley, from a chapter of *Neatness Counts* as an epigraph to *Sedaris* and then later on reading that epigraph in "page proofs" and then even later re-reading it in print. (Not, though, while masturbating.) But soon, perhaps—after she gets this copy of the book, inscribed by me, that I'll send her via regular mail—I'd be Mireille in *Carolyn's* mind as well.

|||

With *Sedaris*—including that second epigraph—about to come out, I continued writing limericks. (The initial epigraph there is by not Proust, anymore, but by David Sedaris: "I tried listening to *The Misanthrope* and *Fontaine's Fables*, but they were just too dense for me. I'm much too lazy to make that sort of effort. Besides, if I wanted to hear people speaking wall-to-wall French, all I had to do was remove my headphones and participate in what is known as 'real life.'") You've already seen some of these in both "G712" and "Kiss and Tell":

> While posing above an abyss,
> Poor Oscar said something amiss—
> > A damnably glib
> > Sodomitical fib:
> "The boy was too ugly to kiss."

> Most audience members cried "Shame!"
> When Vaslav, Diaghilev's flame,
> > Defiled the veil
> > In a pastoral tale.
> But wankers were happy they came.

> "Atonal is straight, tonal gay,"
> Claim students of Miss Boulanger.
> > Take little Ned:
> > Even in bed
> He'd carry a tune all the way.

Some limericks, though, you haven't yet read here:

> A savvy old sapphist named Gertie,
> Considered by many too wordy,
> > Dashed off the Life
> > Of Toklas, her wife,
> While leaving out everything dirty.

"Gertie," there, is Gertrude Stein; that "Life" is *The Autobiography of Alice B. Toklas*—by Stein about *herself*, mainly, in the third person.

> All those who love stunners with smarts—
> If not in real life, in the arts—
> > Should go to a show
> > By surreal Cocteau.
> The guy gave Jean all the best parts.

The Jean Cocteau and Jean Marais relationship paralleled that of Serge Di-
aghilev and Vaslav Nijinsky. While the first two were lovers, Marais starred in
the Cocteau films *The Eternal Return* (1943), *Beauty and the Beast* (1946), and
Orpheus (1949). Unlike the Russian pair, though, the French one remained
friends later on. Whereas Diaghilev never forgave Nijinsky for having chosen to
marry a woman, named Romola Pulszky, and thus for having brutally dumped
him, Cocteau had no problem with Marais seeing other men, including, pre-
sumably, Ned Rorem.

> Architect Mies van der Rohe
> Told Philip to put on a show:
>   "A house made of glass,
>   Surrounded by grass
> Some stripling would then have to mow."

This one, I'd imagine, speaks for itself. But to quote *Wikipedia*: "[Philip John-
son's] early influence as a practicing architect was his use of glass; his master-
piece was a 'Glass House' he designed as his own residence in New Canaan,
Connecticut, a profoundly influential work (1949). The concept of a Glass
House set in a landscape with views as its real 'walls' had been developed by
many authors in the German *Glasarchitektur* drawings of the 1920's, and al-
ready sketched in initial form by Johnson's mentor Mies [van der Rohe]. The
building is an essay in minimal structure, geometry, proportion, and the effects
of transparency and reflection."

> The queerness of opera queen Wayne
> Arose from his feeling the pain
>   Of diva roles juicy
>   As Lammermoor's Lucy—
> A bride who was bloody insane.

Having just been forced—by her brother Enrico—to marry Arturo, with
whom of course the poor woman is not at all in love, Lucia stabs the poor
man, Arturo, to death, loses her mind, and then—still in her nightgown—
wanders back onstage where their wedding festivities continue. (She then
wanders back offstage where she dies. So, too—although onstage—will her
lover Edgardo die. That poor man stabs himself to death.) "Who *wouldn't*
identify with Lucia," asks Wayne Koestenbaum—in *The Queen's Throat*—of
this famous mad scene. Or rather, he corrects himself, who wouldn't identify

with her "wandering voice" in the scene, "careening" as it does "from impulse to impulse?"

Other such limericks include:

Fag-haggery sure worked out well—
For Duncan, that is. As for Bell:
   A broken down heart
   And second-rate art
Bloomsburied by critics from hell.

Virginia Woolf's sister, Vanessa Bell (*née* Stephen), was very much in love with no, not her husband Clive. This poor woman was in love with her fellow painter Duncan Grant. She even had a daughter—named Angelica—by him. Grant, though—the Nijinsky of the so-called Bloomsbury Group—was basically gay. Plus, as a gay man, he was promiscuous—with lovers including, for instance, the biographer Lytton Strachey, who was also Grant's cousin, as well as the economist John Maynard Keynes. (Keynes, although also basically gay, later married a female star—named Lydia Lopokova—of the *Ballets Russes*. And as for that "promiscuity" of Grant, I suppose that I've had sex with even more men than he did. *O tempora, o mores.*) Grant's *aesthetic*—as opposed to mere erotic—success, moreover, has unfortunately far exceeded that of Bell.

Having been raised as a prude,
Julia got wed, then got lewd.
   Hubbie now tips,
   Licking his lips,
"Why don't you get cordon bleu-ed?"

Le Cordon Bleu is the school in Paris where Julia Child (*née* McWilliams), encouraged by her much beloved husband Paul, first mastered *cuisine*. I confess, once again, to having watched an inordinate amount of her television show—*The French Chef*, broadcast from 1963 to 1973—as a child. Not that I myself had yet begun cooking. In retrospect, I consider that fixation to have been both fantasy escape from my mother's cooking and—like my sentimental love of opera—an early sign of my own basic gayness.

And yet even with *Sedaris* including that second epigraph ("*Mais où sommes-nous, au juste, quand nous masturbons? Et qui sommes-nous? Qui, en écrivant? Ou plutôt qui faisons-nous semblant d'être?*") about to come out, and even with my writing all these limericks while imagining myself to be, no, not Sedaris, probably, and clearly not Mireille, and even with my no longer imagining my-self—in class—to be either Florence Dragnet or Joseph Scavone, I was starting to identify—at home—with the only role that has every really been called for (or "interpellated" to quote Louis Althusser) there from me. Not, of course, the role—or path—of either Mary Poppins, and or Auntie Mame, and or Peter Pan. And nor even the role of Uncle Charley anymore. I now identified, at last— nearly fifteen years after my own father's death—with the role of "Dad." This, no doubt, was because "the boys," by which I mean not just Adam, Seth, and Sam but also Seth's friend Keaton—all or whom were teenagers at the time— needed their biological father as well as even "little me" to act like men. (*Little Me* is the very campy book that "Patrick Dennis"—*né* Edward Everett Tanner III in Evanston, Illinois—wrote after the somewhat less campy *Auntie Mame*.) Or rather, they needed us both to act like *grown* men. Or rather, to act like *loving* grown men who therefore know—as does Sedaris, thanks to his mother Sharon, and not to his father Lou—to use shame not destructively but *con-*structively. Who know to use—or "deploy"—it not to abuse people but rather to nurture them. How to use shame, that is, like a *good* father—or in my case a good father *figure*. This was also, no doubt, because David, as both the biologi-cal father of Adam, Seth, and Sam and my own much beloved lover, needed me not just to act like but also to think of myself—only non-"heteronormally"—as a grown and also rather *masculine* man. And yet this was also because, to in-voke Freud's erstwhile collaborator Carl Jung on what he actually called the *persona*, I myself—notwithstanding either the pleasure of camp, and of drag in particular, or the pressure of both feminism and sexuality studies—now finally needed to do so.

After *Sedaris* came out I also started being more of a father figure—or at least a father-*supplement* figure—in class than I'd ever been before. Plus I stopped worrying about what any non-friend but—to me—now son- or-daughter-like scholar, who, as one of their actual targets, needed—I thought—to read those limericks of mine, might themselves think about them. Or rather, I stopped worrying about what he or she might think about my having written them. (Sedaris, once again, is a *mother* figure—in writing—when shaming most other people, as characters there, constructively. He's a father figure, though, when abusively shaming either himself or a couple of people—including Lou—there.)

And so I decided, finally, to publish the limerick series "Wilde," "Nijinsky," "Stein," and so on. Not as a book, though—or just a pamphlet. Nor even in some scholarly journal, as an article. I thought it would be neat, instead, to have an old painter friend of mine—by then somewhat successful, aesthetically, back in New York City—do illustrations for it. He could then, I thought, go get some art gallery there to exhibit us—as collaborators—together. This friend, turns out, was game. But he could think of a much better venue for that work. "Let's submit," he said, "to *Urban Molecule*." This was a brand new—and *soi-disant*—"serial webzine of literature, art, and design." "Fine," I said. But I soon decided—just for fun plus once again as an *obvious* joke—to claim that a brand new and finally *male* alter ego of mine had written the poems. And so "'Gumby' Louis Boots"—a name derived, as you've seen in "Kiss and Tell," from not one, not two, but *three* nicknames that David had given to me and hence if not exactly an autobiographical reference I couldn't yet possibly explain anywhere in public then at least a private "thank you" to him there for his having prompted my Uncle Charley and then Dad identifications at home—would now be one ostensible target. (That posting of our submission in the initial so-called issue of *Urban Molecule*, I should explain, was in the year 2008.) "Kevin Kopelson"—a Charles-Kinbote-like both commentator on and biographer, not to mention colleague, of "Gumby" Louis Boots—would be another. (Evan Wolfson, as you've also seen in "Kiss and Tell," has the—non-anagrammatic—porn name "Boots Beechwood." He's no relation to "Gumby," though.) That biography was brief:

As the author of *Henry James and the Rectal Sublime* and *Notes on Siegfried and Roy*, "Gumby" Louis Boots (1970—2006) was a major player within "the academy." (The nickname "Gumby" derived from this colleague of mine having had "Gilbert's Syndrome"—which made him look green—and also from an unusual flexibility.) Plus he had translated *Jeux d'eau* by Mireille Dujardin. It's a study, inspired by Luce Irigaray, of both the bathroom and sexuality therein. He then translated her second book, called—in English—*Irigaration*. It's on the bidet. Plus at the time of his death (while attempting the "Iron Maiden" move, in yoga) Boots was working on at least two projects I knew of. He was translating Dujardin's next book—to have been called *Les Dentellières lesbiennes au moyen-âge* but left incomplete, unfortunately, at the woman's own death in I think it was 2003. (The title means *Lesbian Lacemakers of the Middle Ages*. Boots joked, though, that he'd call it *Tit for Tat*.) Plus, I knew, he was writing a novel. Its title was to be *Finishing Proust*. It was on some English professor who can't finish writing his own book on why that Frenchman couldn't finish writing *Remembrance of Things Past*. Boots had also been writing poetry, something I learned only when cleaning out his office at work and discovering here, in a desk drawer, this file with about twenty limericks on various twentieth-century celebrities—artists, scholars, and performers, for the most part. But then, at the end, there was one called "Robert Mendoza." (The style of these, as you'll see, is rather clever. The substance, though, is both serious and astute. For this limerick collection—incomplete, unfortunately—not only covers a range of sexual "perversions" but also functions as a "performative" critique of what we now call sexuality studies.) That puzzled me. So I now looked through an address book in another drawer, found the name "Bob Mendoza," called Bob in Manhattan, and through him learned both that he had first met Boots there—years ago—at something called "Boy Bar" and that he was supposed to have illustrated the collection upon its completion. (There were to have been about fifty limericks.) I asked the man to do these illustrations anyway, mainly in order for me to see what at least part of this collaboration of theirs would have looked like but also maybe to display it somewhere. Bob said yes, he'll do them, and in watercolor—but he did not tell me that they'd be so very, as you'll also see, obscene.

The "Mendoza" limerick was of course *very* brief:

Nothing stopped Bob, a *flâneur*,
From hailing some kid as "*Monsieur!*"
    —Only the gripe:
    He's not my type—
Then asking him "*Avez-vous l'heure?*"

As was the commentary on them all. Plus it was both utterly and—I hoped—rather funnily self-regarding if not borderline narcissistic. "Kevin Kopelson," that is, can only ever—for the most part—cite *himself*. See, for instance, his note to "Mendoza":

Clearly, the "perversion" here is cruising. The term *flâneur* derives from both Charles Baudelaire and Walter Benjamin. The question *Avez-vous l'heure?* (Do you have the time?), here, may derive from a deployment of it on page four of D.A. Miller's pamphlet, *Bringing Out Roland Barthes* (1992). For more on cruising, as well as on Barthes, see Kopelson, *Love's Litany*, pp. 129–50. See also Kopelson, *Neatness Counts: Essays on the Writer's Desk* (2004), pp. 51–73, 115, 127, 137.

Bob Mendoza, though—and not at all funnily—died of AIDS just a few weeks ago: on February 18, 2010.

| | |

"Gumby" Louis Boots, you'll have noticed, really did—unlike me—know French, as do Albertine, Michel, Swisher-Tingley, Carolyn, Elisabeth, my brother Bob, Richard Howard, Charles Rosen, Luce Irigaray, Julia Kristeva, and Mireille Dujardin. Or he at least knew the language well enough to—like Richard Howard—translate from it. Another such wish—or fantasy, rather—of mine fulfilled, in that biography from *Urban Molecule*, is that "Gumby," a "major player within 'the academy,'" had been just as famous, when alive, as Mireille when *she* was alive. Because yet another fantasy fulfilled there is that she, too, is now—unquestionably—dead: "He was now translating Dujardin's next book—to have been called *Les Dentellières lesbiennes au moyen-âge* but left incomplete, unfortunately, at the woman's own death in I think it was 2003." (One must confess, though, that—as with Marie-Hélène—the woman still lives on or rather gets *resurrected* by me, or by the three of us, whenever either Carolyn and I or Michel and I now communicate. She is a big part—maybe the biggest one, apart from my crush on Michel—of our own two joint histories.) And yet I am also mocking there—as with Mireille—what is all too frequently the *basis* of such celebrity. The title *Henry James and the Rectal Sublime*, for instance, takes a somewhat mean swipe at—"Is the Rectum a Grave?"—Leo Bersani and not at, say, either D.A. Miller or Eve Kosofsky Sedgwick. (Ellis Hanson, as you might recall from "Kiss and Tell," once took a quite mean swipe at Bersani.) Plus the title *Notes on Siegfried and Roy* takes one at Susan Sontag, or rather at her proto-queer yet homophobic essay—from the year 1964—called "Notes on 'Camp.'" Both "Gumby's" death and that of Mireille, moreover, may fulfill yet another fantasy—that I have finally come to terms with my brother Steve's. More likely, though, they are an attempt—or rather, an *essay*—to accept my own mortality.

Kevin Kopelson, though—you'll have noticed—really did, unlike "Gumby," finish *Finishing Proust*. He did so in Cassis, France, or about a year before beginning *Neatness Counts*. The thing, though, is if not quite "horrible," then at least rather, well, rotten. It's too non-metaphoric for a novel, as well as too non-visual. Of course, that poor man himself—in his own little mind or rather in his little writer's mind's *eye*—is not that visual anymore. Recall, for instance, how he now can't quite picture the fourth-grade teacher—a "Mr. X."—who had him write an essay on some conquistador. Another problem with *Finishing Proust* is that it's really rather maudlin. In fact, it's *morbid*. Nor does it really *address* anyone—other than Kevin himself. Plus maybe his brother Steve. But as you can tell from *this* book—one must hope—I myself, having read and also taught so many other novels by now, am no longer that interested in being, to once again quote James Merrill, "imbued with otherness." ("Young chameleon, I used to / Ask how on earth one got sufficiently / Imbued with otherness. And now I see.") Unless, of course, such imbuement occurs—quite fleetingly—through either classroom rhapsody or such quotation in print. I'm no longer even interested in being, or in *pretending* to be, or in—"*Nous allons marcher ensemble*"—"walking together" with Mireille. Except, once again, when either speaking with or writing to either Carolyn or Michel. I'm no longer even interested—especially now that Bob Mendoza has died—in being "Gumby." Nor even in being my friend Jesse Green—who as you might recall from "My Cortez" first brought that Merrill quote to my attention plus who was the first person I *knew* in person to make me want to write. Nor even am I interested in being my friend Wayne Koestenbaum. Nor even—now that I know *him* in person as well—in being David Sedaris. (Here's a typical and also the most recent exchange between us. Kevin: "Could you tell me, once again, what's the quickest, easiest way for me to get a copy of one of your forthcoming fables to have my class read? I'd have to have it in hand by the end of April." David: "The quickest, easiest way is to have me e-mail it to you. I'm working on rewriting some and should have them ready in a few weeks. You want to just write back and remind me?") Nor even—especially—in being either Bob Kopelson or Steve Kopelson. Being Dad, though—that's another story. Because I'll now probably always—somewhere, somehow—have thought of myself as him.

Clearly, then, Mireille's Way and "Gumby's" Way—like that of Dragnet and Scavone—were both the same Way and not the same one. Both those alter egos of mine were celebrities, plus both knew French relatively well, but only one of them—"Gumby"—wasn't crazy. Plus he alone was only ever *me* alone—unlike Mireille who was at first both Michel and me and then both Carolyn and me. This paradox, no doubt, is a function of how much more complicated than either somewhat paternal or better yet somewhat friendly teaching, *with* graduate students but only *to* undergraduate ones, the so to speak "speech act" of writing—with its both real and imagined readerships—is for me. *Beethoven's Kiss*, for instance, was addressed primarily to my friend Wayne—back in New Haven, Connecticut, and then in New York City—and also of course to . . . well, to who knows whom. This book is addressed to my husband David—here in Grinnell, Iowa—and also to any biological children of mine out there and also to . . . well, to whomever you are. At any rate, I can no longer pretend—here on the page or rather while both working and playing at *this* kind of keyboard—to be any such persona, much as I can no longer pretend here to be either smarter or dumber than I am. As far as you—dear reader—are concerned, I only get—when not quoting others just as in the classroom I might at any point be "rhapsodizing" them—to impersonate my no, not my avuncular self anymore. I only get to impersonate my somewhat paternal or better yet somewhat friendly or even better quite *loving* self.

Does this mean, though, that I also now either transcend or "sublate" what Roland Barthes—as you know from "Hatchet Job"—calls a "two-term dialectic"? (Barthes: "Popular opinion and its contrary, *Doxa* and its paradox, the stereotype and the novation, fatigue and freshness, relish and disgust." Or in my case: Anna Pavlova and Vaslav Nijinsky; Lucia Ashton and Enrico Ashton; Lucia Ashton and Arturo Bucklaw; Florence Dragnet and Joseph Scavone; "Franny" Glass and "Zooey" Glass; Marie-Hélène de Rothschild and Guy de Rothschild; Eve Kosofsky Sedgwick and D.A. Miller; Emmeline Grangerford and Charles Rosen; Avital Ronell and Aviral Tonell; Aviral Tonell and Mireille Dujardin; "Zooey" Glass and "Buddy" Glass; "Zooey" Glass and Seymour Glass; "Buddy" Glass and Seymour Glass; Charles Rosen and Stalin; Richard Taruskin and Stalin, if they're not in fact the same person in this book; Vaslav Nijinsky and Serge Diaghilev; Auntie Mame and Uncle Charley; Mary Poppins and Peter Pan; Mireille Dujardin and "Gumby" Louis Boots. And also: Bob Kopelson and Kevin Kopelson; Steve Kopelson and Kevin Kopelson; Kevin Kopelson and Jesse Green; Kevin Kopelson and Wayne Koestenbaum; Kevin Kopelson and David Sedaris. And so on.) Does it mean—to quote Luce Irigaray—that I have managed, finally, to "thwart" such thinking? No, it does not—as I would imagine you can tell. But nor—and this is my second to last confession here—do I even want to thwart it anymore. Life, you see, has intervened.

Golden Book

Sybil released her foot. "Did you read 'Little Black Sambo'?" she said.

"It's very funny you ask me that," he said. "It so happens I just finished reading it last night." He reached down and took back Sybil's hand. "What did you think of it?" he asked her.

"Did the tigers run all around that tree?"

"I thought they'd never stop. I never saw so many tigers."

"There were only six," Sybil said.

"*Only* six!" said the young man. "Do you call that *only*?"

—J.D. SALINGER, "A Perfect Day for Bananafish"

At age four—or during the same year as my "dying swan" act—I developed life-threatening mastoiditis. It's an infection of the temporal bone behind the ear. This required a mastoidectomy, or removal of that bone. The surgery was to be done by a "Dr. Buchbinder." I recall being on the operating table, then some masked man, probably the anesthetist, said I'm about to fly through outer space. This, in fact, is what now seemed to happen, with both stars and other planets streaming past me faster and faster. With today's drugs, says Dr. David, my husband, this wouldn't happen. I next recall, at any rate, being in some recovery room with Mom and Dad. I could have all the ice cream I wanted, they said, as Dr. Buchbinder, I later learned, had done a tonsillectomy as well. I could also, they said, have any present I wanted.

I asked for a toy fire truck. But they mustn't have been able to find one, at least not in that hospital, for they soon came back with a book. The book, I recall, was—of all things—*Little Black Sambo* (1899). The story there, as you may know, is presumed by many people to be just as racist as the original and then most obnoxious illustrations of it were. It's not, though. Nor were my parents racist. For this wasn't any old edition. It was a new "Golden Book," where Sambo seemed, not like some stereotypical "pickaninny," as both the poet Langston Hughes and my former colleague "Carol" have complained, but like a very cute *real* boy. An *Indian* boy, in fact, as the story was set, by its author Helen Bannerman, not in the American South but in South Asia. It was Bannerman, though, who drew the original illustrations. The ones here were by an I'd guess husband and wife team named Bonnie and Bill Rutherford. Sambo's parents, likewise—"Black Mumbo" and "Black Jumbo"—seemed like a cute young couple. This, too, was how I saw my own parents—by then in their forties just as I have been up until recently. (I am now, as of this writing, age fifty-one.) But the father, Jumbo—I must have sensed—was also pretty sexy.

Yet I didn't like this book, at first. And so nor did I even read it. (Could I read, at four? I think so.) I had wanted that fire truck. But then Mom and Dad found one: a big, beautiful hook-and-ladder truck, bright shiny red, with not one but two steering wheels, front and back. After that I could and did both read or have read to me and love the book. My very own book. My very own first book. In the story, as you may know, Sambo prevails over not six—as J.D. Salinger's "Sybil," at age four, would have it—but four rather hungry, envious, and arrogant tigers. (Why won't Seymour Glass—that "young man," at age thirty-one—correct the girl? Because he's a *good* would-be father figure to her.) Sambo has been forced by them, one by one—so as not to be "eaten up"—to fork over presents from *his* parents: beautiful new clothes, hand-made by the mother, Mumbo; shoes and umbrella that Jumbo got at a bazaar. Each tiger, thus garbed, now thinks himself the "grandest" in the jungle. (So they're all basically "phonies," as Salinger would have it. Or rather, as Holden Caulfield—in *The Catcher in the Rye* [1951]—would.) The reader, though, or viewer, can see they're not at all grand. These clothes, on those animals, are way too small, the shoes worn not on feet but on healthy ears, the umbrella tied by a tail. The tigers, now, see each other, though without also seeing how ridiculous they look. They chase each other around a tree, "fighting and disputing which of them was the grandest"—while Sambo wisely hides. They then rather oddly melt into "lovely butter (or 'ghee,' as it is called in India)." Sambo retrieves the clothes (red coat, blue pants), the shoes (purple and crimson), the little green umbrella. Jumbo retrieves the butter. Mumbo uses this to make "a huge plateful of the most lovely pancakes," twenty-seven of which she herself eats, fifty-five of which Jumbo does, and a hundred and sixty-nine of which—"because he was so hungry"—Sambo does.

Something about this appealed to me, as I'm sure the book has to many. But what it was, in my case, is—one must confess—all the food. Bannerman's morality tale functioned, for me back then, as an *im*morality tale. It seemed to say that if not greed then at least gluttony is good. "Eat all you can," as Lambert Strether, in the novel *The Ambassadors* by Henry James (1903), would certainly not be telling Little Bilham; "it's a mistake not to." I now of course realize—as a literary critic but also as an only somewhat cute real man—that the true moral is: if not gluttony then at least greed is bad. Extortion is bad. ("Very well, I won't eat you this time, but you must give me your beautiful little red coat.") Narcissism, too, is bad. ("Now *I'm* the grandest tiger in the jungle.") Competition, even, is bad—both ridiculous and deadly—when if not purely then at least primarily narcissistic.

What, then, is good? Or if not good, in the story's terms, at least advisable? Perhaps, for someone like Sambo, it's to avoid such a place. ("So he put on all his fine clothes and went out for a walk in the jungle.") Or take your dad there with you. Or having gone alone, ignorant of danger, forfeit anything you have—should trying to keep it keep you in jeopardy—that others over-value. ("Oh, please, Mr. Tiger, don't eat me up. I'll give you my beautiful little red coat.") And then stay out of fights with nothing to do with you.

Needless to say, but I'll say—or write—it anyway: I'd have saved myself a lot of trouble, in academia, if I'd known this all along—or if I'd already known, at age four, how to really read, how not to *mis*read. Then again, I'd have never become a critic—or at least a professional critic—if I did know that. Instead of writing books, then, including this one, I'd have—better yet—chosen, like my first surgeon, in name only, to *bind* books written by others. Bind them beautifully, of course, and yet like Mumbo to do so by hand. Or I'd have chosen, like almost everyone else on the planet, this planet, to just read them—if literary—from time to time, and only then when necessary.